BLACK FASCISMS

BLACK FASCISMS

African American Literature and Culture between the Wars

Mark Christian Thompson

University of Virginia Press
Charlottesville and London

University of Virginia Press
© 2007 by the Rector and Visitors of the University of Virginia
All rights reserved
Printed in the United States of America on acid-free paper

First published 2007

9 8 7 6 5 4 3 2

Library of Congress Cataloging-in-Publication Data

Thompson, Mark Christian, 1970–
  Black fascisms : African American literature and culture between the wars / Mark Christian Thompson.
      p.   cm.
  Includes bibliographical references and index.
  ISBN 978-0-8139-2670-4 (acid-free paper) — ISBN 978-0-8139-2671-1 (pbk. : acid-free paper)
  1. American literature—African American authors—History and criticism. 2. African American authors—Political and social views.   3. Fascism in literature.   4. Politics and literature—United States—History—20th century. 5. African Americans—Intellectual life—20th century.   6. Black nationalism—United States—History—20th century.   I. Title.
  PS153.N5T49 2007
  810.9'358—dc22
                                                                    2007013689

To my family

Contents

Acknowledgments ix

Introduction 1

1. Black Literary Fascism 5
2. The Myth of Marcus Garvey:
   Black Fascism and Nationalism 45
3. George S. Schuyler and the God of Love:
   Black Fascism and Mythic Violence 72
4. "In Turban and Gorgeous Robe":
   Claude McKay, Black Fascism, and Labor 87
5. His Rod of Power:
   Zora Neale Hurston, Black Fascism, and Culture 117
6. Richard Wright's Jealous Rebels:
   Black Fascism and Philosophy 143

   Conclusion:
   Historical Black Fascism, Black Arts, and Beyond 171

Notes 183

Bibliography 201

Index 225

Acknowledgments

No project such as this comes to fruition without a great deal of help, tangible and intangible. I have yet to find the line that divides absolutely these two forms of assistance, and I have no desire to do so now. In that light, I would like to thank my colleagues William J. Maxwell, without whom I would never have had the courage to write this book, and Robert Dale Parker, for asking questions I sometimes did not want to answer. I would also like to thank Eric J. Sundquist, Richard Yarborough, and George Hutchinson for their time, patience, and encouragement all along this way. Nina Baym, Gordon Hutner, Siobhan Somerville, Julia Walker, Nancy Castro, and Michael Rothberg all read various sections of the manuscript at various times and offered important critiques and suggestions; thank you all so much. The Mellon Foundation and the Humanities Research Board at Illinois afforded me time and money for research and writing, and I thank them most gratefully. My deepest thanks to everyone at the University of Virginia Press involved with the development and publication of *Black Fascisms*, especially Cathie Brettschneider. I'd also like to thank *African American Review* for giving me permission to publish a previous version of chapter 5, "His Rod of Power: Zora Neale Hurston, Black Fascism, and Culture," which appeared in *African American Review* 38.3 as "National Socialism and Blood-Sacrifice in Zora Neale Hurston's *Moses, Man of the Mountain*." *MELUS* deserves thanks as well for granting permission to publish material from my article "Voodoo Fascism: Fascist Ideology in Arna Bontemps' *Drums at Dusk*," which originally appeared in *MELUS* 30.3. A version of chapter 3, "George S. Schuyler and the God of Love: Black Fascism and Mythic Violence," appeared in *CLA Journal* 48.2 as "The

God of Love: Fascism in George S. Schuyler's *Black Empire*"; I thank the College Language Association for its kind permission to reproduce the article. Material from my short biographical sketch "Sufi Abdul Hamid," Copyright 2004, from *Encyclopedia of the Harlem Renaissance*, edited by Cary D. Wintz and Paul Finkelman, is reproduced by permission of Routledge/Taylor and Francis Group, LLC. Claude McKay's poem "Sufi Abdul Hamid" is reproduced here courtesy of the Literary Representatives for the Works of Claude McKay, Schomburg Center for Research in Black Culture, The New York Public Library, Astor, Lenox, and Tilden Foundations.

I would also like to thank Perry Meisel, Kevin Bell, Richard Sieburth, Jennifer Wicke, Eva Geulen, Avital Ronell, and Phillip Brian Harper for help and encouragement during the awkward years.

I thank my wife for this and everything else.

BLACK FASCISMS

Introduction

[Black intellectuals] viewed fascism as a blood relative of slavery and imperialism, global systems rooted not only in capitalist political economy but in racist ideologies that were already in place at the dawn of modernity.
—Robin D. G. Kelley, *Freedom Dreams* (2002)

We were the first fascists.
—Marcus Garvey, interview with Joel Rogers (1937)

It seems unthinkable that any African American could have admired European fascism during the 1930s, and many would view the supposition that some African American intellectuals appropriated elements of fascist ideology to foster social change as absurd. As Robin D. G. Kelley makes unequivocally clear, expressing such a thought among "a group of radical black intellectuals including W E. B. Du Bois, Aimé Césaire, C. L. R. James, George Padmore, Ralph Bunche, [and] Oliver Cox" would have been thought tantamount to wishing for the return of slavery (*Freedom Dreams* 56). Outside of this "group," however, some black intellectuals saw things differently. *Black Fascisms* illumines an otherwise dark corner of African American literary history; it shows that some African American authors working during the 1930s turned to fascism to advance their own needs. Authors as diverse as Marcus Garvey, George S. Schuyler, Claude McKay, Zora Neale Hurston, and Richard Wright used fascist ideology to construct the bulwark of fascistic conceptions of radicalism and revolution. With the idea of the fascist state as their starting point, these African American intellectuals appropriated and elaborated on fascist ideology as a means of revolutionary black nation building.

Because the assertion that there existed positive appraisals of fascism within African American literature is bound to be met with understandable skepticism and anger, I would like to make clear from the beginning what this study does not intend to do. *Black Fascisms* in no way seeks to undermine the achievements of black Marxists and Communists working in the 1930s, and it does not seek to condemn the black radical tradition in any way.¹ I do not contend that African Americans formed fascist political organizations, or that African American writers wanted to belong to German fascist groups, the Nazi party, Italian fascism, or any other existing fascist movements. The authors and works examined in this study sought to present a uniquely black form of generic fascism, not to voice allegiance to Germany or Italy, or support genocidal programs. I do not seek to displace canonical readings of African American literary and political history but to supplement them with a little-considered strain of African American political thought. Aside from the scholastic desire to describe as completely as possible an aesthetic and historical moment, the purpose of this study is to acknowledge the multiplicity of African American literary and political thought.

This is not a work of pure historiography or pure political science: it is a literary study that searches novels for political fantasy and the aesthetic form that conveys that fantasy. Cutting across disciplines, *Black Fascisms* engages with a number of fields of inquiry, including African American literary and historical studies, the study of fascism, and critical and political theory. In doing so, *Black Fascisms* combines political theory, historicism, and the close textual analysis of documents of 1930s African American political and aesthetic culture. Taking a rigorous literary-historical approach to the materials along with a comparative literary and political-theoretical structure, *Black Fascisms* delimits a conceptual model with which to assess the histories and cultural manifestations of politically construed African American identity.

The first chapter, "Black Literary Fascism," defines this book's central concepts—black fascism and generic European fascism—and the historical moments that gave rise to black literary fascism. By appropriating what is today called "generic fascist ideology," African American novelists responded negatively to black Marxism and Communism while expressing rage over the Italian invasion of Ethiopia, the U.S. occupation of Haiti, and the 1935 Harlem riot. These events were seen as possible rallying points for the conjuncture of Black Nationalism and fascist revolutionary violence, opportunities to fight fascism on its own terms.

Taking up Paul Gilroy's analysis of black fascism as it pertains to Marcus Garvey's "political style" and fascist affinities, the second chapter demonstrates that Garvey's assertion "We were the first fascists" (Rogers 220) needs to be considered in much wider historical and theoretical fields.[2] What Tony Martin calls "Literary Garveyism" can be rethought in the light of Garvey's fascist political style. This style permeates every aspect of the Garveyite movement and colors Garvey's writings and opinions on the Italo-Ethiopian conflict. Though Garvey's writings are not literary, a model of black fascism can be extrapolated from them, the indirect elaboration and critique of which is found in the work of authors following in his wake. In this sense, each of the novels presented here is a meditation on the fascism implicit in Garveyism.

Chapter 3 considers *The Black Internationale* and *Black Empire* (serialized in the Pittsburgh *Courier*, 1936–38), George Schuyler's bizarre, dystopian vision of an African American world domination movement led by the Marcus Garvey caricature, Dr. Belsidus. Described by Henry Louis Gates Jr. as "the Afro-centrist's dream" ("Fragmented Man" 42), Schuyler's serials are in fact part hoax, part devastating critique of Garveyism; they seek to glorify fascist ideology moreso than Garvey, and better than he had.

Claude McKay's later prose works are the focus of chapter 4, which concludes that McKay's rejection of Communism and embrace of the "Führer of Harlem," the soapboxer Sufi Abdul Hamid, are symptomatic of his admiration for fascist ideology. Concentrating on McKay's essay on the Harlem Riot of 1935, "Harlem Runs Wild" (1935), and an unpublished poem, "Sufi Abdul Hamid" (ca. 1940), I present McKay's support of Hamid as a denial of this self-appointed "Black Hitler's" virulent anti-Semitism. McKay's refusal to see the dark aspects of Hamid's rhetoric allows him to support a black fascist political program in his sociological work *Harlem: Negro Metropolis* (1940) and his autobiography *A Long Way from Home* (1937) without openly admitting to doing so.

Chapter 5 begins with a brief analysis of Zora Neale Hurston's *Tell My Horse* (1937), in which she finds in Haiti a political and cultural model for African American fascist revolutionary praxis. I then deal with Hurston's *Moses, Man of the Mountain* (1939). Through the figure of Moses as well as the Pharaoh, Hurston critiques the ideological premises of National Socialism while at the same time conceding the value of generic European fascism for a program of African American uplift. Indeed, the black cultural nationalism Hurston advocates with her appropriation of the Mosaic myth is achieved along lines similar to the violent creation of the fascist authoritarian state.

The sixth chapter examines the most famous treatment of fascism in African American fiction: Richard Wright's *The Outsider* (1953). Although published outside of the period investigated by *Black Fascisms*, *The Outsider* is Wright's first published novel since *Native Son* (1940) and realizes many of his political concerns of the 1930s. This does not mean that Wright was blind to history. For all its concern with Depression-era African American politics, *The Outsider* is stripped of the historical specifics we find in the other works discussed in this study. In order to accommodate his earlier political reflections while at the same time avoiding producing an anachronistic text, Wright authors a work of political philosophy that sidesteps a highly specified historical context. While including it within the general milieu of Depression-era African American politics, my reading of the novel addresses the book primarily on its philosophical terms. In the novel, Wright explores fascist ideology through the character of the murderer-philosopher Cross Damon. Damon is the logical end point of the development of black fascist ideology traced in *Black Fascisms;* he is the essentially black "essence" of fascism.

Ultimately, *Black Fascisms* asserts that our understanding of African American expressive culture is strengthened by reading political elements both agreeable and odious to current conceptions of "acceptable" and "heroic" African American radicalism. This study believes that to ignore or deny the dark, violent, and ugly political attitudes clearly evidenced by African American writers of the 1930s does the individual thinkers a great disservice. It denies them the full breadth of the human, which includes, sadly, a taste for hate.

1 Black Literary Fascism

My country's tired of me,
I'm going to Germany
Where I belong
—Parody of "America" sung by African American children in the South, ca. 1943

"So you've been to Germany? Well, well! Have they got them radicals in jail yet? Italy's got the dope. Old Moso—what's his name? Mr. Jones was saying the last time I was in the bank, making my weekly deposit—what was it? About six thousand dollars, as I remember—says he, 'John, we need a Mosleny right here in America!'"
—W. E. B. Du Bois, *Dark Princess* (1928)

It is interesting to listen to them and to hear remarks of individuals in the crowd. While not altogether pro-Nazi, they do gloat over the Nazis upsetting the international applecart, and they are not pro-British. Many of them declare that a Nazi victory might be better for the black people. It is not because they imagine the Nazis having any tenderness for black people. But they believe that a Nazi victory would stir the blacks from their present lethargy either to live or to die.
—Claude McKay, *New Leader* (1940)

In 1943 African American children altered the lyrics to "America" to express feelings of severe racial alienation and oppression.[1] The product of this appropriation displays a seemingly unnatural identification with Nazi Germany. No doubt the children had only a vague idea of what they sang. Nevertheless, we must ask how they came to alter "America" in this way. A similar question can be asked of the black bourgeois in Du Bois's romantic novel *Dark Princess* who considers favorably the prospect of an American Mussolini (55–56). As Du Bois realizes with deep dismay (a disappointment, however, he is not afraid of articulating), "Old Moso," or Old fascist Massa, does not pose the same problem to every African American.

Old fascist Massa takes on a very different guise in the rhetoric of Black Nationalist labor activists on Harlem street corners during the 1930s and 1940s.[2] Anti-Semitism and Nazism were prevalent enough in the speeches of the popular soapboxer Sufi Abdul Hamid that both the black and white presses referred to him as the "Black Hitler" and the "Führer of Harlem"—names he reportedly gave to himself.[3] Another Black Nationalist Harlem street agitator, Carlos Cooks, went so far as to form his own group of "Blackshirts" during the Italo-Ethiopian crisis (Naison, *Communists* 196). Claude McKay's justification for the soapboxers' sympathy with fascism—that it stems from a desire to shock blacks into action—rings false when we realize that their reaction to Nazi victories in Europe reveals a profound feeling of admiration for Germany for upsetting the "international applecart." No doubt disturbed by Nazi racial rhetoric, McKay's soapboxers are still able to exhibit pleasure with the Nazi will to power.

In a 1937 interview from exile in London, Marcus Garvey went so far as to say that the Nazi will to power, and fascism in general, originated with him. Garvey claimed, "We were the first fascists" (Rogers 420). By "we" Garvey meant his Universal Negro Improvement Association (UNIA), whose tactics and ideology he believed to be the source of European fascisms. During the same interview, Garvey went on to insist that "Mussolini and Hitler copied fascism from me.... Mussolini and Hitler copied the program of the UNIA" (Rogers 420). While this assertion stretches the imagination, it also speaks to something far more telling in Garvey's position vis-à-vis fascism, namely, that his admiration for Mussolini and Hitler was integral to the UNIA's ideological program. Ultimately, Garvey posits not only the black man's right to devise a form of his own fascism, *but that fascism is essentially black.*

Black identifications with fascism were not limited to marginalized individuals such as Garvey became during the 1930s. A reader of George S. Schuyler's overtly fascistic, wildly popular *Black Empire,* serialized in the *Pittsburgh Courier* in 1936–38, wrote to the newspaper seeking "to understand about this Dr. Henry Belsidus [Schuyler's fascist dictator]. Is his conquest going on now, at the present time, in Africa?" (Hill and Rasmussen 268) Although most readers of the *Black Empire* serials recognized the ongoing story of the African American colonization of Europe as fiction, intense, positive responses to Schuyler's Mussolini figure, Dr. Henry Belsidus, were common among the serial's nearly all-black readership. The idea of Africa "liberated" by an African American Übermensch sold newspapers in the United States as it attempted to quench the thirst for revenge blacks felt over the Italian invasion of Ethiopia.[4] *Black Empire* provided African Americans with a fantasy of Pan-African black collaboration that would fight fascism using its own methods. Paradoxically, European fascism resonated in African America with such negative force as to give rise to positively construed fantasies of black fascism.

Black Fascism in Context

Pan-Africanist sentiment in the United States spiked at the outset of the Italo-Ethiopian war, such that, as Robin D. G. Kelley observes, "Almost overnight an array of support organizations were formed, mainly in New York, Chicago, and Los Angeles, to raise money for relief and medical aid; and men from across the nation volunteered to fight" (*Race Rebels* 129). This avalanche of support marked a singular sympathy with the Pan-African cause among blacks in the United States. Robert G. Weisbord surmises,

> Perhaps no single event in the twentieth century more clearly illuminated the nexus between diaspora blacks and continental blacks than the Italian-Ethiopian war. It is not at all surprising that Benito Mussolini's invasion of Ethiopia in October 1935 stoked passions deep in black Americans. Ethiopia has long held a special place in the hearts and minds of many Afro-Americans. In large measure this has been due to two factors: An impressive cultural tradition traceable to ancient Axum and a uniquely successful resistance to the European intrusion in Africa in the latter part of the nineteenth century. (89)

For diaspora blacks, part of Ethiopia's allure over the centuries stemmed from the ambiguous and provocative *Psalms* 68:31: "Princes shall come out of Egypt, [and] Ethiopia shall soon stretch forth her hands to God." Biblical "evidence," combined with Ethiopia's history of colonial resistance, marked territories of real and mythic proportions in the black imagination, signifying the terminus of black Zionism.[5] As a result, a mixture of "Ethiopianism" and Zionism established itself in transatlantic black consciousness (Jenkins 9). The product of the experience of the middle passage and New World slavery, Ethiopianism and black Zionism mark the division between the real space of colonial oppression and combat and what Benedict Anderson has called an imagined homeland.[6]

Located at the core of the black Zionist myth, Ethiopia's allure as an African American imagined homeland has persuaded African Americans to try its borders for over one hundred years. Perhaps no decade is more important for the development of Ethiopia as a rallying point in African American political thought than the 1890s, which saw the birth of Ethiopianism in the strict sense as a secessionist Catholic church movement internal to Africa that stretched throughout the continent ("Ethiopia" here standing in for all of Africa). The expansion was accompanied by an intense missionary interest on the part of African American clergy (Chirenje 3–4). African American missionary movements sought to educate Africans in both spiritual and cultural matters. Despite the fact that African American missionaries in the 1890s met African congregations caught in the midst of a battle for independence from *all* foreign influence, the New World interest across the black Atlantic in establishing Catholic churches in Africa did not wane (Redkey 23). In fact, Ethiopianism only strengthened, bridging the black Atlantic and defining a specific historical circumstance while retaining a wider, more general Pan-African meaning.[7]

Ethiopianism after the 1890s continued to provide a mythological narrative through which African Americans could identify culturally and ontologically with Africans. Although it responded to specific historical-material conditions, Ethiopianism as myth embraced all peoples of African descent at all times; it cut across the diaspora and in essence identified the problems of one Volk with those of another. As such, Ethiopianism was a mutable concept. As Eric J. Sundquist observes, "In a more radical interpretation [*Psalms* 68:31] could be seen to prophesy a black millennium, a violent seizure of freedom through acts of revolt sanctioned by God and led, literally or figuratively, by a black redeemer from within Africa or, in some interpretations, from America" (*To Wake* 553). Sundquist draws attention to the fact that the biblical basis of Ethiopianism forms the backbone of a Black Nationalist sentiment reared on the idea of Ethiopia as the goal of Christian eschatology. The biblical passage can be read as calling for a "black redeemer," a black Moses to overthrow the colonial powers, return Africa to the Africans, and ultimately advance the inevitable narrative and historical unfolding of holy prophecy. This sense of "nationhood" as a pathway to a privileged, racially coded originary moment characterizes Ethiopia as the site of black independence and glory, civilization and culture, history and immortality. Ethiopia rises in the African American imagination, at least until the Italo-Ethiopian War, to reveal the true nature and unity of all black peoples.

The greatest testament to the validity of Ethiopianism's biblical basis was the successful 1896 defense, led by Menelik II, of the African nation against Italian incursion. Menelik's victory, which was to be "avenged" by the Italian Fascists, inserted itself neatly into the mythohistorical understanding African Americans possessed of Ethiopia. It enhanced that understanding to such a degree as to make it secondary to the simple fact of an outright black victory over a colonial power. As Sylvia M. Jacobs understands it, "Ethiopia was a symbol of black independence and successful black self-government years before Menelik's victory over Italy. . . . Black identification with Ethiopia reached a high point with the victory of the Ethiopians over the Italians in March of 1896. . . . Black American interest in Africa in general, and in Ethiopia in particular, was heightened during these years" (192, 193). However, Ethiopia's military victory did not prevent African Americans from maintaining a sense of superiority over the mythically charged yet inevitably "backward" continent. Despite Ethiopian martial success, African Americans continued to hold the seemingly contradictory image in their collective imagination of the African as savage and savior (Berghahn 190). Conversely, these images of Ethiopia allowed African America to envision itself as both redeemer and redeemed. Ultimately, then, Ethiopianism in the United States was a mode of African American exceptionalism, which took a terrible blow when Mussolini invaded Africa.[8]

Not only was black greatness measured over and against the defeat of colonial forces in Ethiopia, it was measured over and against the defeat of Italians. When Italy returned to Ethiopia for its revenge, it attacked both a single, sovereign nation and the heart of the idea of black greatness, undermining the contemporary needs of African America. If Ethiopianism expressed the essential core of the "contemporary needs" of Black Nationalism in the United States, then the 1935 Italian invasion of Ethiopia caused an eruption of Pan-African sentiment in America perhaps unequaled since Menelik's victory in 1896 (Dawson 194).[9] With this explosion of interest in the war came frequent, violent assaults on Italians in Harlem. Seeking retribution for the loss of the foundational text of Black Nationalist mythology and ideology, blacks in Harlem attacked Italian Americans with a ferocity that bordered on a fascist celebration of violence for itself.[10] As Mark Naison recounts, "nationalist street orators . . . spoke of Ethiopia as a race war, encouraged attacks on Italian-Americans, and affected a paramilitary air reminiscent of European fascism" (*Communists in Harlem* 196).[11] Accusations of fascist violence within African America were not limited to reprisals for the Italian invasion of Ethiopia. The Harlem soapboxer and putative "Black Hitler" Sufi Abdul Hamid and his "Don't Buy Where You Can't Work" boycott campaign were also blamed for fomenting anti-Semitism and the destruction of the 1935 Harlem riot.

Adam Clayton Powell Jr. most often receives the credit for originating, organizing, and executing the 1934 "Don't Buy Where You Can't Work" Harlem jobs campaign, a boycott directed against Harlem's large department store owners who refused to hire African American clerks despite having overwhelmingly black clienteles.[12] Sufi Abdul Hamid is usually relegated to the role of assistant to Powell. Yet, as Jervis Anderson describes it, the Sufi "did more than aid Powell with the campaign before being relegated to the role of little more than a footnote of the labor movement's history in Harlem." Instead, Anderson says, "Powell—along with John Johnson, the pastor of St. Martin's Episcopal Church, and Sufi Abdul Hamid . . . led a boycott against department stores along 125th Street ('Don't Buy Where You Can't Work') which forced these stores to end their policy of refusing to hire black salesmen and saleswomen" (293).

Hamid's role in the boycott was even more extensive than Anderson indicates. After having success with a similar campaign in Chicago in the opening years of the 1930s, Hamid, an inflammatory orator and ex-cultist now working the streets of Harlem, brought the "Don't Buy Where You Can't Work" slogan to prominence once again in 1933. The Sufi captured Harlem's attention with his outrageous dress—Hamid appeared beturbaned and in a mélange of national costumes—and with his rhetoric of black pride and virulent anti-Semitism. It was his anti-Semitism that, as mentioned before, earned Hamid the title of "Black Hitler" in both the black and white presses. In the October 9,

1934, *New York Times,* Hamid is purported to have said that "the war is on" against the Jews, and that he was the "only one fit to carry on the war against the Jews" (2). This rhetoric resulted in charges of disorderly conduct and intent to ignite a race riot. Indeed, the blame for the March 19, 1935, Harlem riot found its way to Hamid's doorstep, occasioning Claude McKay to take up the Sufi's cause in the pages of the *Nation* with "Harlem Runs Wild." "In assessing the underlying causes of the riot," Cooper allows, "McKay discounted the influence of Communist agitation and emphasized instead the recent efforts by the Harlem community to force the larger merchants along 125th Street to hire black clerks. This movement, McKay pointed out, had not been initiated by either the Communists or by traditional black leadership; it had been started by a strange, turbaned black man 'in gorgeous robes' who claimed Egyptian origin and called himself Sufi Abdul Hamid" (306).[13] According to Cooper, McKay admits that Hamid caused the riot, apparently because Hamid's fascistic agitation over the year and a half before the riot primed Harlem to react violently to the disinformation stating that police killed a boy caught stealing a ten-cent penknife from Kress's. However, the assessment Cooper offers of McKay's position vis-à-vis Hamid neglects to mention that McKay spent a good deal of time with the Sufi before and after the riot, and that McKay had nothing but admiration for the man. McKay adored Hamid because the soapboxer used his skills as a cultist to mobilize the masses in an effort to advance the aims of black labor. Yet despite Hamid's work for the cause of black labor, charges of labor racketeering always dogged him. One such instance was in 1932, when Hamid, then called "Harlem's Egyptian Negro," attempted to run for the Assembly in Manhattan as a democrat. His bid to remain on the ballot was denied because it was believed that most of the two thousand signatures required were forged.[14]

By contrast, the concerns of the popular Harlem cultist Father Divine had less to do with the improvement of the material conditions of his followers then with his own (Levering Lewis 300).[15] Still, Divine and Hamid found common ground on the issue of the need for black clerical jobs (Weisbord 134). Hamid's racism and anti-Semitism, as well as his own relentless ambition, eventually proved too much for Divine, as well as the Jewish organizations the Minute Men and the Harlem Merchant's Association. "Jewish store owners in Harlem," Cheryl Lynn Greenberg details, "having helped form the Harlem Merchant's Association at the time of the initial pickets, first complained of Hamid's anti-Semitism in 1934. They accused him of repeating Nazi propaganda, and called him 'Black Hitler.' . . . He was brought to municipal court in 1935 on charges of disorderly conduct and 'instigating a race war.' He denied the charges and was released with a warning" (126). The merchants had a vested interest in discrediting Hamid, who maintained throughout his relatively short-lived career that anti-Semitism and racism held no place in his thought. Yet, as Winston C. McDowell opines, "Hamid's culpability was stronger than he admitted. There were indeed powerful business interests pushing for Hamid's conviction on the disorderly charge. . . . He was known to spew ethnic slurs quite freely: Italian and Greek businessmen were referred to as 'spaghetti slingers' and 'swine herds,' respectively. Hamid was probably not shy about utilizing anti-Semitic remarks in order to attract followers, particularly those frustrated by the inability of African Americans to establish an economic foothold in areas dominated by Jewish businesses" (228–29). Whether anti-Semitic or not, Hamid lost organizational control of the boycott, finding himself on the outside as Powell's Citizen's League, a relative latecomer to the game, began to take control of the black labor movement in Harlem. The Sufi's attempt to regain control of the boycotts partly explains why the Citizen's League did not achieve its ultimate goals. According to Solomon, "Shortly after the victory over Blumstein's, the Citizen's League began to fracture. It was attacked from the outside by Sufi Abdul Hamid, who saw his dreams for a lucrative labor agency punctured by the coalition that 'stole' his campaign" (267).

The Sufi's motives for organizing and then tearing down a radical black labor movement remain fodder for speculation. It is certain that McKay's admiration for Hamid, his growing racial chauvinism, and his distaste for the Communists and the black intelligentsia stem from the same source. As Tillery notes, "McKay's defense of Hamid underscores his continuing retreat to racial chauvinism" (165), as well as his further withdrawal from the Communists. "In fact," Giles claims, McKay came to view "the Communists in 1935 as a sinister, but rather ineffectual, force in Harlem. In the last chapter of *Harlem: Negro Metropolis,* McKay also deals with the destruction of the Sufi Abdul Hamid movement; but, while the black intelligentsia is still treated harshly, the Communists are seen as a much more dangerous and powerful force" (143).

McKay held the conviction in the 1930s and 1940s that the Communist Party (CP), as an interracial champion of all workers' rights, was ideologically incompatible with the specific needs of black labor.[16] Cooperation with the CP made the black intelligentsia impotent and exploited what McKay perceived as the talented tenth's desire for white acceptance and black assimilation. This resulted in gross incompetence at the level of black labor's leadership and retarded the goal of improving the material conditions of black workers. In McKay's view, the riot and the ongoing condemnation of Sufi Abdul Hamid were pressure points that revealed how the combination of black and white liberals and radicals, powerful though effeminized by the groups' interracial makeup, attempted to suppress black labor. Hamid used the language of fascist ideology to help break Communism's grip on black labor concerns because it offered a radical alternative to radical interracial activism.

Along with the invasion of Ethiopia and Harlem labor practices, Haiti inspired fascistic fantasies in the popular imagination of African Americans in the 1930s. During the latter half of the decade, there was a dramatic increase in works about, and romanticizing, Haiti and Haitian history.

When the U.S. occupation of Haiti ended in 1934, the heroism of Haitian history, of successful black resistance, was ostensibly validated. The United States had occupied the island since 1915, originally as a peacekeeping mission. But, as late as 1934, it was, according to the Roosevelt administration, the threat of foreign intervention in the Caribbean that necessitated the continued marine occupation of Haiti. As Emily Greene Balch's 1926 "disinterested" report on the occupation noted, for all intents and purposes, that danger did not exist: "It seems . . . that there was virtually no danger of foreign intervention, and that if the authorities in Washington believed that there was, the cause was in the state of their nerves rather than in any actual menace" (21). Haiti's inability to pay an enormous debt owed the United States, combined with a profitable agricultural industry, probably accounts for the United States' often brutal occupation of it.[17] What is certain is that during the years of the occupation, all vestiges of an independent Haitian spirit came under relentless attack as a matter of U.S. policy.

This violent response to Haitian cultural difference and economic independence informed a great measure of Black Nationalist sentiment throughout much of the first half of the twentieth century. An early champion of the Haitian will to independence and visitor to the "troubled island" in 1920, James Weldon Johnson stimulated, by his own immodest admission, much of the U.S. literary response to the occupation. In his autobiography *Along This Way* (1933), Johnson makes his claim for the sudden influx of literature on Haiti, asserting that "What I said and wrote was in some degree responsible for a new literary interest in Haiti" (352).[18] Dash supports Johnson's claim: "After Johnson's visit black American contacts with Haiti, personal, literary and political, intensified" (51). This intensification grew in tandem with a national trend in the arts. At this time, Haiti as a cultural product had value equal to that of Haiti as producer of sugarcane. The image or idea of Haiti held as much allure as a malleable commodity advertising the exotic as it did as the representation of U.S. imperial power. The marines' "presence in Haiti, and the resistance it engendered," Renda observes, "called attention to the 'black republic' in the United States. And as U.S. citizens (and consumers) took an interest in Haitian affairs, Haiti became not only a point of protest, but also, with new vigor, an object of cultural fascination—indeed, an object of desire, a valuable commodity" (185).

Opened up for cultural consumption by visits such as Johnson's and consciously exploited by books like *Black Majesty* (1928) and theatrical productions like Orson Welles's "Voodoo *Macbeth*" (1931), the Haiti of the occupation underwent a literary treatment that signaled a shift in the island's representation in African America that still allowed vehemently racist perceptions and representations to hold sway.[19] The various genres of writing that came to bear on Haiti—anthropological, travel, fictional, poetic—constructed their object from a growing need in African America for a more versatile image of Black Nationalism than had previously existed (Plummer 127).

Haiti's postoccupation government served as such a model. African American cultural production with regard to Haiti did not flourish despite distaste for, but because of admiration for Haitian president Sténio Vincent's authoritarian regime. (Renda 185–228). Vincent ruled a Haiti in which, as David Nicholls points out, "there was considerable sympathy . . . for European fascism, among a number of different groups. They saw in fascism . . . an alternative to the liberal democratic model which had widely been accepted as the one which should be followed in Haiti. Many *noiristes* of this period, with their anti-liberal and authoritarian rhetoric, were advocating a kind of fascism for Haiti" (179). Positive evaluations of fascism were, at minimum, part of Haiti's postoccupation public political dialogue. The Haitian constitution of June 2, 1935, is itself an authoritarian document that, as Robert Debs Heinl and Nancy Gordon Heinl note, "allowed the president [Sténio Vincent] to dissolve the legislature and govern by decree, abolished the separation of powers, proclaimed the executive 'sole authority of the State,' and . . . gave Vincent outright power to name ten of twenty-one senators, the remainder to be chosen by him from slates presented by the legislature. Most important, a 'Unique Article' invested Citizen Sténio Vincent with a second term commencing 15 May 1936" (492).

Not unaware of the problematic nature of Haiti's postoccupation government, many African American writers and artists set their pens to Haitian resistance of the past as a way of distorting yet still valorizing the Haitian present. The events artists and writers often treated were from the early years of the Haitian War of Independence. For the African American political imagination, this war signified race pride and the possibility of black revolutionary change. The conception of Haiti as the site of an indigenous black revolutionary consciousness is what allowed W. E. B. Du Bois, as late as 1961, to invest the island with the doctrinaire communist position he adopted near the end of his life: "In after years, the successors of Toussaint, Dessalines, and Christophe developed communalism, and made the Haitian state independent and owner of its land and crops" ("Toussaint L'Ouverture" 300). Du Bois's claims for the content of Haitian history describe an internecine period of revolution marked by the names Toussaint, Dessalines and Christophe, followed by a time of relative prosperity under the system of "communalism." Having taken one of the great events of a globally construed black history, the Haitian War of Independence, and transformed it into a proletarian revolution, Du Bois contents himself with establishing early independent Haiti's history as a form of communism that seems to come naturally to blacks.

However, as Dash has shown, "The disturbing political realities of Haiti meant that the dream of racial solidarity would now have to take into account nonracial, historical factors which made instinctive identification between blacks of different societies increasingly difficult" (Dash 54). "The disturbing political realities" of independent Haiti presented African American authors, including Langston Hughes, with a troubling identification. In *I Wonder as I Wander*, Hughes writes, "When Dessalines was killed, Christophe carried on the building of the Citadel.

Three thousand feet above sea level the fortress rose stone by stone, cannon by cannon, passed by hand up the steep slopes. When Christophe died, Haiti became a republic. But its upper classes developed a political caste that ruled badly—yet no worse than many another ruling class in other lands" (*IWW* 27). African American intellectuals in the 1930s, such as Bontemps, and in the early 1960s, such as Du Bois, performed the paradoxical task of embedding within the early days of independent Haiti an indigenous, instinctual drive to "communal" political life. But Haiti as it lived and breathed removed itself so far from such an image that the politics of the island nation made it almost impossible to match it to its history. The experience of this disjuncture between the ideal Haiti and the material reality of Haiti's class structure shocked Hughes into a crucial realization: "It was in Haiti that I first realized how class lines may cut across color lines within a race, and how dark people of the same nationality may scorn those below them" (*IWW* 28). Before this time, Hughes labored under the assumption that race defined categorically political sympathies. Haiti taught him that the revolutionary class presents a diverse popular front, as does its antagonist, fascism.

Zora Neale Hurston goes farthest in admitting the deficiencies and inequalities of Haiti's political system, challenging directly the notion that Haitian history reveals the ontological imperatives of the black radical subject:

> Of course Haiti is not now and never has been a democracy according to the American concept. It is an elected monarchy. The President of Haiti is really a king with a palace, with a reign limited to a term of years. The term republic is used very loosely in the case. There is no concept of the rule of the majority in Haiti. The majority, being unable to read and to write, have not the least idea of what is being done in their name. Haitian class consciousness and the universal acceptance of the divine right of the crust of the upper crust is a direct denial of the concept of democracy. (*Tell My Horse* 75)

Hurston sees Haitians as servile and desirous of monarchical leadership. Haitian "democracy," which does not follow "the American concept," amounts to little more than the people choosing in corrupt elections who shall rule them like a king. In fact, Hurston ignores or neglects to mention the fact that Haiti's president at the time of her visit,

Sténio Vincent, effectively eliminated the next election when he wrote an automatic second term for himself into the Haitian constitution of 1935. This omission allows Hurston to avoid admitting that Vincent's dictatorship may have had something in common with the fascist dictatorships of the 1930s, which in turn enabled her to romanticize Haiti's political and martial strivings.

Many African American artists and intellectuals negotiated Haiti's political present by omission; they avoided creating politicized works that spoke directly of Haiti's authoritarian regime. Instead, as in the case of Arna Bontemps' *Drums at Dusk* (1938), or Jacob Lawrence's Toussaint cycle (1939), artists favored the romantic and heroic time of Toussaint, which fits more easily into the morally and heroically enlightening narrative movement from bondage to freedom. A quasi-fascist Haiti was exchanged for a heroic past with no apparent connection to the present. By locating their works in Haiti's mythic past, these writers could revere Haiti's revolutionary history without having to reference directly its present government. In this way, intellectuals celebrated contemporary Haitian resistance while sidestepping its fascistic aspects.

To Richard Wright's mind, however, the problem of fascism was not limited to Haiti or Africa or even to African American labor movements; it was a very real, pressing issue for all African Americans. In the *Daily Worker* description of his new journal, *New Challenge,* Wright lists as one of the journal's explicit goals the presentation of "the literature and conditions of life of American Negroes in relationship to the struggle against war and Fascism" (Fabre 142). By this, Wright did not mean that "the struggle against war and Fascism" was to be fought solely against whites, but also against similar tendencies within African America. He did not see fascism as radically incompatible with black life but instead understood it as one side of the political coin. Believing that Communism and fascism were African America's ultimate political horizons, Wright posited that African America's political future lay exclusively with one of these two choices. Indeed, Wright always considered the problem of Bigger Thomas to be inextricably bound to Bigger's fascist potential. In 1940's "How Bigger Was Born," Wright reveals fascism as one of Bigger's midwives:

> In 1932 another source of information was dramatically opened up to me and I saw data of a surprising nature that helped to clarify the

personality of Bigger. From the moment that Hitler took power in Germany and began to oppress the Jews, I tried to keep track of what was happening. And on innumerable occasions I was startled to detect, either from the side of the Fascists or from the side of the oppressed, reactions, moods, phrases, attitudes that reminded me strongly of Bigger, that helped to bring out more clearly the shadowy outlines of the negative that lay in the back of my mind. ("Bigger" 444)

As early as 1932, Wright watched the Nazis and learned from them. Instead of seeing them as an irreducibly alien force to black life, however, he saw in them an analogue to a given and a potential situation within the United States. According to Wright, American racism had issued an ultimatum demanding of African Americans that they choose between Communism and fascism. This political mandate allowed for no other alternative to these two choices and saw no inherent contradiction within the logic that states that an African American can be a fascist. It seems, then, that some African American intellectuals found satisfying the thought of an alliance or at least an alignment with European fascism before World War II.

Viewing African American political culture of the 1930s within a wider spectrum reveals that positive assessments of fascism made by African American intellectuals were neither unheard of nor aberrant. This view of 1930s African American intellectual life maintains what Cornel West has called "the specificity of Afro-American oppression" while articulating its political and cultural manifestations and points of contestation as hybrid in character (17). The product of this reading is a new understanding of 1930s African American literature that incorporates the disruptive and disturbing politics of noncanonical texts by well-known Harlem Renaissance authors. On the rare occasions that texts such as George Schuyler's *Black Empire* have been approached critically, they are subsumed under the heading of either black conservatism or unreadable anomalies. Since they are exiled from the wider, ongoing dialogue of radicalism in African American fiction of the 1930s, these novels appear to exist merely to reinforce the idea of African American political insurgency coming from the right as either an aberration or an unseemly addendum to an otherwise normative structure of radical African American political belief. The general design of this normative structure details a coherent collective leftist political unconscious operative throughout African American history. This tradition encompasses the history of blacks in the West in general to the exclusion of all other definitions of black radical tradition.

Black Fascism and Black Radicalism

Cedric Robinson defines the black radical tradition as "the continuing struggle for liberation motivated by the shared sense of obligation to preserve the collective being, the ontological totality" (171). It is the "ontological" sense of the black radical tradition that divided Garveyites and Communists in the 1920s. Believing that Communists put class warfare above the specificity of black concerns vis-à-vis inherent racial difference, Garvey saw Communism as another, less profitable manifestation of white oppression. In turn, Garveyism showed the Party that blacks could be mobilized on a grand scale along racial lines. Attempting to win black hearts as well as minds, the Party set out to satisfy both the racial and economic concerns of blacks. At the Fourth Congress of the Comintern in Moscow in 1922, with McKay and Harry Huiswood in attendance, a Negro Commission was formed to address the Negro Question. Discussing the UNIA and how to mobilize Black Nationalist sentiment on behalf of Communism, "The Negro Commission suggested that the UNIA's was only a particular form of race consciousness and that it was possible for race consciousness to be transformed into a progressive force. A world-historical race consciousness, recognizing the exploitation of Blacks as Blacks, but part of and related to the exploitation of other workers could develop from the earlier form" (C. Robinson 223). Race-first rhetoric was adopted, which included the eventual formation of a "Black Republic" that would be beholden only to the Comintern.

Ultimately, "The Party wanted to present itself as the legitimate heir of Garveyism, particularly in communities like Harlem and Chicago" (Kelley, *Race Rebels* 120). Yet, throughout the 1920s and early 1930s, as Garveyism waned and economic depression set in, a shift in the Party's approach to African America and the black world took place. Having been incapable of galvanizing the multitude of blacks that Garvey had during his heyday, the idea of the "Black Republic" succumbed to that of the "Black Belt" nation within a nation theory. An independent black state would not be established; instead, Black Nationalism would be subsumed under the rubric of culture. The result was that "[a]fter 1935 black nationhood clearly faded from Communist rhetoric" (Solomon 86). Replacing the rhetoric of nationhood was the idea of black culture as inherently nationalistic, but not divorced from class struggle. The goal of replacing the national front with the cultural front was to create a seamless connection between class conflict and Black Nationalist sentiment. Whereas before 1935 the Party line described Black Nationalism as a development in the awakening of class consciousness, after 1935 Black Nationalism *was* class consciousness. With this shift in emphasis, "Race and class converged in an ideological comfort zone where expressions of fierce racial opposition to the dominant society meshed with passionate class partisanship. Simple facts did not have to be articulated: The bosses were white, the lynchers were white, the landlords and merchants were white. Smoldering racial feeling could be vented through contempt for a *white* ruling class" (Solomon 183). The artists and intellectuals this study considers could not help but notice that most Communists were also white. The Party's strategy was to recode class struggle with a lexicon of race. In eliminating white difference among the white Party bosses and owners, Communists ran the risk of excising all but essentialist differences and becoming the true heirs to Garveyism. Unable to draw the line between white oppressors and white Communists, black intellectuals like McKay, Wright, and Ellison perceived the ontological imperatives addressed by the black radical tradition as betrayed by the very logic of the tradition itself. No matter how it was packaged, interracial cooperation as envisioned by the Communist Party was outside the parameters of racial-ontological imperatives of the black radical tradition. In this sense, the Party fell into the pit of racial essentialism with no means of getting out. As Kate Baldwin believes:

> Although the Soviets may have provided a useful analytic framework for deciphering the workings of capital, a Soviet belief in the use value of black Americans to accommodate the fomenting of racial consciousness nonetheless lay in a critical misperception of race. This misperception was based on an assumption that black Americans were . . . nevertheless ineluctably linked to Africa. The situating of the Negro question as fundamental to communism's future was grafted onto a continuing racial essentialism. (48)

Just as the Party's attempt to maintain nationalism without nationalism resulted in the essentializing of whites, it essentialized blacks. The old problem persisted, namely, the inability to meet the racial needs of discrete black populations. It is true, as Mullen points out, that the "American Communist Party's 1935 shift in policy toward an expanded 'cultural front' with special emphasis on black culture likewise reflected and coincided with an ongoing revision among African-American artists and intellectuals leading a national reconsideration of a black aesthetic and political program" (9). However, it is also true that this shift in policy deterred some African American artists and intellectuals from participation. Seeing the contradiction at the heart of the Party's attempt to reconcile Black Nationalism with class conflict, the writers this study examines decided that race indeed must come first. If we consider that the black radical tradition is bound to ontological imperatives, then black literary fascism as a variant of "race first" ideology is not entirely outside of the black radical circle.

I am, of course, making a claim for a definition of radicalism that includes forms of political agitation in addition to Marxism. I am not, however, making a plea for the redefinition of the term *radicalism* outside of its leftist sense.[20] On the contrary, I seek to introduce fascism into the discussion of black radicalism as a positive form of black political engagement. My purpose in doing so is not to glorify fascism but to widen the critical terrain of Marxist critique by exploring Marxism's negations. The negations of black Marxism (not everyone fell in with the Party line), of which black fascism marks but one possible effect, must be accounted for. The very notion of a black radical tradition defined along ontological lines and that excludes every radically negative political gesture, such as anarchism, syndicalism, fascism, and so forth, does not foreclose on the possibility of their occurrence, but on our ability to recognize and prevent their taking hold. This is not to say that African American conservatives or centrists haven't been given their due in the thinking on the African American political tradition. Any general account of African American political thought would have to acknowledge Booker T. Washington, and so the central place of conservatism in its narrative. But to present a more complete picture of the African American political imagination, spaces for radical black negation must also be made in the onto-genetic narrative structure that describes as well as embodies the form and content of black radicalism.[21]

The problem with the appraisal of the conscious black radical mind as entertaining solely leftist thoughts comes when we attempt to account for nonleftist radical belief outside of but in direct reaction to the field of Marxist political intellectual endeavor and social agitation. Just as any general history of the Left in the United States during the 1930s recognizes fascism as a radical "counterculture" to the counterculture of modernity, considerations of black Marxism and the black Left during the same period must suggest that at the very least quasi-fascist agitation against Marxism existed within African America.[22] The alternative calls for the belief that, by dint of race and socioeconomic position, an African American could not entertain a fascist thought—not even as a fantasy. In black fascist texts, a large degree of disenchantment with Marxist paradigms of revolutionary action stems from the idea that Marxists and Communists privilege class over race. The call for "race first" dislocates the Marxian centrality of class and offers instead the seed of racial nationalism as the generative basis of a "classless" Volk. For example, Marcus Garvey, who prized race above class, deeply hated Communism; this can be explained by his belief in the positive, intimate link between private property and fascistic notions of communal cohesion and healthy Volk existence.

In his essay "Black Fascism," Paul Gilroy extends the analysis of generic fascism beyond its European and Euro-American manifestations into the intellectual apparatus of the Garveyite movement. Gilroy defines Garveyism as quasi-fascist because the "political style" of its leader displays fascist "brutality and masculinity" as its main characteristics. This does not mean, however, that Garvey or any ideologue who falls in the Black Nationalist category necessarily espouses brutality, hypermasculinity, or other fascist beliefs aside from nationalism. Nationalism (and brutality and masculinity, for that matter) need not be fascist, but for an ideology to be considered fascist, it must contain a strong nationalist, or ultranationalist, component. The Garveyite movement possessed a nationalist sense of the unity of black peoples considered globally and racially. As a racially construed nationalist position that eschews class altogether, it pits itself against Marxism insofar as it descries race as the agent of history over and above class consciousness. This is not to say that Garvey saw no possibility for proletarian revolution, but instead that his understanding of race and nationalism sought *to prevent* the revolution from occurring.

Garvey's position on proletarian revolution follows the classical Marxist account of the rise of fascism, which hinges on a reading of nationalism as derived from a crisis in capital brought to bear on an otherwise impending proletarian revolution.[23] This analysis of fascism's causes and functioning sees fascism as a reactionary implementation of state power to crush the rising tide of proletarian revolution. Within this understanding, fascism is not an ideology in itself but rather a blunt instrument with which to implement another ideology. This classical Marxist understanding of fascism fails to apprehend its object as anything other than a repressive state apparatus utterly dependent on class struggle for its existence. Although fascism negates Marxism and Communism, it combats both by appropriation, as Ernst Nolte's "fascist minimum" makes clear.[24]

Because the Marxist account of the rise of fascism sees fascism as a reactionary bourgeois movement, it fails to explain black fascism. Du Bois's attack on the greed of the black bourgeoisie points to one area of support for fascism within African America. Other areas of support for black fascism in the 1930s were Black Cultural Nationalists, Black Nationalist labor agitators, and blacks who tried but failed to be Communists. Capable of listening to the full range of African America's voices, the liberal-humanist theory charting fascism's rise resonates well with the historical situation of African Americans from the failure of Reconstruction to the start of World War II.[25] Liberal humanism interprets fascism as the petit bourgeois reaction against rapid modernization, and its articulation of frustration with what it perceives as its impotence before the ascendance of big business and laissez-faire mass democracy. Insofar as African Americans could cite their experiences in a recently enslaved society undergoing rapid industrialization as a cause for espousing fascism, the advent of black fascism traces an economic and psychological conflict within a form of nationalism integrated with that of white America, yet exalting racial exclusion. This form of nationalism enjoyed a high level of militancy in the aftershocks of World War I. As evidenced by the huge popularity and martial quality of the Garveyite movement in the latter teens and early twenties, America's refusal to acknowledge the heroism of black soldiers, as well as the Red Summer of 1919, caused African American cultural pessimism and the perceived need for violent revolt.

Responding to this, the Jamaican-born Marcus Garvey played a major role in shaping black fascist thought. Although his impact was global in scope, I limit the field from which I create a working theory of black fascism to artists working in the United States. In doing so, I concede that politics across the black diaspora vary greatly and that any conception of black fascism must account for local knowledge and the specific material and historical circumstances of a discrete group of people. Of course, this does not mean that geographical borders created monadic political and cultural institutions. My theory of black fascism in the United States specifically relies on the general premise of Paul Gilroy's *The Black Atlantic* and Sieglinde Lemke's *Primitivist Modernism* that there exists a racial and cultural cross-pollination across the Atlantic and Caribbean that informs African American intellectual history in general and that of the interwar period in particular.

The essential characteristics of black fascism, then, cannot be thought of as an imitation of a purely "white" political form. There are no purely "white" political forms. All political ideologies are open to appropriation and improvisation across racial lines, even if only as political fantasy. In this light, the very idea that African Americans a priori could not have been attracted to fascism is absurd. Blacks can and did develop a fascist ideology of their own. The question is not whether black fascism exists, but how one can recognize it.

This problem of recognition is complicated by the fact that no black fascist political party as such ever existed. Again, this study neither suggests nor proves that African Americans organized fascist political groups, either for themselves or in support of European fascisms. The work of black fascist ideology was done instead almost exclusively on the individual level as a political and aesthetic fantasy of collective action. This fantasy appealed to a sense of dissatisfaction with Marxism while maintaining a revolutionary socialist political thrust, charting a "Third Way" between Marxism and capitalism that insisted on a heightened Black Nationalism and segregation.[26] The Third Way profited from the "core myths" within African American history: the liberating forces of a black Moses, the cultural and political autonomy of Ethiopia as the ancient arbiter of African identity and racial pride, and a reverence for the Haitian revolution as the single instance of a successful slave revolt and ensuing black republic.[27] It also addressed the "sense-making crisis" African Americans experienced as a result of their growing disdain for the "decadence" of the Harlem Renaissance, as well as the fact that the New Negro intelligentsia was laid low by the Great Depression.[28] Finally, the Third Way recognized the birth of a yet newer "New Negro," whose redress of the shortcomings of the renascent New Negro took the form of a series of fascist negations born of World War I and the crisis of democracy it exposed and exacerbated.

The thought of a black radical tradition dominated by political systems derived, even if only in part, from Marx's writings constituted the manifest content, or political conscious, of the radical dreams of black intellectuals. There is, however, also a complex and evasive subterranean black radical unconscious that manifested some of its otherwise critically repressed darkness. If indeed we can speak of "freedom dreams," then we must also be prepared to entertain the unavoidable, dystopian images of freedom nightmares in our troubled sleep of reason.

This troubled sleep is one reason why fascist ideology enjoyed widespread success among European artists and intellectuals during the 1930s, and why fascism found a place within the American cultural context of the interwar period as well. From the doctrine of Huey Long and Father Coughlin; to the Klan and Brownshirts mobilizing in Atlanta and across the country; to the similarities between FDR's early New Deal policies and those the National Socialists used to reinvigorate the German economy; to Ezra Pound's political and aesthetic agitation on behalf of Mussolini, American politicians, artists, and intellectuals appropriated fascist ideology to suit their specific needs.[29] Expressing the zeitgeist of a cultural milieu that extended across the Atlantic, fascist ideology could no more escape the cosmopolitan reach of the African American political imagination than it could that of white Americans. The refusal to concede that African American artists and writers could find some use for elements of fascist ideology betrays, in part, a desire to endow radical African American politics with a congenital leftist position. Where discourses on African American intellectual history currently trace lineages stretching across an Atlantic that disseminates Marxist and Communist ideologies, the routes end before reaching unflattering political conclusions. The supposition that Marxist ideology traverses the black Atlantic without its fascist antagonist is untenable.

Paul Gilroy's black Atlantic presents counterhegemonic, potentially utopian spaces in which black artists and intellectuals maneuver to perform their displacement and to displace dominant, oppressive political discourses. This does not mean, however, that *all* the various physical and intellectual de- and reterritorializations that occur on the black Atlantic have a utopian potential. The interpretation of black cultures, as Gilroy argues in *Against Race,* cannot be limited to positive accounts of cultural adaptation and elaboration. In tailoring dominant cultural discourses to suit black needs and unique forms of expression, black intellectuals necessarily negotiate and at times incorporate the very ideologies charged with the task of annihilating black resistance. James Clifford's "predicament of culture" names precisely the cultural forms and structures of belief that escape domination and representational hegemony as they engage in the seemingly ceaseless activities of cultural barter and exchange. Black culture, while involved, as Michael North has shown, in a dialectical, productive relationship with transatlantic modernism, does not escape modernism's darker aspects. If fascism and modernism possess a kinship demonstrated in part by writers such as Ezra Pound and Wyndham Lewis, then black modernism understood in dialogue with European and Euro-American modernisms opens itself to at least the possibility of such a charge.[30]

American culture between the wars, as Walter Kalaidjian and Michael Denning have brilliantly observed, encompasses a much wider field of operations than that of high modernist narratives of cultural production. Seen with a greater sense of cultural dialogism, it becomes clear that African American political positions were negotiated within high modernist aesthetics. The high modernist appropriation of a racialized voice smuggles in discourses of race and identity on the level of dialect and speech, and signals not simply a borrowing of what can be called "racial form" but also and inevitably the political content that manifests itself in and as such forms.[31] Appropriations of dialect and speech, both black and white, bring with them the political assumptions they carry in their "original" contexts. They displace racial identity as they symptomatically reveal the existence of an unexpected political unconscious. In this sense, heterogeneity, the impossibility of a "pure product," outlines the predicament of a culture whose contours include a politics of apparent self-annihilation as a form of "mimicry" that does not remain silent as it undoes the work it seemingly parrots.[32]

Thinkers such as Cary Nelson and William J. Maxwell, who seek to recover the intense interplay between modernism, African American literary and cultural production, and the radical politics of the Depression 1930s, rightly point to the influence of Communism and Marxism on African American aesthetics of the period and beyond. I believe, however, that we must also uncover the intellectual histories of the splintered political schools of thought brought into being by African American cultural investment in radical politics.[33] In this regard, Kalaidjian's idea that proletarian literature and culture were formative of the American avant-garde and American modernism as a whole resonates with this study insofar as it establishes the existence of American aesthetic movements in harmony with the relation of race to radical political thought. This class-based articulation of race and aesthetics is what black fascist texts identify as the problem of African American Leftist politics. Instead of a classless society brought into existence by proletarian revolution, black fascist texts eliminate class, offering in its place the racialized, hegemonic totalization of power requisite to the stabilization of the authoritarian state. As Stuart Hall argues, the total racialization of state and economic power subsumes class under the heading of race, obscuring class conflict completely, articulating the racialized state untroubled by internecine class warfare.[34] Black fascism, then, seeks to disarticulate institutionalized racial subjection and reinscribe it with its poles reversed via a pronounced anti-Marxist stance, maintaining the hegemonic structures of class and race that Marxism strives to undo. It does so not by articulating an existent, national manifestation of fascism, but by appropriating "generic fascism."

Generic Fascism

Like many European and American artists and cultural critics, African American intellectuals felt as if they were being forced to make an absolute choice between two forms of authoritarian government: fascism and Communism.[35] These intellectuals either perceived no essential difference between the two forms of government, as would happen with Richard Wright, or apprehended the nationalist bias in fascist ideology as superior to the ostensible internationalism of Communism, as did George Schuyler. As opposed to Communism, fascism's nationalist program extolling the organic unity and virtues of a disenfranchised Volk offered a powerful panacea for economic and social ills to the African American intelligentsia as well as to their European and Euro-American counterparts.[36] The position of the African American artist and that of the European or Euro-American writer were not, of course, the same. Whereas fascism's virulent racism was in many cases in the European and Euro-American contexts alluring, it was a great deterrent to the African American intellectual considering the embrace of fascist ideology. However, the writers this study considers were able to negotiate this problem. Although ultranationalist belief—which must be present in a system of ideological apparatuses if it is to be considered "fascist"—always entails racism, the racist element of fascism need not be virulent, as in the case of Franco's Spain.[37] Black Nationalism of the 1930s implied some degree of race privilege, which was not out of keeping with Spanish racism or that of very early Italian Fascism. Schuyler's *Black Empire* relishes in the programmatic genocide of whites, and Claude McKay backhandedly defends Sufi Abdul Hamid's anti-Semitism as heroic. Indeed, Depression-era Harlem was rife with anti-Semitic sentiment. In any event, it is illusory to believe that some African American intellectuals were neither racist nor anti-Semitic. One need not establish a nonracist definition of fascism in order to accommodate African American cultural life. Like members of any historically constructed "race," African Americans are capable of virulent racism and anti-Semitism, or at the very least, being attracted to them. The historical conditions of the creation and execution of the particular form and content of African American racism will be unique and thus different from those of European fascisms.

What this study calls "black literary fascism," or "black fascism," saw within fascist ideology elements other than racism that could be of use for "purely" literary representations of various forms of radical sociopolitical change. Having perceived all of the possible applications of fascist ideology for African American life, black fascist writers then, without recourse to any specific fascist program, infused their works with elements that can now be defined as fascist. An introduction to "generic" fascist ideology will be helpful in understanding this process. *Generic fascism* and *generic fascist ideology* are the operative terms of the current scholarly discourse in which characteristics of the various fascisms present before and during World War II are synthesized or discarded in order to create a working theory of fascism in general.[38] Generic fascism operates under the precept that in however many diverse national manifestations the various European fascisms appeared or how contradictory their impulses and ideologies were within a single, national political milieu, they nonetheless propounded certain consistent principles and ideological precepts. Historians and theorists of fascism gather these principles under the heading of "generic" fascism as a correlate to the study of any one given form of historical fascism, and as a field of study in its own right. In other words, "generic fascism" means no specific manifestation of the phenomenon, such as Italian Fascism, or Nazism. There has been considerable debate in the study of fascism as to whether Nazism can be considered a form of fascism, owing usually to the virulent racism central to Nazi ideology. This study treats Nazism as a form of fascism. As Roger Griffin asserts, "[t]o treat Nazism as a form of fascism is not to deny its uniqueness, but to claim that some of its causal factors and empirical aspects are thrown into relief if it is seen as a permutation of a generic phenomenon called 'fascism'" (*Fascism* 96).[39]

Removing the national specificity and virulent racism of a general notion of fascism informed solely by Nazism, Stanley G. Payne lists six characteristics of generic fascist ideology under the heading "Style and Organization," five of which will be central to this book: "1) Emphasis on esthetic structure of meetings, symbols, and political choreography, stressing romantic and mystical aspects; 2) attempted mass mobilization with militarization of political relationships and style and with the goal of mass party militia; 3) positive evaluation and use of, or willingness to use, violence; 4) extreme stress on the masculine principle and male dominance, while espousing the organic view of society; 5) specific tendency toward an authoritarian, charismatic, personal style of command, whether or not the command is to some degree initially elective" (*FCD* 7).[40] To create a flexible but rigorous working theory of fascism with which to understand black fascism, I combine Payne's list with several major critical theories of fascist ideology. Of these, the most important for this study is Walter Benjamin's identification and analysis of the means of fascist power as the aestheticization of politics.[41] An "emphasis on aesthetic structure" underlies Benjamin's conception of the mass-produced work of art, which fascism invests with myth instead of history. For Benjamin, the "essential" condition of mass-produced art is to function as a vehicle for either Communist social consciousness or fascist social delusion. Working at the level of mass psychology, the fascist appropriation of art allows for the militarization of the body politic, as Ernst Jünger celebrated, Adorno and Wilhelm Reich lamented, and the Freud of *Civilization and Its Discontents* intuited.[42]

The implied militarization of the masses contained in the work of art was not lost on Benjamin, either. In his 1930 "Theories of German Fascism," a review of a collection of essays edited by Jünger, Benjamin writes, "And the point is this: War—the 'eternal' war . . . is said to be the highest manifestation of the German nation. It should be clear that behind [this] 'eternal' war lies the idea of cultic war." (122). The cult of the warrior and the embrace of war as a first principle form the ideological armature of fascism and the work of art as fascist. In this sense, war is an ontological proving ground for the nation. When Benjamin asserts that "In the parallelogram of forces formed by these two—nature and nation—war is the diagonal" (127), he means that the medium this line traverses, the white space against which the diagonal makes itself visible, is the work of art. The mythologized nation can only appear as such in one place: not on the battlefield, as Jünger believed, but in and as the work of art as both fascist cultic mystification and its critique—as its dialectical image.

Extolling war and violence as virtues, the foundational myths of the various European fascisms celebrate the aestheticization of blood, soil, and sacrifice. Violence and war as the means of affirming the myth of the fascist state become not only requisite but desirable. This positive evaluation of violence stems from what Klaus Theweleit identifies as fascism's linked principles of masculinity, desire, and socio-organic unity. According to Theweleit, the protofascist is an ex-soldier who understands the experience of World War I as essentially male, communally binding, and spiritually purifying. For the protofascist, women are "the feminine": pacifistic, unclean, fragmenting, and ultimately annihilating. In reaction to this, argues Theweleit, the protofascist attempts to create and maintain the structural integrity of his ego through violent, misogynist means. If women are construed by fascist ideology as agents of psychical fragmentation and the ultimate dissolution of the male ego, then the unified ego is essentially male and constituted outside the body of the protofascist over and against women.

Theweleit's genitive model of fascism reflects the general tendency of fascist ideology's extreme antifeminist stance. As Kevin Passmore has noted, "Fascism is as deeply opposed to feminism as it is to socialism. Historic fascists generally argued that women's primary function was domestic and reproductive" (123). Feminism is coupled with socialism, and so with a politics against which fascism is positioned. Misogyny in fascist ideology runs deep enough that feminism is viewed as an external political threat, an anti-ideology that promises to rend the fabric of the fascist state in two. The seam along which feminism tears is the normative connection between traditional gender roles. Because women had to enter the work force in large numbers during the First World War, gendered subject positions fell into question in terms of earning potential. This confused economics of gender engendered a crisis of masculinity and, by extension, social decay. "The alleged crisis in gender relations," Passmore continues, "was seen as a sign of social decay. Radical workers or turbulent national minorities were thought to be affected with 'feminine' passions" (123). On the surface, the blurring of economically determined gender roles indicated a wider social sickness. That women could leave the domestic sphere and earn as much as their male counterparts bespoke of nothing less than the decay, or degeneration, of society. The point was not that women were getting stronger but that men were becoming weaker. The weakening of the phallus metonymically signified the weakening of culture.

It was a short step from this misogynistic understanding of culture to a reading of national minorities as both destructive agents and themselves feminine. As they seduced the hegemonic cultural body with feminine wiles, national minorities infected this body with the disease of the feminine. In exhorting that women know their place and remain at home, fascists by proxy ordered the strict separation of the nation proper from the national minorities festering within it. If the hypermasculine national majority were to regain its potent phallic stature, national minorities, too, would have to know their place and stay there.

For as clear-cut as fascist misogyny seems, it was not without its ambiguities. "There was, however, a contradiction in these policies, for fascists wanted women in the home yet politicized functions once regarded simply as 'domestic': reproduction, education, and consumption all became national duties" (Passmore 126). Restoring traditional gender roles was not simply a matter of cultural hygiene. The body of the nation depended on clear, anachronistic gender positions if it were to function as an organic whole. Women had national duties to perform; their clear understanding of their place in society and culture made it possible for them to discharge these duties properly. The contradiction arose because often women were required to execute their tasks outside of the home.

"National duties" extended beyond shopping for dinner, consisting as well in political education and participation. In 1930s Germany, women's groups were formed with the goal of advancing the aims of Nazi ideology. The work women performed did not challenge male economic power; women earned little to nothing. Instead, they accrued intangible wealth on behalf of Nazi propaganda and ideology. The primary effect women's work had was to embody the traditional gender roles espoused by the Nazis. The work of women was to show concretely and emphatically that women do not work. As Gättens relates: "The significance of women's employment in the political discourse of the thirties . . . is not so much based on the economic impact of women's work but on the potential in altering the definition of what is male and what is female" (33). Far from fascism's ostensible victims, women who participated in fascism's concretizing of its ideology created and bolstered fascist power. In the case of Nazi Germany, "The question of women's involvement in the Nazi machinery can be seen from two sides: officially women were excluded from the party leadership . . . but unofficially they helped both to bring the Nazis to power and to maintain it there" (E. Martin 20). Convinced that the performative nature of gender was nature itself, many women under fascist regimes willingly played their oppressed parts. The misogynist revulsion Theweleit finds in the fascist mind-set became for many women desirable. Woman's desire allows the fascist to transform his loathing into a positive means of identification. In reestablishing traditional gender identities, masculine self-loathing is masked as heroic masculine potency. This means that the external, feminine object of identification is essential for the fascist seeking a structural model on which to base his misogynist strivings for ego coherence.

Most important for fascism were the means of identification themselves, independent of such particular manifestations as fascist misogyny. As Lacoue-Labarthe and Jean-Luc Nancy recognize in their essay "The Nazi Myth," the charismatic (male) ruler supplies the image for this identification and provides what Lacoue-Labarthe and Nancy call *the means of identification*. By this, they mean that myth (the myth of the Führer and the Volk), like art, provides the means, or narrative, with which the myth's audience creates subjective identity. The Nazi myth translates the subject into the ideological apparatuses structuring and elaborating the belief, racist in essence, in the nation as sacred. Lacoue-Labarthe and Nancy identify the subject of modern philosophy as identical to what they call the Nazi Myth, such that "the [Nazi state] is to be conceived as the Subject-State. . . . [I]n the last instance it is in modern philosophy, in the fully realized metaphysics of the Subject, that ideology finds its real guarantee" (294). For Lacoue-Labarthe and Nancy, the realization of the metaphysics of the subject is the task assigned to myth. Myth provides a teleological narrative in which the subject finds itself, one that needs no justification beyond its own premises. The Nazi state depends on this work of myth; the state cannot be identified separately from it. According to Lacoue-Labarthe and Nancy the state as myth operates as the mechanism of identification by which individual and collective subjects recognize themselves. Myth as the Nazi state elaborates, in effect, a work of art. This is why Lacoue-Labarthe and Nancy write that "the problem of myth is always indissociable from that of art, not so much because myth is a collective creation or work . . as because myth, like the work of art that exploits it, is an instrument of *identification*. It is, in fact, the *mimetic* instrument par excellence" (298). The recognition of the Nazi myth as the instrument of identification means that we find at the shared heart of art and the Nazi state the work of myth as implicated in the history of modern philosophical thought. For Lacoue-Labarthe and Nancy, the Nazi appropriation and deployment of the power of myth constructs the ultranationalist sentiment that provides the cohesiveness of the Volk.

This conception of myth informs Žižek's point that not only is there no "ideology without a trans-historical, 'authentic' kernel, but rather that it is only the reference to such a trans-ideological kernel that renders ideology 'workable'" (98). Myth and ideology share the same "authentic" essential feature that invests each with a quality of individual subjective transcendence and national apotheosis. Žižek goes on to place this observation within the context of Nazi myth: "This aesthetic suspension of the political . . . was at the very core of the fantasmatic background of the Nazi attitude: at stake in it was something more than politics, an ecstatic aestheticized experience of Community best exemplified precisely by the nightly rituals during the Nuremberg rallies" (98). Myth as ideology is the aesthetic form of fascism par excellence, in that, as Laclau believes, myth is essentially an empty vessel to be filled with whatever political ideology matches the goals of power. Laclau's notion of ideology as composed of free-floating signifiers that have no intrinsic meaning but are given substance by their position in a wider ideological structure underscores the fact that the fascist appropriation of myth can be tailored to accommodate any system of political thought, regardless of race. Race does not prohibit fascist ideology from, as Roger Griffin concludes, "draw[ing] its internal cohesion and driving force from a core myth that a period of perceived national decline and decadence is giving way to one of rebirth and renewal in a post-liberal new order" (*Nature* 14). Providing "a core myth" of rebirth and renewal for a nation as racial group, the fascist work of art stages the union of myth and ideology as it creates the mythic experience of an "imagined community."

Finally, my study assumes that fascism constructs, echoing Bataille, a matrix of rigorous social interdiction, homogeneity, and latent transgression. This matrix both gives rise to and supports what Deleuze and Guattari understand in *Anti-Oedipus* as fascism's eradication of the state as a "body without organs." In other words, fascist ideology seeks to direct the flow of the various branches of ideas that make up the almost amorphous network of communal thought into a single tributary: the mythic Volk. This Volk signifies a subservient body politic created, as Foucault states in his preface to *Anti-Oedipus*, by tapping into "the fascism in us all, in our heads and in our everyday behavior, the fascism that causes us to love power, to desire the very thing that dominates and exploits us" (xiii). Fascism begins as a desire, a misogynist fantasy of power capable of being actuated in aesthetic representations of unadulterated power. I understand fascism, then, as more than a historical phenomenon subject to theoretical analysis and synthesis into a generic quantity. Following the thinkers whose theories of fascism I've just briefly sketched, I see fascism as a psychological event that is symptomatically represented in historical-material reality as well as in fantasy and myth. Behind any fascist pageant and work of art, fantasies and myths of power lurk and inform all of their partial representations.

Fascist Aesthetics

The greatest "pageant of power" to come out of a fascist regime is Riefenstahl's *Triumph of the Will*, which Berman views as representative of fascist aesthetics: "*Triumph of the Will* defines a fascist rhetoric as the displacement of verbal by visual representations: the power of the image renders scripture obsolete" ("Written" 61). For Berman, even fascist literary aesthetics privileges the visual over the verbal. The image in the text takes precedence over the function of the image in a system of writing. Proposing something like Imagism's incorporation of the aesthetics of the plastic arts, Berman sees fascist modernism as constructed around the production of the Imagistic ideogram. The ideogram conveys fascist ideology without transmitting it through a phonological meaning. The challenge, then, for the fascist literary text is to manufacture in ideograms a practice that Berman defines as "the insistence on the priority of image over writing as a stratagem of fascist power" (62). Finding itself in a seemingly paradoxical situation, the fascist literary text denies its own textuality to express something it inherently lacks. The combination of the idea and the picture shatters the written word in order to reconstruct, from archetypical as well as stock images culled from the politically charged pop-cultural atmosphere, an ideogrammatic-ideological premise. The main referent for the fascist ideogram is for Berman the Führer: "Without doubt, fascist modernism, at least in the German context, invokes images of leadership figures toward which an unmistakably homoerotic desire is directed" ("Written" 206). The fascist literary text functions on two distinct, yet tangential levels. First, the text must evoke homosexual desire and then cathect that libidinal energy onto the idea of the leader. The image of the leader must not necessarily be presented, as long as the chain of signifiers leading to that image is followed by the reader. Therefore, fascist modernism provokes a sexual response that it then directs toward the leader. Beginning inside the reader by presenting images that arise from within her own thoughts and her life-world, the fascist text guides these libidinal impulses into the political arena, where they are devoured by a preexisting iconography of dictatorial power. What Berman describes is essentially the aesthetic as a means of identification that draws its strength from the sexual desires of the forming subject.

Once the masses have, through the work of art, libidinally invested in the persona of the Führer, they are then prepared to comprehend the ideologically overdetermined, propagandistic manifest content of the text. This content narrates the myth of the Volk: "The idiosyncratically conservative character of German fascism and its ideological appeal to the antiurban sympathies of the urban masses generates images of a premodern community of the folk" ("Written" 206). The "antiurban sympathies" of the urban masses find their measure in fascist primitivist fantasies. These fantasies essentially superimpose the city on the country, the past on the present, and allow the urban masses to escape internally their "unnatural" existence. This escape into a primitive purity is achieved only communally; it is not attainable for the atomized, city-dwelling individual of modernity. The fascist work of art, then, presents a temporally distorted urban rustic and achieves this effect not through the linguistic force of the writing but the "dream work" performed by the reader bombarded with images (here understood as ideograms). The fascist literary text functions like a Freudian dream in that it plumbs the depths of a preverbal unconscious in order to cathect the idea of the leader with sexual and political libidinal energies. Once this is done, the text then analyzes itself, highlighting its primitivist strains and offering a mythologically charged, communally shared narrative.

In this sense, the fascist aesthetic eradicates material history in favor of a mythohistorical, teleological progression. As Hewitt surmises, it fills history emptied of its contents with the propaganda of myth: "As the moment of full unfolding, the avant-garde, no less than fascism, could think itself as both the completion and liquidation of historical sequentiality. If a modernist history promises such plenitude, it must nevertheless within its own progressive logic defer that moment. In making good on that promise, Fascist Modernism both realizes and de-realizes the modernist logic of history" (7). Linking "the modernist logic of history" with fascist aesthetics, Hewitt finds that both proceed along the same historical trajectory. Fascist modernism deviates from modernism "proper" only in that it presents history as completed in myth, and not as a process of becoming without end. Whereas modernism gives values to its metaphors to show how these values deconstruct themselves, "Fascist aestheticization would be the movement beyond any systematic encoding of values into the realm of metaphor" (165). Thus, fascist aesthetics produces the effect of the completion of history in myth by saying nothing. The fascist text remains a series of cryptic images that cannot be systematized and thus accrue concrete, deconstructable meaning. These texts function like chameleons, constantly taking the form of whatever is at hand to achieve their aims and protect themselves from stable definition. The reason the fascist aesthetic is so difficult for critics to limn is because it utilizes any aesthetic means necessary in an attempt to remain indefinable. Without context and contour, the fascist text annihilates the words with which it is written and appeals directly to the unconscious. In so doing, its propaganda speaks "unmediated" to the emotions of the reader and cannot be reasoned with.

However, the indefinable character of the fascist text does not mean that, as Falasca-Zamponi believes,

> fascism's identity was always in flux; certainly a core of assumptions and values, although loosely structured, continuously operated within fascism. Indeed, no movement can ever be said to be fixed, an objectified and objectifiable entity. Nor do self-proclamations, such as Mussolini's denial of a permanent political stance, necessarily convey the truth or postulate reality. But the moment proclamations become public and are shared intersubjectively, they acquire a power of their own, they cast and frame prospective actions, and they make the speaker liable to its referent, whether it is to embrace, retract, eradicate, or assail it. (4)

Falasca-Zamponi correctly points out that fascism, no matter how amorphous its ideological premises, maintains a basic structure from which it develops its various positions. More important, the mode by which fascism creates its subjects, through intersubjective experience and shifting yet appropriable referents, determines the nature of its political praxis. The work of art is one way in which an intersubjective identity of the Volk is established. Thus, "the power of discourse, including its nonlinguistic forms (rituals, myths, and images), as an essential element in the formation of the fascist regime's self-identity, the construction of its goals and definition of ends, the making of power" (Falasca-Zamponi 3). Discourse in and as the work of art determines the nature and extent of fascist power. In this formulation, fascist aesthetics is a malleable discourse capable of assuming whatever forms necessary to achieve the goals of power. Such an aesthetic hinges on forces determined wholly outside the realm of the aesthetic, treating internal developments in literary history as superfluous to the work of art. In effect, the fascist work of art is not a work of art but propaganda presented as art and maintaining art's primary means of identification, the psychological actualization of myth. There is, then, no fascist work of art, only fascism disguised as art.

That's not to say that art cannot be fascistic, as in the case of the modernists Pound, Lewis, and others. Indeed, fascism and modernism shared a number of themes. As Mark Antliff explains, "Common denominators uniting modernist aesthetics and fascism include concepts of cultural, political, and biological regeneration; the use of avant-garde techniques, such as montage; notions of 'secular religion'; primitivism; and anticapitalist theories of space and time" (2). The points of commonality Antliff identifies do not merely entail an affinity between modernist aesthetics and fascist ideology; rather, they indicate a much more intimate relationship between fascism and modernism in terms of their shared theoretical aims.

This recognition of shared aesthetic and political visions sometimes led artists to support fascism openly. Pound and Lewis saw in the politics of Mussolini and Hitler, respectively, viable solutions to cultural ills. "Pound's fascism and anti-Semitism," Morrison suggests, "have their origins in a profound and potentially revolutionary dissatisfaction with the liberal establishment; the anticapitalist, antibourgeois fervor that motivates both need not have assumed the reactionary form it did" (4). Pound shares with the fascists the same general dissatisfaction with the liberal establishment. Morrison is careful to note that such dissatisfaction does not necessitate the development or embrace of fascist ideology. Pound's turn to Mussolini was motivated by more than surface distinctions; he found in Italian Fascism and in the figure of Mussolini in particular the combined aesthetic and political solution to what he understood as an otherwise irrevocable cultural decay.

This conflation of the aesthetic and political in Pound's life and thought highlighted his conception of the artist as Duce, and the Duce as artist. For Pound, the promise of Mussolini was to be realized in the absolute fusion of aesthetics and politics, art and life. With this conception of the Duce as artistic genius in mind, Pound, before meeting with Mussolini for the first time, "sent ahead to *il Duce* a copy of his first 30 cantos, and Mussolini was looking at them when Pound was ushered into his presence" on January 30, 1933 (Redman 95). In essence, there was no one more qualified than Mussolini to judge the *Cantos,* in that the *Cantos* sought to do in poetry what fascism attempted to achieve in politics. This is not to say that the *Cantos* are, as a whole, a fascist poem simply on the basis that fascism and Pound's aesthetic project sought to achieve the same goals in ostensibly separate media. But still, one cannot so easily exonerate Pound's poem on the same aesthetic grounds. Hatlen proclaims, "I do not believe that the *Cantos* can accurately be labeled a 'fascist poem,' simply because Pound's political ideology undergoes a radical decomposition—or, if you like, a deconstruction—as it is transmuted by Pound's ideogrammic method" (Hatlen 146). The logic behind Hatlen's dismissal of the *Cantos* as "fascist poem" lies in the belief that the modernist aesthetic in its formal properties is radically separate from fascism. That is to say, modernist form, and by extension form in general, is not ideological. Yet, as discussed earlier, the ideogram is the aesthetic tool par excellence in fascist aesthetics. In fascist aesthetics, the marriage between form and ideology, image and text, is completed in the figure of the ideogram. Therefore, the very formal aesthetic practice that would seem to excuse, if not Pound himself, but his mode of aesthetic production leads further to his culpability.

Lewis's relationship with fascism, too, is more complicated than a purely political belief. As Sherry believes, "What decides Lewis's preference for fascism over democracy is not the putative difference between the values of oppression and liberality; it is an aesthetic standard defined primarily in visual terms—for him the clarity and directness available (mainly) to the eye. His choice represents a distinction between better and worse states of perception, not between States founded on creeds either admired or disapproved" (102). As with Pound, Lewis's attraction to fascism is related to the visual. Through fascist "clarity and directness" Lewis discerns an aesthetic of political responsibility and action. What interests Lewis in fascist aesthetics are precision of representation and acuteness of vision. In this sense, Lewis raises fascist aesthetics to the level of an epistemological imperative. If the aesthetic becomes the site par excellence for the speaking of truth, then the political depends on the aesthetic to realize its potential. The aesthetic mediates between event and context and makes ideology and action consumable at once. For Lewis, the only essential distinction fascism can claim from, for example, democracy is the nature of its representations. Fascism's defining characteristic is aesthetic form. Thus, "fascism differs from current democratic method mainly or only on the matter of linguistic directness. Fascists at least say what they do, and that, Lewis claims, is the least we can hope for" (Sherry 102).

The difference between fascist artwork and the fascistic work of art is precisely this concern for the internal movement of the work itself in its wider place in literary history and aesthetics. The fascist work of art is essentially propaganda that uses the means of identification inherent in art to advance the goals of power and create the subject-state. These were not the goals of the avant-garde; however, this does not mean that their works do not contain fascistic elements that could have been and were appropriated by fascism. As Adamson points out, "regardless of [the avant-garde's] intentions, their creation of a potent rhetoric of cultural renewal ultimately played into the hands of fascism, which, in need of intellectual credibility, appropriated this rhetoric and adapted it to more politically explicit but also more culturally impoverished and dangerous ends" (262). While fascist aesthetics has the ability to transform itself to suit the needs of power, it also is capable of appropriating other works of art and transforming them to meet its needs. One key aspect of fascist aesthetics would be, then, the appropriation of the rhetoric of the modernist work of art. This process begins with fascism's recognition in the work of art of affinities, or homologies, between the aesthetic and political realms. Though without fascistic intent, a "potent rhetoric of cultural renewal" in Eliot's *The Waste Land* (1922) could later easily lend itself to the same purpose in fascist political rhetoric and life. When approaching the fascistic work, the task of fascist aesthetics is to strip the work of art of the aesthetic itself and maintain the rhetoric. Thus, Nazism could denounce the aesthetics of modern art as degenerate while maintaining many of modernism's cultural claims.

Cultural ills could be cured through fascist aesthetic principles of the work of art as inherently unstable, hence easily appropriable and transformable. Through "aesthetic overproduction" the fascist work of art is overburdened with a stockpile of images it may deploy in any form or structure that is capable of functioning as a means of identification. "If an 'aesthetic overproduction' is necessary to compensate for fascism's 'unstable ideological core,'" Golsan suggests, "then that overproduction must be expected to possess and provide a certain cohesiveness lacking in the ideology itself" (*Fascism, Aesthetics* xii). The infamously nebulous quality of fascist ideological systems takes clear shape in the work of art. A lack of ideology is supplemented by the aesthetic. Therefore, fascist ideology cannot realize itself without the work of art. We recall that fascist aesthetics marshals an army of metaphors but invests concretely in none of them. It says nothing while saying something to the emotions of the masses, leaving enough empty space in its presentation for the creation of the subject and the subject-state. The creation of the subject is for fascism self-reflexive in that fascism finds itself in its own fantasy. Fascism succumbs to its own means of identification, basing its ideological premises and the cohesiveness of its logic on its fractured mirror image. Fascist aesthetics, then, serves the purpose of creating the fascist state. The work of art is not merely a propaganda tool used to create the mythological-ideological core of the Volk; it creates this core for the state as well. The fascist state is always trapped in a reverie.

The Black Fascist Aesthetic

While the ideogram is not a feature of black fascist aesthetics, the priority of the image as a "vortex" of meaning plays a dominant role. The concern in the black literary fascist text is for effect over coherent, accessible meaning. That is not to say that the images presented in texts such as *Black Empire* or *Moses, Man of the Mountain* are ideologically incoherent, empty signifiers. Images in these texts attempt to perform the same tasks as those in the fascist aesthetics of Pound and Lewis, and in Riefenstahl's propaganda films. They seek to cause the reader to invest libidinally in the figure of the Führer without presenting its aims as such. This sexual, often homosexual, investment in the embodiment of fascist rule is effected by the image's lack of stable content. As in fascist aesthetics, the "open architecture" of the image-laden black fascist text instigates a process in the reader whereby she may insert herself in the text not merely as a participant in a fantasy but as a forming subject that is completed by a textually induced delusion.

In black fascist aesthetics, this "delusion" is conjured by the form of the texts themselves in collusion with the images each text deploys. Every text under consideration in this study is in its way incomplete. From Garvey's loose musings on the nature of power in *Message to the People*, to Wright's monolithic but unrealized *The Outsider*, each text contains its own unique lack. Claude McKay's novel *Harlem Glory* remains an unfinished fragment. Hurston's *Moses* is, as will be discussed, a wild heteroglossia of elements that she herself was deeply unsatisfied with. Although the reasons for the "incompleteness" of each text can be found in practical concerns of composition—for example, *Black Empire* was serialized over a long period of time and Schuyler was unable to tie up all the loose ends—that does not belay the effect of the fragmentary nature of each text. This, combined with overdetermined images that cathect libidinal energies into the figure of the Führer, helps to identify black fascist texts as practicing a form of fascist aesthetics.

Another element of black literary fascism is the presentation of a mythological narrative of the greatness of the Volk. This narrative recasts the Volk as it creates the bonds that unite black communities as a single Volk. To achieve this effect, the myth destroys material history and replaces it with various mythological points of reference that the reader must then string together. It is this work of the reader that helps to form the individual and collective subjects, and attempts to bring mythological teleology to fruition. The task of the black fascist aesthetic is, then, threefold. First, it interpolates the individual subject through a sexual identification with the Führer. Through a guided but loosely defined reading process, it then leads the individual identification to the communal identity found in the mythology of the Volk. With regard to the means of identification, this is the text's ultimate goal. The initial, individual identification acts as bait to hook the reader into group identification. In absorbing the reader into the group though myth as means of identification, the black fascist text then makes good on its historical promise in fantasy. History in the black fascist text is the medium through which the means of identification justify themselves. By learning a new history or by misrecognizing myth as history, the collective and individual subjects cathect not only the Führer, but the state. The state is the instrument through which the Führer will realize the greatness of the Volk as promised at the beginning of mythological time. The end of history comes with the realization of the goals of the black subject-state.

Only latently in accord with Du Bois's belief that all art is propaganda, the black fascist text is ostensibly antipropagandistic. It does not seek to enlist the reader in an existent political program or to galvanize the public to address a specific social ill. Its goals are much more open and fluid: it seeks to create subjects. This is not to say that art as propaganda does not address the subject but that it speaks to an existent subject that it tries to sway. Once again, the difference between fascist art and fascistic art pivots on this axis. Fascist art is propaganda; fascistic art creates subjects that will then be ready to accept the directives of fascist propaganda. The task of the black fascist text is not to cause the reader to embrace Nazism or Italian Fascism but to lay the psychological basis for the creation of a totally new fascist entity. Black fascist subjectivity is not a copy of Italian Fascist subjectivity; it is for itself.

The infusion of fascist ideology and fascist aesthetics into the black fascist text produced an open text in which the subject enters in order to become a different, other subject. This process of becoming reflects itself in the texts' form. Black literary fascism did not favor socialist realism's insistence on materialist representation. Often fantastical, black literary fascism could not present itself in a mirror image of reality. The world it would reflect did not exist. In *Black Empire,* Schuyler depends on a near-future narrative as a means of placing a black fascist state in the realm of possibility, and as a way of bringing to fruition a latent, unformed black fascist subjectivity. *The Outsider's* Cross Damon leads an implausible life not because Wright failed aesthetically but because Wright's objectives were incompatible with the realm of the possible. Hurston retells the story of Moses because in her estimation there was no contemporary, or even historical, black Moses on which to base her fascistic musings. The "black Moses" Marcus Garvey directs his vague political pedagogy and speculations to an ill-defined audience, leaving enough room in his *Message* for misrecognition, misprision, and reflective subject-formation. By presenting their works as open and constantly in flux, black literary fascists created a space in which the reader's directed "becoming" could take place.

While necessary to the work of becoming, this ambiguity produced a variety of fascisms. Each author this study considers understood fascism in a slightly different way. Although each text shares a core of ideological premises that allows for the text's identification as fascistic, the primary concerns of all black fascist texts are not the same. Just as there were several different European fascisms, there were various black fascisms. The reason for this is that there was no black consensus regarding fascism, no black fascist political party to create consensus, and ultimately no unified vision of Black Nationalism to form the basis of a black fascist party. In the 1930s, the closest figure to achieve unanimity on the question of Black Nationalism was still Marcus Garvey, even though he had fallen from the public eye. The memory of Garvey lingered, and, if fascism depends on ultranationalistic sentiment, Garvey was directly invoked. The black fascist use of Garvey was neither uncritical nor unproblematic: Garvey himself took a black fascist position that had to be negotiated. Also, Garvey's Back-to-Africa project, as well as the man himself, was seen as a failure. Although the strongest model for the presentation of the charismatic back fascist leader, Garvey also posed the greatest obstacle to this presentation. One of the tasks of the black fascist text was to revere Garvey while reviling him, to glorify certain aspects of his movement while disavowing others. Because Garvey was such a pivotal figure for black literary fascism, the next chapter is devoted to the question of his fascism and can be read as a supplemental discourse on the nature of black literary fascism.

Using Marcus Garvey as both model and foil for a black fascist aesthetic, the authors here under consideration created a fictive world in which a black fascist state could be realized. In doing so, they constructed a political ontology of black fascism centered on both the charismatic leader and an aesthetic imperative. However, if fascist aesthetics ultimately helped foster obedience to a normative, "classless" state and a charismatic, deified ruler, then individual instances of black fascist aesthetics cannot be said to have performed the same task. Instead, the black fascist text created the state and the charismatic ruler to which it sought to subject the reader. In short, the black fascist text laid the groundwork for the possibility of black fascism.[43] Theories of the Volk; of race chauvinism; of an extreme masculinist politico-cultural praxis and aesthetic; of ultranationalism; of racial militarization and violence; of the subordination of reason to vitalism in quest of recapturing a mythic, originary, essential moment of definition of and for the racially coded people: all of these fascist ideological imperatives exist in the literary output of a considerable number of black authors working on the United States during the Depression. If we understand the Harlem Renaissance as an artistic movement of diverse political ideologies that gave way to Depression-era radicalism, then the assumption holds that the period directly succeeding the Harlem Renaissance—officially dating the Renaissance's end with the Harlem Riot of March 19, 1935—must have entertained a far wider field of radical political difference than previously believed.[44] Inasmuch as the end of the Harlem Renaissance and the onset of the Great Depression gave birth to a new, positive, and exhilarating chapter of a black radical tradition defined by Marxist political engagement, it also begat monsters.[45]

2   The Myth of Marcus Garvey
Black Fascism and Nationalism

> We had disciplined men, women, and children in training for the liberation of Africa. The black masses saw that in this extreme nationalism lay their only hope and readily supported it. Mussolini copied Fascism from me but the Negro reactionaries sabotaged it.
> —Marcus Garvey, interview with Joel Rogers (1937)

As overt as Garvey's admiration for the fascist dictators was, his relationship with fascism remains largely unexplored. In an effort to downplay negative aspects of his complex political thought, critics usually characterize Garvey's fascination with fascism as the product of "naïve identification," a lamentable infatuation. For example, Robert A. Hill, in his introduction to *Marcus Garvey: Life and Lessons*, says that Garvey "identified with the rise of both Hitler and Mussolini from lower-class status, and admired the power manifested in their nationalistic brand of leadership. He praised both men in the early thirties as self-made leaders who had restored their nations' pride, and used the resurgence of Italy and Germany as an example to blacks for the possible regeneration of Africa. He admired in particular the remarkable ideological stamp the fascist leaders had succeeded in imprinting on the world" (Hill and Blair lvii). Edmund David Cronon also takes up the Garvey-fascism gauntlet, albeit briefly, in his *Black Moses*. As with Hill's assessment, the answer lies in Garvey's naïveté: "One may question whether Garvey was aware of all the connotations of either fascism or Communism, but certainly his UNIA, with its fierce chauvinistic nationalism and strongly centralized leadership, had fascist characteristics" (Cronon 199). The implications of these "fascist characteristics," aside from the fact that they exist, Cronon never examines.

The desire to suppress the more disturbing aspects of Garvey's philosophy and opinions, such as his anti-Semitism and fascism, accounts for why Rupert Lewis condemns "some historians" who find sympathy between Garvey and his fascist contemporaries. "A by-product of

Garvey's stand on the Italo-Ethiopian war," Lewis argues, "is that some historians have allowed superficial comparisons between Garvey's oratorical style and those of the fascist leaders, Hitler and Mussolini, to mask his efforts to rally support for the Ethiopian cause and his clear-cut anti-fascist position" (174). If bringing to bear anti-Semitic rhetoric against Ethiopia's emperor at the time the African nation succumbed to fascist Italy does not in some way impugn notions of Garvey's "clear-cut anti-fascist position," then the fact that Garvey himself expressed open admiration for Mussolini and Hitler while accusing them of stealing his political style should. But even if it does not, then Garvey's claim that "Mussolini and Hitler copied fascism from me. . . . Mussolini and Hitler copied the program of the UNIA," however improbable, speaks to something far more collusive in his position vis-à-vis fascist ideology.[1]

Hardly the invention of insidious or insane historians, Garvey's admiration for Mussolini and Hitler was overt and integral to his ideological program and African colonization scheme. As Lawrence W. Levine has remarked, "Even as [Garvey] denounced Benito Mussolini for his rape of Ethiopia, he openly admired aspects of his regime." (136). Tony Martin adds that "Garvey hoped that the black race would produce a Hitler and that black people would acquaint themselves with Hitler's ideas. By 1934, however, mindful of his own experience in the United States, he concluded that a black Hitler could be permanently successful only in Africa, for Africa afforded a far greater opportunity for an appeal along nationalistic lines than areas in the African dispersion" (*Race First* 60–61). Clearly evincing a deep investment in fascism, Garvey's identification with Mussolini and Hitler can be read accurately if one takes into consideration what Paul Gilroy refers to as Garvey's fascist "political style" ("Black Fascism" 71). The point in examining Garvey's political style in relation to fascist ideology is not, as Gilroy puts it, "to undermine the extraordinary achievements of the Garveyite movement, nor to discount the very real antiblack racism of European fascists." Instead the goal is to highlight "affinities between Garvey and the fascists" (70). Garvey shared, however, more than "affinities" with the fascists. As Wilhelm Reich recognizes, "To the detriment of genuine efforts to achieve freedom, fascism was and is still conceived as the dictatorship of a small revolutionary clique. The tenacity with which this error persists is to be ascribed to our fear of recognizing the true state of affairs: fascism is an *international* phenomenon, which pervades all bodies of human society of *all* nations" (xiii). Once critics view fascism as more than a strictly European phenomenon, Garvey's enthusiasm for, and strategic investment in, fascist ideology becomes visible. Indeed, his didactic *Message to the People* (1937) knowingly adapts fascist ideology to the rhetoric of the Garveyite movement in an effort to instruct his acolytes in the art of mass manipulation as well as racial uplift. As Garvey knew and Adorno makes clear, "Fascism, in order to be successful as a political movement, must have a mass basis. It must secure not only the frightened submission but the active cooperation of the great majority of the people" (Adorno, "Introduction" 230). It would be the task of Garvey's faithful to win the hearts and minds of the masses and create a fascist base.

Garvey offered his *Message* to the few students in attendance—all the remaining faithful and elite of his movement—at an intensive, weeklong session of the "College of African Philosophy" conducted in Canada. Here the students learned every aspect of Garvey's philosophy, including his fascistic understanding of the exercise of political power under the aegis of a dictator. In addition, aside from demonstrating a great deal of admiration for Hitler and Mussolini, Garvey's nuanced discourse in *Message to the People* reveals a philosophical affinity with the fascist power of subjection, which embeds state apparatuses in a transformative myth of the Volk as the body politic of the absolute subject-state of mythical history. As this chapter shows, it is in myth and in the Idealist philosophy of the subject that Garvey's *Message* goes beyond admiration for, and identification with, fascist dictators and appropriates their ideas for the ideological apparatus of the Garveyite movement. I begin with an examination of Garvey's negative reaction to Emperor Haile Selassie during the Ethiopian crisis, which was counterbalanced at this time by his admiration for Mussolini. I then consider similarities in Mussolini's and Garvey's theories of the state. Ultimately, I find that Garvey in the later 1930s describes a political project of black uplift that owes a great debt to fascist ideology and provides the backbone for subsequent aesthetic attempts to envision a black fascist state.

The Line of Solomon

Marcus Mosiah Garvey was a forgotten man by the time of his death on June 10, 1940. Robert Hill notes that the public lost track of him to such an extent that an "erroneous report of his death circulated in May [that lead] to printing of obituaries in newspapers around the world" (*Life and Lessons* lxviii). How could the most influential leader of the early 1920s black diaspora become, in the span of a decade, so marginalized? Unable to return to the United States owing to his 1923 conviction, 1925 incarceration, and subsequent 1927 deportation for mail fraud, Garvey lived in London during the latter half of the 1930s, where he edited and published the periodical the *Black Man*. It was in 1935 in the pages of the *Black Man* that Garvey launched his untimely and ill-considered attacks on the Ethiopian emperor Haile Selassie, who was also exiled in London. Garvey's lack of consequence in black political life of the latter half of the 1930s can be traced to this untimely and ill-advised criticism of Ethiopia's negus (Nembhard 236).[2]

Blaming Selassie for Mussolini's conquest of the spiritual center of his dream of a black Zion, Garvey also felt embittered toward the emperor because of the popularity he enjoyed in Garvey's native Jamaica, where Selassie was revered as a god (Jah) by the Rastafarians.[3] Also, while in London, Selassie refused Garvey an audience, a slight that Judith Stein rightly sees as the provocation for the sustained critical posture Garvey adopted toward the Ethiopian emperor (271). One cannot, however, understand the reason for Garvey's vitriolic attacks on Selassie at such a crucial juncture in Pan-African politics as singularly personal. Doing so relegates the later Garvey to the role of childish fool and ignores the consistent nature of his philosophy, which Stein characterizes as knee-jerk "mercurial politics" that express "personal relations." The personal and the political in Garvey's thought neither contradict nor lack relevancy to one another. Garvey did not hastily condemn Selassie as a means of revenge at a time when such an act would be tantamount to political suicide: for better or worse, his comments were made after reflection; they calculated carefully, and wrongly, the political effect of a denunciation of Ethiopia's rightful sovereign that Garvey believed was correct and warranted.

The miscalculated attack on Selassie was not the first time Garvey overestimated what his public would and would not tolerate from him. He won no blacks to his cause with statements like: "Between the Ku Klux Klan and the Morefield Storey National Association for the Advancement of 'Colored' People group, give me the Klan for their honesty of purpose towards the Negro. They are better friends to my race, for telling us what they are, and what they mean, thereby giving us a chance to stir for ourselves, than all the hypocrites put together with their false gods and religions, notwithstanding" (60).[4] Such ill-conceived pronouncements are more than the mercurial politics of a rash man driven primarily by personal considerations and one-sided scores to settle. They are also, as Tony Sewell believes, expressions of a man who "argued that it was pointless to fight the Klan because they not only represent the totality of white America, but the common UNIA desire for the black man to make something of himself, separate from white people" (45). Garvey saw no contradiction in arguing this point with as much conviction as he possessed while extolling the virtues of the black man and exhorting him to follow the Garveyite movement back to Africa.

European fascism meant much the same to Garvey, if not more, as the Klan did; his attitude toward Haile Selassie shows us his acceptance of fascist ideology's emphasis on the importance of power tailored to the modern world. As A. James Gregor puts it, by 1923, fascism, not at all an antimodern utopian movement, "could be—and was by a considerable number of contemporaries—recognized as a modernizing and industrial movement" (132). Garvey was no exception, believing that modernization and colonization accompanied one another and were desirable.[5] In this respect, Garvey espouses what Geoffrey Herf calls, in the case of Germany, "reactionary modernism." According to Herf, "Reactionary modernism was not primarily a pragmatic or tactical reorientation, which is not to deny that it transformed military-industrial necessities into national virtues. Rather, it incorporated modern technology into the cultural system of modern German nationalism, without diminishing the latter's romantic and anti-rational aspects" (2). Garvey's appropriation of a reactionary modernist stance—his high appraisal of industrialization and modernization, and his incorporation of technology in his nationalistic scheme—play a crucial role in his denunciation of Selassie. To Garvey, Selassie's flight from the Italians was due to his failure to usher the modern age into Ethiopia, leaving the African nation open to attack from fascist powers that exalted modernization and, as a result, displayed an insatiably bellicose desire for colonial conquest (T. Martin, *Hero* 143). The industrial nation prepared technologically to meet the modern world also carried within it a desire to conquer that world. In failing to prepare Ethiopia for the rigors of modern life and modernity, the emperor of the technologically backward nation also neglected to prepare for an essential aspect of fascist modernity: colonial aggression.

Fascist colonialism spelled ruin for Africa only insofar as Africa had yet to enter, in Garvey's estimation, the modern age. Garvey foresaw the fall of Africa to a fascist power not because fascist ideology in itself demanded such a thing but because fascist ideology as embraced and practiced by Hitler and Mussolini had no equivalent in Africa to match it. This is not to say, however, that Garvey's political style did not approximate that of the fascist dictators, and the comparison does not end there. C. L. R. James expanded the range of similarities between Garvey and his European analogues when he claimed, "The only person I know who can be compared to what Garvey did is Adolph Hitler. Adolph Hitler came forward and upset the traditions of Western civilization. They had the growth of democracy, 1789 and everything and Adolph Hitler said 'No! Race and blood matter' and the Germans upset completely the mentality and outlook of Western civilization" (qtd. in Sewell 56). James later insisted that he was not "comparing Garvey to Hitler. I am comparing one historical movement and another historical movement. There were these two men who upset the mental conception of modern history" (qtd. in Sewell 56). But despite his insistence to the contrary, the comparison has been made. The emphasis on race and blood has value for James insofar as it disrupted the complacency of Western institutions and opinions vis-à-vis the black man. The fascist turn Garvey takes evinces a de facto anti-Western position, negating the "mentality and outlook of Western civilization" and thus negating humanist as well as antihumanist Western political philosophies in toto. What James gestures toward in his comparison of Garvey with Hitler is what Linz calls "the 'anti' character of fascism" (15). Seeing fascism as an "anti-movement," Linz defines it as a "hypernationalist, often pan-nationalist, anti-parliamentary, anti-liberal, anti-communist, populist and therefore anti-proletarian, partly anti-capitalist and anti-bourgeois, anti-clerical, or at least, non-clerical movement" (12). In other words, the anti-Western sentiment James understands as the achievement of the Garveyite movement brings with it a set of negations that James does not adumbrate but which Garvey promoted.

But the most important feature of Linz's definition is not a negation per se but its invocation of ultranationalism, the very cornerstone of the

Garveyite movement. According to Moore, Garvey began by espousing a "positive" form of nationalism, which throughout the 1930s degenerated in content into "reactionary nationalism," or fascism. "Progressive and positive nationalism," Moore asserts, "expressing the right of the African, as of all other peoples, to self-determination, self-government, and self-realization, now gave way in Garvey's consciousness more and more to unrestrained and reactionary nationalism" (231). Moore believes "reactionary nationalism" must be defined in light of its positive counterpart: "By contrast repressive [reactionary] nationalism is evident in Mussolini's fascist Italian nationalism" and "Nazi nationalism" (232). If positive nationalism represents racial pride and the desire for black self-determination, then Garvey's reactionary or repressive nationalism seeks the negative moment, the manifest destiny of the decolonized, politically enfranchised black state. This form of Black Nationalism would follow the very model of colonial aggression pursued by Mussolini against Selassie. According to Knox, wars of imperialism were "linked to revolution.... Foreign adventure was . . . internal forward policy, not the mere 'social-imperialist' defense of order at home characteristic of more staid authoritarian regimes" (302). Fascist imperialism is distinctive in that it is linked to a period of national revolution and subsequent stabilization. In other words, Garvey values the *idea* of colonial force Mussolini puts into practice against Ethiopia because, as was the case for Italy with Italian Fascism, black fascist imperial aggression would help to consolidate the revolution and concomitant black nation (Moore 233–35).

Another aspect of Garvey's ultranationalism is its belief in the biblically portended, divine nature of the black state. The Bible was Garvey's primary source for the proof for many of his accusations against Selassie, and for his ideology of black supremacy. This is why Garvey teaches in his *Message for the People* that the greatest favor one could do for oneself is to "Read a chapter of the Bible every day; old and new testaments. The greatest wisdom of the age is to be found in the Scriptures. You can always quote from the Scriptures. It's the quickest way of winning approval" (10). Recognizing that to create a form of totalitarian government, as Hannah Arendt observes, "the masses have to be won by propaganda," Garvey's biblical exegesis provides his ideology of the Volk with precisely the propagandistic basis of his attempted conquest of the black masses (*Origins of Totalitarianism* 341). Garvey's bible is a means to the end of fascist social control and dictatorial power. It probes what Garvey refers to as "Negro psychology," which he understands as conducive to fascist coercion. As Erich Fromm suggests, the fascist mindset inserts itself into a hierarchy "in which everyone has somebody above him to submit to and somebody beneath him to feel power over; the man at the top, the leader, has Fate, History, Nature above him as the power in which to submerge himself" (235–36). The Bible offers Garvey and his subjects a Fate, History, and Nature in which to submerge and become hierarchically ordered.

The originary point of Garvey's biblical triumvirate of Fate, History, and Nature is *Psalms* 68:31: "Princes shall come out of Egypt; Ethiopia shall soon stretch out her hands unto God." Using this passage, Garvey maintains that Ethiopia was the chosen nation of biblical prophesies. However, to fulfill its destiny, Ethiopia required a "prince" capable of such greatness. In this matter Ethiopia could not, as Garvey insists in a 1936 article for the *Black Man,* expect help from above: "For God to maintain his equilibrium He cannot take sides in human political differences between peoples and nations, otherwise He would cease to be the God of all" (A. Garvey 231). Despite having favorites, God must remain ostensibly neutral, putting the onus of prophecy-fulfillment on the Ethiopians themselves, and Selassie in particular. Garvey concludes with the opinion that "God was not on the side of the Italians and Fascist Mussolini dropping incendiary bombs and mustard gas from the air on defenseless people in their own country" (*Garvey and Garveyism* 230–31). Displaying what de Felice calls fascism's "mystical concept[ion] of life and politics based on the primacy of irrational activism" (R. Griffin, *Fascism* 301), Garvey invokes an ill-defined and ultimately fascistically mystical idea of God's activity, or inactivity, in the world. Unmoved by Ethiopia's plight, and as a means of remaining available to all, Garvey's God refuses to take sides. Here, Garvey would seem to be caught in a contradiction. If Ethiopia is a chosen nation, hasn't a side already been taken? Garvey is aware of the apparent slippage in his logic. For him, it is not that God can not intervene, but, in this case, will not. Garvey believes that God will not protect the African nation of prophesy because it is led by an emperor who traces his lineage from Solomon, a Jew.

Garvey himself traces Selassie's biblical lineage from Solomon, decrying, "The new Negro doesn't give two pence about the line of Solomon . . . Solomon has been long dead. Solomon was a Jew. The Negro is not Jew. The Negro has a racial origin running from Sheba to the present, of which he is proud. He is proud of Sheba but he is not proud of Solomon".[6] Garvey judges Selassie unfit for Negro support because of the Emperor's status as a Jew. With this condemnation, Garvey also reveals the anti-Semitic bent of his thought. Even if Garvey looked to Mussolini rather than Hitler for inspiration, by 1935 Italy's concordance with Germany on the so-called Jewish question was clear.[7] As Garvey condemns Selassie as a Jew, he does so with full knowledge of the white supremacist ideological implications of fascism in general and Italian Fascism in particular.[8]

For Garvey, then, race and history are constructed a priori through Christological-mythological narratives. Race cannot be conceived without myth understood as history; mythological history is the truth of race. The true Christians are the chosen race and the privileged agents of this mythohistory; Selassie is not one of them. To be black, then, is to be Christian; Christianity is essentially black. This is not to say, however, that Garvey sought to place the church above the state. Neocleous points out that fascism "required the creation of the nation by a universal force which could challenge the moral and spiritual power of the church. For this reason the state had to assume the guise of a new spiritual community alternative—the power of the Church. The state, then, is a moral unity" (24). Garvey offers an alternative to the church and achieves his moral unity by reinvesting the church's lexicon and iconography with meanings beneficial to his politico-secular goals. An example of this is Garvey's biblical genealogy of "the Black Race" in *Message to the People*: "It was the Black Race through Simon, the Black Cyrenian, who befriended the Son of God and took up the cross and bore it alongside of Him, up to the heights of Calvary. . . . The cross is the property of the Negro in his religion because it was he who bore it" (15). Eliding Christ with Simon, Garvey insists that because a Negro bore the cross, the "Cross is the heritage of the Black man. Don't give it up" (58).

It is through, then, what Emilio Gentile has called the fascist "sacralization of politics," the creation of a politics that is also a religion, that Garvey ultimately justifies his attack on Selassie. Garvey's sacralization of politics and concomitant emphasis on aestheticized political structures and relationships fashion the backbone of the fascist mythological beasts he creates with the Bible. What Garvey proposes is a

Christian-based theology that claims that Christianity belongs in its essence and by way of the one true Cross to the Negro. Conversely, if one is not Christian, one is not Negro. Garvey condemns Selassie as a Jew to dispossess the emperor of the one true Cross, which signifies the Negro race, and so his sovereign rights.

To do otherwise would be tantamount to admitting that Jesus Christ was a white man: "Never admit that Jesus Christ was a white man, otherwise, he could not be the Son of God, and the God to redeem all mankind. Jesus Christ had the blood of all races in his veins, and tracing the Jewish race back to Abraham and Moses from which Jesus sprang through the line of Jesse, you will find Negro blood everywhere; therefore, Jesus had mostly Negro blood in him" (*Message* 15). Following a bloodline different than that of Simon, Garvey submits that because one can find Negro blood everywhere, it must have flowed through the veins of Jesus Christ. The bloodlines of Jesus and the Jews split at their origin. Jews and Jesus may have sprung from Abraham and Moses, but they did not develop along the same line.[9] Garvey lets enough Negro blood to prove its priority and ubiquity, but not enough to confuse the biologically based theological difference between Negro and Jew. Although containing trace amounts of his blood, the Negro stands outside of the line to which Selassie belongs, that of Solomon. In following Biblical bloodlines, Garvey gives theological narrative content to his version of fascist biological mysticism.

Through his appropriation and cultivation of Jesus's racial origin, Garvey plants the seed of the Negro family tree. This seed blooms into the very mythological genealogy that endows the Negro with full rights to the fruit of Christianity. Because of his privileged lineage, the Negro is the subject of Christian eschatology. To increase the Negro's domain, Garvey conflates Christianity with "civilization" in general—a rhetorical move that positions blacks at the very origin of all culture. In Garvey's opinion, Christianity signifies the universal as it confounds the secular and the sacred. Embraced by Christianity as its rightful subject, the Negro becomes the first and final arbiter of what now amounts to sacred culture, a cornerstone of fascist ideology. If, then, "All civilization goes back to the Black Man in the Nile Valley of Africa" (16), it all goes back to the Negro. That Africans did not practice Christianity until exposed to European Christendom makes little difference to Garvey's fascistic myth of Africa. The Negro's Christianity awaited the catalyst required to make it manifest beneath the surface and as his essence. Furthermore, the development of Christianity by Europeans merely betrays the fact of the Europeans' African origin. It is this origin that manufactures the Negro's biologically mystified racial purity as holy spirit. Regardless of appearances, in his spirit Selassie is not a Negro because he is, as far as Garvey is concerned, a Jew, outside the purity of the "Black Race."

Despite Paul Gilroy's point that for Garvey, "racial purity is a project not a condition" ("Black Fascism" 72–73), Garvey's fascistic myth and sacralization of race situate the extreme limit and originary moment of the very idea of "racial purity." In other words, racial purity exists as possibility; it must be achieved. This is why Garvey demands that blacks marry only within the race. Garvey believes that "[f]or a Negro man to marry someone who does not look like his mother or is not a member of his race is to insult his mother, nature and God, who made his father. The best tribute a race can pay to nature and God is to preserve its species; when it does otherwise, it is in rebellion" (25). Aside from insulting one's mother, nature, and God, to marry outside of the race would, should children be born, pollute the racial bloodline. If the achievement of racial purity is one of the offices of the state, then miscegenation amounts to the slackening of the ideological hold of fascist state power. Propagating his version of what Foucault calls "Bio-power," or the attempt by "political rationality ... to increase the scope of power for its own sake by bringing the bodies of the state under tighter control," Garvey's ideal, procreative citizen reproduces racial perfection conditioned by state power (*Discipline and Punish* 137).

The highest manifestation of racial purity is the sovereign. If the sovereign exudes racial purity on every level of comportment and appearance, then a child outside this image and concept will be by nature subversive to the state. For the health of Garvey's fascist state, one must

> [i]nsist on a campaign of race purity; that is, doing everything moral and social within the race. Close ranks against all other races. It is natural that it is a disgrace to mix your race with other races. To split up the race is unwholesome and does not tend to morally dignify the race. It will be a beautiful thing when we have a standard Negro race. (25)

Racial purity must be preserved if the very basis of Garvey's fascist state and the authoritarian leader's power are to be maintained. Without this zealous adherence to the achievement and preservation of the purity of the race, the fascist state falls into disarray. Because of this danger, Garvey's program of racial purity is so rigorous that even to think of the race in abstraction necessarily entails thinking properly racist thoughts and attributing their authority to the divine prerogative of God. For Garvey, proper thinking means proper living; to think fascist racial purity cannot be distinguished from the attempt to achieve it. Thus, one must "think of the race in the highest terms of human living. To think that God made the race perfect, that there is no one better than you; that you have all the elements of human perfection and as such you must love yourself" (28). If God made the race perfect, if "God made you beautiful" (28), then to think otherwise blackens His name. Ethiopia was clearly a case in which an inferior racial bloodline produced an inferior "Jewish" state. Selassie's light-skinned appearance enabled Garvey to justify his exhortation not to marry outside the race, resolve the issue of interracial breeding, and preserve his fascist myth of the Volk based on the image of the ruler. This racial thinking, Lacoue-Labarthe's and Nancy's "Nazi myth," ensures the authenticity of a reading of racial origin that stipulates the superiority of Garvey's Blackman. It does so by clearly outlining a type of Pilgrim's Progress toward the ultimate goal of the racial redemption of the Blackman by the racially absolutist black fascist state.[10]

The Negro honors God and helps the race achieve purity through the body as well as the mind. Garvey instructs, "You must live so clean that everybody can see the cleanliness of your life" (*Message* 60). Garvey's idea of racial "hygiene" captures the body in a conceptual framework of racial morality.[11] If one is kempt, one is clean in every aspect of life. Proper racial thinking shapes outer appearance and situates the body within an intellectual racial economy that can be viscerally apprehended. To be in possession of a "filthy" body means one is the owner of a dirty mind. "Most of the deformities in a community," Garvey suggests, "are the result of immoral and loose people cutting loose. Sick people never produce good children. Disease in man is destructive. It destroys the species and wrecks the mind of man" (63). The appearance of disease in a community points to previous immoral acts, which, of course, are not the products but the manifestations of improper, immoral, and inherently anti-black—in Selassie's case, Jewish—thoughts.

One must learn to think proper black thoughts and not Jewish ones. Racial purity in Garvey's philosophy is not only written on the body but can also be read in one's demeanor and as the mark of a man's breeding. Garvey exhorts in his *Message*, "You must never stop learning. The world's greatest men and women were people who educated themselves outside the university . . . read and study" (1). The goal of self-education is to accumulate a wealth of knowledge pertaining to the race that cannot otherwise be had. Such information, as a positive evaluation of the past and potential of blacks, has been systematically suppressed by state-sanctioned, orthodox secular training. This is why Garvey's citizen must "[r]ead history incessantly until you master it. This means your own national history, industrial history, the history of the world, and the history of the different sciences; but primarily, the history of man" (2). Garvey commands voracious readers to recoup marginalized and suppressed black history through the archaeology of knowledge. The well-rounded black man and woman begin digging with the history of the world. Such an inquiry does not merely mark a neutral genealogical appropriation of the past.[12] Garvey hopes to appropriate as well what Althusser has called "the knowledge effect," which "is produced as an effect of the scientific discourse, which exists only as a discourse *of the* system, i.e., of the object grasped in the structure of its complex constitution" (*Reading Capital* 68). The knowledge effect offers up knowledge as for and of the system to which it pertains. Knowledge is, then, subservient to something both outside of itself and integral and a priori to its self-presentation. It is knowledge pro- and pre-scribed, pre-scripted to serve a specific ideological purpose. In this case, Garvey hopes to deploy the reading apparatus for the coming to self-knowledge of the well-rounded black man and woman as subjects in and of black history. Garvey hopes this reading will engender not only a tradition of reading but black tradition in itself.

Creating the black tradition as he discovers it, Garvey's well-rounded reader is the model for his new fascist man. As George Mosse writes of Italy, "the new 'fascist man' is, on the one hand, set within the Italian patriotic tradition, and, on the other, supposed to live a superior life unconstrained by space and time. He must sacrifice his personal interests and realize that it is his spirituality that gives him human values. But his spirituality must be informed by history, meaning Italian traditions and national memories" ("Towards a General Theory" 32). Just as Italians must generate and venerate their patriotic tradition, so, too, must the black man. Just as for Italians, history signifies the teleology of progressive national self-becoming and perfection, so, too, must history for the black man. Garvey's new fascist black man creates and enriches his spiritual life through endless hours of reading the Bible and history. History here does not purport to mean objective world history, but black history understood as the history of the world. Historical materialism reinforces mythic historiography.

At the very moment Garvey's ideal subject seeks to layer himself with Biblical and historical knowledge, he becomes what Herbert Marcuse describes as a one-dimensional man, "a pattern of *one-dimensional thought and behavior* in which ideas, aspirations, and objectives that, by their content, transcend the established universe of discourse and action are either repelled or reduced to terms of this universe" (*One-Dimensional Man* 12). Prescribing every individual desire in advance, Garvey's Biblical framework nurtures its one-dimensional men as it "obliterates the opposition between the private and public existence, between individual and social needs" (*ODM* xlvii). In his attempt to create his paper-thin subject, Garvey seeks to frame the public in a mythohistorical narrative of racial imperatives. The most important book to read to gain a "proper understanding" of the racial past is the Good Book. The Bible is Garvey's urtext of Machiavellian machination; in it he finds the justification for any historical-political contingency that arises, including disenfranchising the emperor of Ethiopia not only of his place at the head of state but of his race. Garvey's bible provides a discourse on and of princely power in the sense that Althusser reads Machiavelli: The Prince is "a specific political form charged with executing the historical demands 'on the agenda': the constitution of a nation" (*Machiavelli* 13). Because Emperor Selassie as Jew is excluded from Garvey's Christian-based theosophy, he is radically outside the race and therefore in no position to negotiate the historical demands "on the agenda": the constitution of the black nation. Furthermore, as part of the European development of Christianity that helps to reveal its own African origins and the chosen status of the Negro, Mussolini, by invading Ethiopia, paradoxically purges the continent of its Jewish element (Selassie) and paves the way to the future recognition of the Negro's Christian greatness, which is to say, Garvey's princely sovereignty.

Garvey and Mussolini

As evidenced in poems he wrote for his London exile journal *Black Man,* such as "The Smell of Mussolini," Garvey's hatred of Mussolini appears to have been unequivocal.[13] This apparent hatred did not, however, prevent Garvey from emulating the odiferous dictator. Indeed, Garvey's political style did not differ that much, at least in ideological content, from that of "the Beast of Rome." As we have seen, Garvey shares certain affinities with the Duce.

One such affinity is a belief in the absolute power of the state. "Government should be absolute," Garvey believes, "and the head should be thoroughly responsible for himself and the acts of his subordinates" (*Life and Lessons* 30). Garvey's call for an absolutist government echoes the description of the colonial fascist state Mussolini and Giovanni Gentile offered in the widely translated 1932 *Enciclopedia italiana* article "La Dottrina del fascismo." Mussolini writes, "The cornerstone of fascist doctrine is its conception of the state: of the state's essence, its functions, and its ends. For fascism the state is [an] absolute, while individuals and groups are relative. Individuals and groups are thinkable to the degree that they operate within the state" (58).[14] Individuals and groups are "thinkable" (*pensabili*) only with regard to the absolute state ("*Per il fascismo lo Stato e un assoluto*") and the charismatic, authoritarian ruler, who inevitably embarks on a project of empire. According to Mussolini, "The fascist state expresses the will to exercise power and to command. Here the Roman tradition is embodied in a conception of strength. Imperial power, as understood by fascist doctrine, is not only territorial, military, and commercial. It is also spiritual and moral" (60). Imperialism is the manifest essence of the fascist state. Centered on the charismatic ruler, the fascist state heeds a spiritual and moral drive to claim foreign territories. Garvey's imperialist vision for Africa mirrors Mussolini's doctrine of fascist imperialism. Indeed, the very imperial violence Garvey attacks in his poem "Mussolini—Scourge of God" he advocates in what he calls "the Empire Urge" (*Poetical Works* 82–83).

With the term *Empire Urge* Garvey identifies the drive in the black body politic to "[l]et no religious scruples, no political machination divide us, but let us hold together under all climes and in every country, making among ourselves a Racial Empire upon which 'the sun shall never set'" (*Life and Lessons* 5). Racial-national unity and imperial expansion are here understood as a single compulsion. Under the sway of the Empire Urge, Garvey's ideal state devours everything in sight. With this hunger for imperial conquest, Garvey conceives of a common bond between all diaspora blacks, such that each member of a black diaspora transcends him- or herself and merges with the totality of blacks worldwide. Garvey's Pan-Africanism as Empire Urge is also a form of pan-nationalism advocated in fascist ideology. As Linz reminds us, "Many fascist movements were also characterized by pan-nationalist ideas which represented a challenge to the existing states and account for much of their aggressive expansionist foreign policy" (15). As an element of his fascist ideology, Garvey's pan-nationalism helps to constitute a racialized totality of the Volk. This totality is understood by Garvey to be a collective entity that manifests itself fully as an empire only when it realizes itself in the racial consciousness, and political unconscious, of its constituent parts. When Garvey asks that blacks "hold together under all climes," he suggests that, to date, the necessary condition for the creation of the incipient Empire has yet to occur. At the same time, however, he portends the fulfillment of his imperial project. To place the desire to build an empire in the realm of instinct by dubbing it an "urge" endows imperialism with an irrepressible, essential element of racial-national determination.

The idea of the racial-national determination of all black peoples plays a dominant role in proper racial thinking. The fascist state determines and expresses the collective thought of the people. As the realization of essentially black fascist thought, Garvey locates the site of this future state, of course, in Africa. Indeed, as he states in *Message*, "The national aspiration of the race is to find expression, not in revolution where you are established when you are under other people's government, but to accomplish this end in Africa" (71). Once back in Africa, the mission of the Garveyite movement will be "*To assist in civilizing the backward tribes of Africa*" (29). Eschewing any thought of revolution in the United States, or in any other nation in which an oppressed black population lives, Garvey understands his project as ultimately imperialistic and maintaining the basic assumptions of European and American colonial interests already present in Africa. "Africa," for Garvey, "is the motherland.... Therefore, it is necessary to help the tribes that live in Africa to advance to a higher state of civilization" (29). More than anyone else, Africans must be taught how to think proper African thoughts. Only then will they participate fully as members of the black collective and empire.

Because of their reliance on imperialism as a fundamental mode of nationalism, Garvey's and Mussolini's conceptions of the fascist, corporatist state were rigorously anti-Communist and anti-Marxist.[15] This is not to say, however, that either Garvey's or Mussolini's economic beliefs within a fascist frame can be reduced to a negation of Communism and Marxism. As Zeev Sternhell believes, "Fascism... seems an expression of a rupture signaling a crisis of civilization, and ... was no mere reflection of or reaction to Marxism, but on the contrary a phenomenon with considerable intellectual independence" (*Birth of Fascist Ideology* 2). Independent of their negation of Communism and Marxism, Mussolini in practice and Garvey in theory sought to create global economic hegemony through the investment of vast sums of individual income allocated to discretionary funds of the corporatist state.[16] Garvey had no qualms with Mussolini's belief that the "fascist state claims the right to rule over the economic domain no less than over the other domains" (59). As Garvey theorized, "No individual should be allowed the possession, use or the privilege to invest on his own account, more than a million, and no corporation should be allowed to control more than five millions. Beyond this, all control, use and investment of money, should be the prerogative of the state with the concurrent authority of the people" (*Philosophy* 72). His antipathy toward Communism and Marxism well known, Garvey excoriated black and white Communists and Marxists in his writing and speeches, accusing them of attempting to disenfranchise blacks of the very thing that would gain for them political power: private property.

Perhaps the most important thought Garvey attempts to get his College of African Philosophy students to think revolves around capital. The economic component of the *Message to the People* is dominant from the *Message*'s beginning. Capitalist zeal enhances Garvey's speculative, fascist-mythological idea of race by supporting it with practical advice on how to make the desire for wealth work for the race as a whole.[17] Garvey calls on the people to spend wisely, meaning that a race's economic productive power should stay *within* the race: "Never give your money away outside of your race. If you are called upon to give it to God, ask yourself if God is really going to get it.... [A] good cause in his [sic] name may need it and you should first find out if there really is a cause" (88). God finds a place in the economics of race, and in placing Him there, Garvey elevates economics to a mythological principle.

The exhortation to spend within the racial community assumes that the community already exists. And yet, the question of the existence of the community remains suspended throughout the *Message*. Garvey speaks to the creation and futurity of the community; his *Message* is the community's blueprint. The *Message* speaks of, not to, a "people." It creates the people as a performative gesture and as the act of the will that thinks the Negro world. Garvey's community is, then, the ideal Negro community. Tarchi observes that the "fascination of the ideal community envisaged by the nascent fascist movements is twofold: on the one hand, it presents itself as the agent of dissolution for the social bonds judged to be anachronistic, such as one's profession or 'class'; on the other, it is to act as a binding force in the name of a reality which is no longer and not only material" (269). The desire behind Garvey's drive to create the ideal Negro community articulates a need to eliminate "class" and "profession" in the corporatist state. He does this by consolidating the ideal Negro community as an independent, segregated entity, unified and given meaning solely by racial identity. This is why Garvey advises, "He [the Negro] should segregate himself residentially in that community so as to have political power, economic power and social power in that community.... In this respect segregation is good. To do otherwise is bad" (30). The fact that such segregation and subsequent economic investment has not come to pass defines the assumption behind Garvey's advice. The individual accumulation of wealth marks the only way for blacks to gain enough money to form the essential spiritual basis of the Volk that will lead to collective economic and so political independence.[18] "Therefore," Garvey insists, "the Negro should indulge in every kind of business that is necessary to earn profit; because it is by profit that he will be able to obtain life's necessities for himself and his race" (32). Individual wealth must precede the wealth of the Volk; without the black entrepreneur, there can be no black fascist corporatist state in Africa. In other words, the community proceeds from the wealthy individual, and not vice versa. As the work of the wealthy individual, the corporation shapes the community, and eventually, the ensuing black fascist state.

As Roger Eatwell notes, "The most consistently advocated socioeconomic institution by fascists in Europe was corporatism... Corporatism was meant to institutionalize social unity by aligning workers, management and the state" (199). Garvey's fascist corporatist state unfolds in this manner: the individual grows wealthy by any means necessary; he then offers substantial funds to an organization (the UNIA) devoted, indeed called on by God, to create the black spiritual community and subsequent corporatist state; the money required to create and maintain the corporatist black state circulates entirely within the race—but at this point there is no division of wealth.[19] Garvey's economic scheme fascistically preserves and depends on class divisions; he is deeply invested in Mussolini's belief that fascism "denies the immutable and irreparable character of the class struggle as the natural outcome of [the] economic conception of history" (Mussolini and Gentile 54). When Garvey writes that "[p]roperty in community is evidence of your status in the society of the community" (70), he maintains the divine prerogative of the Duce. If Garvey's fascist state excluded the quest for wealth, the Duce himself could not claim to exist beyond the pale of the average man. Thought is material; he who possesses the highest thoughts and the greatest intelligence, and so the greatest material wealth, rules. The rest carry the Blackman's burden through the march of Garvey's racially coded, speculative idea of history that realizes itself in his eschatological Christian ideal of the Duce

Granting the validity of Max Horkheimer's dictum *"State capitalism is the authoritarian state of the present"* (96), in Garvey's state, capitalism still requires a Christian face. As Mussolini insists, "The fascist conception of life is a religious one." It defines "a spiritual community" and "a system of thought" (Mussolini and Gentile 48).[20] It is therefore essential that Garvey's economic juggernaut, the Volk, be unified under one set of religious beliefs and practices. This is why Garvey points out that because "there are so many different religious thoughts, the Negro should be brought under the influence of one system of religion and the belief in one God" (31). Unification can and will be achieved, according to Garvey, because Christianity is the very essence of all Negro religions, no matter what form they take. Moreover, Christianity as the final manifestation of Negro religious and spiritual belief and practice must occur if the Negro wishes to return to the scene of his former greatness, an event that never took place.[21] The greatness of Garvey's Negro remains always a Hegelian Idea, something that will follow the logic of the fascist absolute subject developing itself in and as a racialized history, and will meet itself for the first time at the end of time.

Garvey's *Message* reflects what Roger Griffin calls Giovanni Gentile's "ponderous Hegelian gloss to the principles underlying the Fascist state," just as Mussolini describes a "people, perpetuating itself in history, a multitude unified by an idea and imbued with the will to live, with the will to power, with a self-consciousness and a personality" (R. Griffin, *International* 238; Mussolini and Gentile 49). Without doubt, the *Message* offers a speculative idea of history and the Volk. Garvey thus writes in bad faith when he insists that "[t]here is no speculative idea behind his [the Negro's] religion" (31). Garvey's myth of racial origin is a speculative idea in a Hegelian system detailing the black subject of history dialectically coming to absolute self-knowledge. However, the impersonal, racialized speculative idea coming to self-knowledge through the dialectics of *Aufhebung* is subject to personal forces. Garvey's call to the history books and his Nietzschean insistence on persistence as truth marks the existence of a level of discourse in his text that never lets go of the aesthetics of the will. The truth of history is engendered by the creative act of the subjective will. The speculative idea (the Nazi myth) that lurks beneath the surface of Garvey's image of Christianity qualifies his theology as a cult of personality. History here is little more than one man's fantasy imposed on what Lacoue-Labarthe and Nancy call the collective "subject-State." Emptied of its content, history determines sovereign power and completes the aestheticization of politics Benjamin diagnosed as indicative of fascist propaganda.

To call Garvey's subject-state a mere collective does not give due justice to the full spectrum of Garvey's vision. More than a group of people bound by common mythology and racial origin, what Garvey envisions is the black nation. By prophesizing that this nation would take its rightful place as sovereign over the earth, Garvey transformed Black Nationalist thought into a rigorous internationalist racial ideology of black power.[22] Indeed, for Garvey,

No race is free until it has a strong nation of its own, its own system of government and its own order of society. Never give up this idea. Let no one persuade you against it. It is the only protection for your generation and your race. Hold on to the idea of an independent government and nation as long as other men have them. (34)

Until the day all nations become obsolete under the aegis of the imperial black state, the black nation will be the only entity capable of ordering black society and protecting black sovereignty. The nation provides blacks with a space in which to cultivate their past as the promise of the future black imperial corporatist state. Cultivating the mythological and ideological kernels Žižek sees as productive of fascism, the black nation provides the ideal space in which the Negro may grow and take shape in the image of the dictator. Again, it is Garvey's God that forges the physical tie between the body politic and the body of the Duce: "God never could have intended to make you look as you look and as you are, and make your king, president, emperor or ruler of a different race than you are" (34).[22] The black nation is ruled by an autocratic, authoritarian ruler who is the physical ideal of a diverse community. The Duce must exhibit all the characteristics of the ideal of the race, but in himself he must be no one and nothing but this ideal; he must allow for the fascist mythological self-identification of each of his subjects with him. "Fascist man is not only an individual," Mussolini contends, "but also a nation and a country. He embodies the ideal" (Mussolini and Gentile 47). Garvey echoes this when he exhorts "See only yourself in everything. Make your nation the highest expression of human idealism" (37). The highest expression of this ideal human type is the Duce himself. Agamben perceives this ideal as the state's primary means of subjective identification and subject formation, and so of Nazi mythological power. The ideal sets in motion, "along with the disciplinary process by which State power makes man as a living being into its own specific object, another process . . . in which man as a living being presents himself no longer as an *object* but as the *subject* of political power" (Agamben 9). For Garvey as for Agamben, the state's ability to embody and reproduce the human marks both the advent and perpetuation of its sovereign power.

The essence of the state is realized in the person of the sovereign. As the perfect charismatic leader, Garvey sees himself as the embodiment of the collective subject of the racialized state.[24] Garvey's state manifests its own nature, insofar as it is his own. The Volk's essential link to its leader, and so to the state, can only be maintained if the state is viewed as organic. The fascist state, then, is not a man-made entity but a man-making animal. It is nature bestowing on its children ontological homogeneity, in the sense of Bataille's analysis of the fascist state as an organic entity reproducing itself as the "homogenous" or totalizing being of the Volk. In eliminating difference and replacing it with the body of the leader, the state elaborates the authoritarian psyche.[25] The subject under fascist-authoritarian rule identifies with the ruler completely, eliding the ontological difference between the two while maintaining ontic distance. Whereas Bataille laments this fact, Mussolini revels in it, positing that the state "is always, at least potentially, an organic conception of the world" (47). The racialized state is the highest manifestation of nature, depending, of course, on the race. Garvey's natural state, or state of nature, can make this claim because "Man is made of mind and matter. Matter is manifested through nature, and mind is the connecting link with the spirit of God" (105). The state as the highest expression of the essence of the black man is the tangible expression of a collective mind that establishes itself in the world as sovereign above all other states. This belief allows Garvey to exhort: "Fear no other man but God, for God is your superior, but man is always your equal, so long as you rise to his attainments. You may rise to his attainments through the extraordinary use of your mind. *Mind is matter, mind is king, when it goes wrong, it loses its scepter*" (106). Garvey's claim to the mantle of the Duce confounds mind and matter, in so doing, concretizing thought, making it material. The thought of the subject as the chosen agent of history leaps from mythopoeia to historical fact.

The Duce operates in the sphere of myth transformed into material history. Because he is the primary agent of history, he is superior to his followers. "To lead," Garvey says, "suggests that you must have followers. For others to follow you, you must be superior to them in the things that they must follow you for" (19). With this, Garvey exhibits a basic tenet of fascist ideology, what Stanley Payne describes as the "general tendency to exalt the function of leadership, hierarchy, and subordination, deferring to the creative function of leadership more than to prior ideology or a bureaucratized party line" (Payne, *Fascism: Comparison* 14). Garvey stresses the leader's superiority as the precondition of his

Duce's creative task. All that the Duce does is a truthful interpretation of reality because he creates reality. This is why the superiority of the Duce goes without question. Because the Duce is the ideal human, he is the only one in the position to dictate, to speak reality. The Duce is both the end and means of fascist identification.

In order to facilitate fascist identification with the leader, Garvey simplifies the qualities he believes must be clearly articulated in his Duce: "A leader must have personality; he must be clean cut in his appearance so as not to be criticized. An untidy leader is always a failure" (19). The Duce must be clean (we recall the Smell of Mussolini), and have personality. It is not clear what personality traits Garvey's leader should have. In whatever he does, however, he must present himself to the people as the paragon of virtue and racial purity. This may mean that Garvey's leader must "[k]eep smiling with the world even though [his] mother is dead" (21). The recommendation to smile in the face of the death of one's mother articulates Garvey's belief that the Duce must practice self-annihilation so he can project the image of absolute confidence and moral-racial authority. In fact, the illusion of moral authority is more important than its presence. Ever the political pragmatist, Garvey opines, "If you have to do something that you know you will be morally and socially ashamed of if some one else knows; never do it, but if you have to do it, see to it that you are careful that no one else knows" (20). The moral relativism Garvey displays confirms the fact that evasion, elocution, and evocation determine moral right in his fascist system. The limits of what can be considered ethical conduct are always in flux. When Garvey announces that "[w]hen your followers see that self-confidence they will believe in you and follow you" (21), he pushes his version of the fascist metaphysics of the subject determined by a morally relative Christian theosophy. For Garvey, God is not dead, He is flexible.

Far from granting the subject personal freedom, this malleable theosophy subsumes the subject immediately in the personality of the Duce. Garvey's speculative idea of mind as matter serves only to create and subjugate the black subject in the leader's image. What Garvey's *Message* describes, then, is a universe created and controlled by proper thinking: "*It is thought that created the Universe. It is thought that will master the Universe.* Man must therefore use his thoughts to the limit to get the best results from the Universe. No thinking, no knowledge. Proper thinking may lead you suddenly into the conquest of that which heretofore was mysterious" (111). This conquest of the mysterious is the most troubling aspect of Garvey's formulation of the universe as thought, for the quest for the mysterious signals the apotheosis of Garvey himself.[26] This apotheosis amounts to little more than Garvey's mystification of the concept of Negro "man" as a fact of nature. It also signals his complicity in the logic of totalitarian development in the project of enlightenment described by Horkheimer and Adorno as the putative demystification of nature that "dares to transcend the false absolute, the principle of blind domination," to become the "wholesale deception of the masses" (42).

Through this wholesale deception, Garvey has not only the power of a god over the masses, but power over God. Garvey teaches that "[m]an in his excellence lifts himself highest to God by his mental industry, and the man who has no mental industry forfeits that mentality to the useful servant who climbs in his excellence to the most excellent" (111). Garvey describes the excellence of man as that of God; because of this, man's sovereignty is divine. In Garvey's estimation, the divine possesses no hidden value, no hidden mystery. God succumbs to "proper thinking" in man, revealing that the divine never existed in the first place. A construct, God formed the outlines of an ideal of perfection constructed to give man a target at which to aim his ambition.

Garvey, however, is cognizant of the fact that he advocates a dangerous atheism. This is why he writes, "It is when you reach up to it that you approach God's elevation. Not in rivalry of God, but as coming to God to whom you were always a part, but for the darkness of your own soul" (112). This rivalry not only banishes the "darkness in your own soul" separating you from God but recasts the genial, humble "coming" to God as confrontational and ultimately superfluous. Man (Garvey) does not rival God, he surpasses Him. As God on earth, Garvey claims the dual monarchy of Ethiopia's rightful emperor and Übermensch among Übermenschen.

As the ideal human, Garvey believes, "The sovereign of a people is in the nation." The body of the sovereign is the fascist negative of Deleuze and Guattari's "body without organs." The fascist body descries an authoritarian principle that ideologically prescribes and forecloses on the possibilities of self-governance and the achievement of ends desired independently of state needs. "It is the result of a people forming a society of their own to govern themselves and to achieve their ends" (36), Garvey believes, even if the means include killing:

When it is said "Thou shall not kill," it means you must not kill the soul of man. This is how warriors such as Napoleon, the Emperors, Pharaohs and the old religious warriors who fought battles among men interpreted it. . . . This is how it shall ever be because man shall ever be at war with man in the fight of good against evil. (58)

Here Garvey takes on the mantle of benevolent Duce who must wage constant perpetual warfare against evil. Invoking only to refute the biblical interdiction that prohibits killing, Garvey sanctions the use of terminal force for the purpose of his cause. The violence he recommends—indeed, that the Good requires—follows the dictates of race; racial differences align with moral positions. Violence, then, reveals the being of a people, and, as Mussolini believes, culminates in war: "War alone keys up all human energies to their maximum tension and impresses the seal of the nobility upon those peoples who have the courage to face up to it" (Mussolini 53). Garvey's Negro has more than enough courage to face up to his essential violence.

This positioning of race within a violent, Manichean logical framework asserts that one race falls on the side of the good, the other on that of evil. However, the moral conduct of each race cannot be distinguished from that of the other in any other way than by race itself. Thus, with no other evidence than his understanding of the Bible, Garvey can make the claim that the "white man is Cain transformed, hence his career of murder, from Cain to Mussolini" (104). Garvey invokes yet another biblical lineage, this one ending with the Beast of Rome. Seeing no inherent contradiction in his argumentation, Garvey asserts this brief history of the white man without taking into account that much of what he recommends in the *Message* can be construed as justification for a career in murder. Setting up Mussolini as his unsympathetic straw man, Garvey interprets of the line of Cain so that he can take his place as the true Duce and thus the first fascist. By appropriating and denigrating Mussolini at the same time, he annihilates the man without harming the fascism for which he stands. Garvey has done the same thing to Mussolini that he did to Haile Selassie: he dispossesses them of that which defines them, and then he asserts that it is inherently his own. Hence, Mussolini and Selassie are Marcus Garvey imposters. Establishing this fact is the only way Garvey can claim to have been among the first fascists, and the only way he can be the rightful heir to the crown of Ethiopia.

Garvey's *Message* contains within it his own coronation and apotheosis: anyone who listened sympathetically to his words could not help but become embroiled in the work of Nazi myth. Ultimately, Garvey seeks to invest in the written and unwritten histories of blacks the mechanism of fascistic identification described by Lacoue-Labarthe and Nancy as the Nazi myth. Once Garvey's Nazi myth effectively deploys its interpretive strategies and ideological models, it forms the basis of black fascist historiography. Racial purity depends on this reconstructive historiography, not just for Nazi mythology, but for the myth of Marcus Garvey as well. At the heart of Garvey's "Back to Africa" project lurks the fascistic constitution of a black Volk based on a mythological understanding of the race as ontologically superior to all others. This canvas of representations of mythological events acts as the backdrop against which the teleological unfolding of the race's perfection presents itself. Garvey endeavors to elaborate a speculative idea of the total black fascist state as the product of his fascist appropriation of the means of identification. The speculative idea of history that lurks beneath Garvey's image of Christianity does not alter that surface more than to mirror individual and collective subjects, and to convert Christianity into a cult of personality for profit. History and religion are here little more than variations of the Nazi myth Garvey imposes upon the collective black subject of history. It is no small wonder, then, that Garvey, after disseminating his message, said in 1937, "I am trying to make everyone a Marcus Garvey personified" (*Message* xxi). Each of us has a Marcus Garvey within; he would be precisely what Foucault called the fascist in us all.

For African American authors working in the latter half of the 1930s as diverse as Hurston, Wright, McKay, and Schuyler, the Garvey within provided an aesthetic model from which to imagine black fascism. Each of these authors engaged with the myth of Marcus Garvey as an aesthetic-ideological form. When looked at as a whole, it can be seen that the tacit reflection on black fascism taking place in the latter 1930s describes an artistic and intellectual developmental narrative that begins with Schuyler and his near future fiction *Black Empire*, and recedes in fictive time, ending with a Wright's outsider as the essence of black fascism. This retrograde motion traces a continual rethinking of the black fascist paradigm from contemporary politics through established historical narratives. Whereas McKay's reflections on Garvey and fascism in *Harlem Glory* are easily recognizable, Hurston dissembles her black fascism by placing it in biblical time. Wright removes his analysis of black fascism altogether from historical and theological chains of signification. As we shall see, this allows Wright to represent a fascist essence in which blacks, too, can easily participate.

3 George S. Schuyler and the God of Love
Black Fascism and Mythic Violence

> George S. Schuyler is a joke;
> His brain must be like sausage pork.
> —Marcus Garvey, "George S. Schuyler Again" (1934)

> Naturally, large numbers of Negrophiles will violently disagree with me, but an orderly, dispassionate and objective survey of the facts will convince even Marcus Garvey that I am right.
> —George S. Schuyler, "The Negro and Nordic Civilization" (1925)

> [George S. Schuyler] is the supreme advocate of Uncle Tom Do-Nothingness.
> —Claude McKay, "McKay Says Schuyler Is Writing Nonsense" (1937)

No one identified less with Marcus Garvey than did George Samuel Schuyler. Throughout his long career as a Menkenesque, iconoclastic journalist, Schuyler disparaged Garvey and Garveyism at every turn. A special target of Schuyler's vilification was Garvey's Pan-Africanism. Yet after the 1935 Italian invasion of Ethiopia and Garvey's denunciation of Haile Selassie, it was Schuyler who, in the pages of the *Pittsburgh Courier*, vigorously supported the emperor and growing Pan-African sentiment in the United States. In addition to launching vitriolic editorials against Italy and in favor of Pan-African counterattack, Schuyler's serialized *Courier* fiction, *Black Empire*, envisions an African American Mussolini retaking not just Ethiopia but all of Africa. Thus, although Schuyler and Garvey almost never found themselves on the same side of an argument, the one thing they did agree on was the positive potential of fascism for Africans and African America. Radicalizing Garveyism to an almost absurd degree, Schuyler's *Black Empire* engages with, and finds positive use for, fascist ideology.

Serialized in the *Pittsburgh Courier* from 1936 to 1938 as "The Black Internationale: A Story of Black Genius against the World" and "Black Empire: An Imaginative Story of a Great New Civilization in Modern Africa," Schuyler's *Black Empire* is a utopian vision of a black secret society's quest for world domination led by the morally ambiguous genius Dr. Henry Belsidus. Belsidus decides to begin his conquest with Africa. Landing in Monrovia and, in effect, slapping Garvey in the face, Belsidus wipes Africa clean of white influence. In this sense, *Black Empire* acts out a revenge fantasy aimed at Italian aggression against Ethiopia. However, this revenge is not antifascist per se. Belsidus fights fascism with fascism itself: as such, the revenge *Black Empire* exacts from Italy and other colonial powers heeds the "call of Ethicpia" by replacing one fascist dictatorship with another.

New Fascist Negro

Perhaps the suggestion that Schuyler finds a use for fascist ideology does not come as a surprise to those familiar with his well-deserved reputation as a right-wing journalist. Schuyler's early political thought during the 1920s, however, has a decidedly leftist bent, betraying a loose socialism combined with a touch of Pan-Africanism. For example, one finds in Schuyler's 1925 essay "The Negro and Nordic Civilization" his positive association of Africans with "a crude form of communism":

> Take housing, for instance. Here again the Africans are hopelessly behind the times. No massive modern tenements greet the eyes of the traveler in that unfortunate land.... They are still at the primitive stage where only one family occupies a habitation. Instead of a couple toiling forty or fifty years to pay off the mortgage or meet the landlord every thirty days, I am informed that the whole tribe pitches in and erects a home for every couple of their wedding day! How can a real spirit of thrift exist in such an environment? Though I cannot place much credence in a rumor so terrible to contemplate, I have heard it reported that these people practice a crude form of communism. (NNC 5)

The biting sarcasm and social satire are typical of Schuyler. This positive notion of Africa, however, as practicing "a crude form of communism" resembles nothing in Schuyler's oeuvre written after 1931. In that year, Schuyler journeyed undercover to Liberia to report, in his book *Slaves Today* (1931), on socioeconomic conditions in the putative independent state. What he saw there negatively altered his perception of blacks in Africa. Indeed, the contrast between his descriptions of Africa after the trip and the passage just cited from "The Negro and Nordic Civilization" creates a striking impression. Writing for H. L. Mencken's *American Mercury* in 1933, Schuyler reports in "Uncle Sam's Black Step-Child" that, "The Aframerican who goes there a resolute advocate of Liberian independence is more than likely to come away convinced of the necessity for American intervention. Arriving in Monrovia, the capital, enthusiastic over being at last in a country ruled by black men, he is shocked by the lack of common sanitation, the unpaved, rock-strewn, meandering, weed-grown, unlighted streets, the swarm of rats, and the general atmosphere of shiftlessness and decay" (USBS 17). The society marked by a crude form of communism gives way to one in dire need of capitalist intervention and colonization. Schuyler here envisions a fate for Liberia not dissimilar to that of Haiti during the United States' occupation. He also signals the demise of whatever Pan-African sentiment he may have felt before reaching Monrovia. Only the severity of the Ethiopian crisis was a heavy-enough blow to resurrect within Schuyler a feeling for Pan-Africanism, and in particular Ethiopianism, if not for socialism.

After the Italian invasion of Ethiopia, Schuyler reconsidered his hatred of Pan-Africanism, writing in the *Courier* that there can be "no excuse this time that any Negro community can give for not having a branch of the Friends of Ethiopia," and that, "what Ethiopia needs is money. She has man-power, grit, determination and intelligence" ("Views and Reviews").[1] The war not only raised Schuyler's ire over imperialism in Africa and kindled his sense of humanitarianism in the service of Pan-Africanism, but it also instilled in him a sense of diasporic racial solidarity, which included a desire for African Americans to take to the battlefield in the cause of Ethiopia's sovereignty (Hill, Introduction 14). As Joseph E. Harris notes, Schuyler's publisher sought to place African Americans on Ethiopian battlefields: "Observing that many African Americans were interested in enlistment, Robert Lee Vann, the publisher of the Pittsburgh *Courier,* requested information from the State Department on regulations governing the enlistment of citizens of the United States in foreign armies. The department did not deviate from the position it had adhered to throughout. It cited the relevant statutes of the United States, stated the purpose of the neutrality legislation, and stressed the security risks in Ethiopia" (45).

Blocked by the U.S. State Department from participating in the physical defense of Ethiopia, Schuyler's readers had little recourse to vent their rage over Italian imperialism in Abyssinia.[2] In the *Courier*'s July 27, 1935, "Views and Reviews," Schuyler stoked the flames of his readership's frustration, writing, "And yet there is something dramatically appealing about the idea. As an old soldier, I would certainly like to participate in such an adventure and press a machine-gun trigger on the Italian hordes as they toiled over the Ethiopian terrain. It is one of the few wars in which I could participate with enthusiasm" (17). Feeding African American anger over Italian aggression, Schuyler fantasizes along with his public about the battlefield, his finger on the trigger, felling scores of bloodied, Italian soldiers.[3] Unable to write columns containing factual accounts of African American valor on the battlefields of Ethiopia, Schuyler manifests in fantasy what African Americans had been barred from doing. Schuyler enacts in fiction the very militancy and violent desire for revenge that he recognizes in his 1938 *Crisis* essay, "The Rise of the Black Internationale," as the defining quality of the New Negro. In a section of the essay entitled "Beginning of Revolt," Schuyler insists that, "In America, in Asia, in the islands of the sea the darker men became critical and condemnatory of white civilization where once they had been worshipful and almost grateful for shoddy castoffs" (35).

The next section, "The New Negro Arrives," begins, appropriately, with the claim, "The New Negro is here. Perhaps no more courageous than the Old Negro who dropped his shackles in 1863, and fought against ignorance, propaganda, lethargy and persecution, but better informed, privy to his past, understanding of the present, unafraid of the future" (35). Excused from what Schuyler considered to be the hokum definition of the New Negro as primarily a producer of authentically black cultural products, his New Negro arrives and is ready to kill. Born on the battlefield in 1863, the New Negro's character reveals itself to be essentially that of a soldier and not an artist, or rather, the New Negro combines the two positions. Schuyler's aestheticization of violence sets the limits of what Benjamin calls fascism's "cult of war." Schuyler's clarion call to arms signals a moment in his oeuvre in which racial militancy fused with an aestheticized vision of warfare comes to the fore, defining itself as essentially warlike and revolutionary. The New Negro is tantamount to a violent New World Order. In light of his "The Negro-Art Hokum" (1926), in which he caustically insists that "the Aframerican is merely a lampblacked Anglo-Saxon" (52), to find Schuyler positing the arrival of "the New Negro" in 1938 as versed not in the literary, theatrical, or plastic arts but in the art of war, is not only shocking but also indicative of the high degree of racial militancy and solidarity felt in African America in the wake of Mussolini's invasion of Ethiopia.

The Rise of Black Fascism

The notion of a people, a race, a nation born in battle was an idea with some currency at the time Schuyler wrote "The Rise of the Black Internationale," iterating as it does the fascist conception of the new men and nation who, led by a charismatic, authoritarian ruler, find their essential beings in war.[4] At its heart, Schuyler's vision of the New Negro as born on the battlefield echoes fascism's advocacy of a rigid militarized hierarchy with a dictator/general/father figure at its zenith. This *Führerprinzip* dominates generic fascist ideology; it also takes center stage in *Black Empire*.[5] From the murderous moment that we first meet the suave, violent criminal genius Dr. Henry Belsidus, it is clear that Schuyler has something on his mind different from the satire contemporary critics might expect of him, or the value-free escapist pulp fiction his audience may have craved. *Black Empire,* labeled by Henry Louis Gates Jr. as "the Afrocentrist's dream," is not so much a dream as a revenge fantasy that employs fascist ideology as a means to defeat European fascism ("Fragmented Man" 42). With "The Black Internationale" and "Black Empire," Schuyler begs the question: What if there had been a "black Mussolini"?

When Marcus Garvey chose to identify himself with the fascist dictators of his day, Schuyler agreed with Garvey's self-appraisal. In his 1966 autobiography *Black and Conservative,* Schuyler opines that "Garvey anticipated Hitler, who was then unknown save by a handful of followers" (120). Considered as a meditation in fiction on what Garveyism done right would accomplish, *Black Empire* does not shy away from Garvey's suggestion that his movement may have taught the fascist powers something of both political style and ideological content. Indeed, far from a purely parodic vision of Marcus Garvey, the would-be black Mussolini, Dr. Belsidus, cleaves his way through *Black Empire* with a preternatural tactical genius that lends itself equally to mass psychology and the battlefield. He signifies, as Gates observes, "Du Bois, Booker T. Washington, George Washington Carver, and Marcus Garvey rolled into one fascist superman" ("Fragmented Man" 42). In his foreword to *Black Empire*, John A. Williams also recognizes clearly Belsidus's role as fascist dictator. "Dr. Belsidus," Williams writes, "in the final analysis, is a dictator, a fascist, though his goals are established as moral ones. . . . If we substitute national origin for race in these works . . . their fascist assumptions become quite clear" (xiv). Where Gates provokes but does not substantiate the charge of fascism in Schuyler's text, Williams correctly decides that if we consider Belsidus's dictatorship and racial militancy in the light of fascist nationalism, valid comparisons may be drawn. In ascribing moral goals to him, however, Williams implies that Dr. Belsidus's fascism cannot be grouped with Mussolini's. Williams also assumes here that "nation" and "race" do not overlap in fascist ideology, which is not the case.[6]

It may also not be the case that Schuyler was in any substantial way serious when he created his great dictator. Certainly, the author of *Black No More* (1931) had a penchant for devastating satire. Using *Black No More* as a template, Schuyler's critics identify the entirety of his literary oeuvre under the rubric of "satire." However, this conception conflates *Black No More* with every fictional text Schuyler wrote and dismisses his journalism and essays of the latter half of the 1930s as either aberrations in an otherwise brilliant but solidly conservative journalistic career, or satire so deeply encoded that the satiric elements escape notice (Tucker 145, 146; Gruesser 110). The problem with reading *Black Empire* as satire shows itself when we consider that Schuyler espoused a genuine and virulent anti-Italian rhetoric during and after the 1935–36 Italo-Ethiopian War. If in fact Schuyler intended the serials to be read predominantly as satire, then he used "the rape of Ethiopia" as the frontline of a satirical attack on racial chauvinism. How is it that at such a time Schuyler disparaged tout court a Pan-Africanist position in his fiction, if he voiced in his journalism an extreme sense of outrage over Italian imperialist aggression in Africa? Readings of *Black Empire* as an overwhelmingly satiric text also tend to ignore the serials' wider politico-historical context within Schuyler's nonfiction of the period.[7] Seen from within this context, it cannot be maintained that satire operates as the dominant discursive mode in Schuyler's *Black Empire* (Gysin 177). To do so would be to negate Schuyler's deep commitment to direct political engagement and commentary.

Another possible interpretation is that Schuyler wrote an elaborate hoax. While this is reading is probable, *Black Empire* does not proceed in the usual fashion of a hoax. A hoax attempts to convince someone that something that is not real is real. The duration of Schuyler's work on *Black Empire* might mitigate the effect of this type of hoax. To maintain a hoax over a few years' time would have presented Schuyler with issues of credibility he could not overcome. The aim of such a hoax as this would have been to convince fraudulently the reading public that Dr. Belsidus's machinations were the actions of a real man, and that his conquest of Africa was actually taking place. While some readers did in fact believe this, there is no evidence that the majority of Schuyler's audience subscribed to this point of view over a long period of time.

However, there could be a second type of hoax at work in *Black Empire*. Schuyler's goal may simply have been to write a fascistic text and have people like it, whether it was taken as fiction or journalism. In this sense, *Black Empire* was a hoax. That is to say, Schuyler composed *Black Empire* with the intention of writing a text whose main objective was to sway unwitting readers to find fascist ideology attractive. If this indeed was the case, which I believe it very well may have been, it does not mitigate the fact that the genre in which Schuyler realized his hoax is not satire. Schuyler does not simply satirize the characters in his serials, he subjects them to melodrama.

Pulp melodrama dominates *Black Empire*. As Robert A. Hill and R. Kent Rasmussen observe, "Schuyler's newspaper fiction, which lacks the droll humor characteristic of *Black No More,* his signed columns, and his *American Mercury* essays, clearly belongs to the 'pulp' fiction genre, with all its attendant limitations: clumsy melodramatic plotting, stereotyped characters, stilted dialogue, and so on—all of which contrasts with the seeming care he invested in his books and essays" (269). "In fact," Hill and Rasmussen add, "the stories about Africa and Africans make use of the melodramatic elements of intrigue, love, and adventure that characterized the 1930s pulp genre; as used by Schuyler, however, the stories formulate a coherent allegory of African resistance to white domination" (270). Hill and Rasmussen point out that Schuyler's serialized fiction contains a wide array of rhetorical strategies, including satire, yet falls primarily within the purview of melodrama. Highlighting his choice of genre and venue of publication, Hill and Rasmussen see Schuyler interjecting his newspaper fiction with social and political commentaries. If viewed as satiric, the visceral anger over the Italian invasion of Ethiopia that Schuyler expressed in the serials and shared with his readers would be undermined. It is this anger that led Schuyler to create his own great Duce, Dr. Henry Belsidus.

Anatomically Correct

At the focal point of the charismatic, authoritarian ruler, nation and race merge in Schuyler's text in a fascist biological mysticism instantiated by state religion. Not so much man as the myth of man, Belsidus takes his place in the office of head of state, at the altar as high priest of the Black Internationale, and in the ether as the movement's god. He achieves these ends by merging political and theological authority in the institution of the Temple of Love.[8] In Schuyler's fictive United States before the Italian invasion of Ethiopia and in his Africa after the continent has been purged of the white colonial powers, Belsidus erects hundreds of so-called Temples of Love that serve as the fundamental building blocks of the communities into which the Black Internationale inserts them. Within the standardized walls of each Temple, the body politic of Belsidus's empire is formed. The religious ceremony performed manufactures blind faith in the state as it indoctrinates the masses into Belsidus's program of black empire.

The Temples of Love do not merely fashion religious sentiment; they erect the groundwork for a new society. The Temples' high priest, Reverend Binks, "is making the church what it was to ancient times . . . a center of everyday life and activity, of amusement and instruction, conforming to, yet shaping society" (58). The church becomes both a throwback to an invented, inaccessible earlier age and the harbinger of a future that will be at once the redemption and the alienation of black history. Believing they are the ancestors of the Egyptians and Babylonians, the congregations profess an ontologically black faith, and an ontogenetic propaganda of black empire and racial superiority. The standardized ceremony performed in each Temple articulates and promotes the Black Internationale's ideology of racial exclusivity, which amounts to the promotion of a chosen people. The serials' narrator, Dr. Belsidus's secretary Carl Slater, describes firsthand and in detail the various means of indoctrination devised by the Black Internationale for use in the Temples:

> Then an amazing thing happened. A great bell tolled from somewhere. A stentorian voice boomed, "Rise, All Ye Within! Rise, All Ye Within! Rise and worship the God of Love, Ruler of black men and women. Rise to greet Him!" The dancers stopped, transfixed.
>
> All the lights seemed to die or concentrate themselves in one great spotlight, and this shone upon the huge 50-foot statue of the nude Negro. (61)[9]

The God of Love rules black men and women; he conquers all others. Exhorted to rise, the congregation finds itself inculcated first and foremost with a racial pride that underscores the status of blacks as universally oppressed but able to revolt under the sway of a powerful influence. When Reverend Binks introduces the God of Love, he presents a fascist ruler who buttresses his power with the religious faith of the masses in the race, insofar as Dr. Belsidus *stands in* for the God of Love. The statue of the God of Love is but a thinly veiled simulacrum of Dr. Belsidus, his *means of identification* to facilitate mass subjectification. The statue is what Siefried Kracauer calls the "mass ornament": a ritual object that is "an end in itself." But even after the "ritual meaning" of such objects is discarded, "they remain the plastic formation of the erotic life which gave rise to them and determined their traits" (146). The mass ornament is emptied of its ritual content and plenitude and re-cathected with an erotics of power that seeks to control the masses' libidinal urges by converting them into an iconic religious outpouring. This is why Schuyler's mass ornament is depicted as "a huge statue of a nude Negro standing with legs apart, gazing sardonically downward with arms crossed. It was all of 50 feet high and every part of the body was clearly depicted" (58). The bearer of the sardonic gaze cannot be mistaken. "Sardonic" is, after all, one of Schuyler's favorite adjectives for the good Doctor and his notorious gaze. Also inescapable in this mammoth fifty-foot statue of a male Negro is an anatomical accuracy that surpasses the bounds of decency. If one wondered whether Dr. Belsidus's movement followed the fascist phallocentric logic of male ego-reintegration Theweleit theorizes, the appearance of the fifty-foot "God of Love" in all his anatomical glory removes all doubt.

But aside from adding yet another lurid quality to Dr. Belsidus's empire (a superfluous endeavor), the statue also operates in a different manner. It is not merely a static work of sculpture; it is also a hypno-robot that uses mind control to indoctrinate the masses in Belsidus's political program. "Now the great arms which had been folded slowly unfolded and stretched out full length. The great breast began to rise and fall. The huge eyes became luminous and the great head began slowly to nod up and down. It was awesome indeed. The singing ended. The eyes continued to blaze. The great head moved up and down" (61). A hypnotic device produces the awesome effect of the robot's eyes, an effect that does not pass unnoticed into the narrator Carl Slater's unconscious. This illusion has, however, the force of the real despite the fact that Slater "knew it was hokum. I knew Binks had rigged up this robot and I knew approximately just how it worked, and yet for the life of me I could not but enter into the spirit of the thing and obey the commands of the voice" (61).[10] Carl and all those who are present enter into the spirit, one that contains, or fabricates, a fascistic communal bond of race, blood, and self-sacrifice. Knowing Belsidus's quasi-theological pyrotechnics to be hokum, Carl nevertheless finds his Foucauldian inner fascist.

Within the Temples of Love, a society births its inner fascist under the irrefragable direction of a fascist ruler. The Temples create racial and communal sentiment in the service of the great dictator, opening the minds of the congregations they service to Dr. Belsidus's fascist teachings. What the congregations learn during the ceremonies, at least before liturgy degenerates into orgy, is summed up by Reverend Binks: "Follow the Black Internationale. Obey its commands and all the world will be given to you" (65).[11] In an absolute psychological identification with the mass ornament of the God of Love, the masses are ready to be filled and fulfilled with the God's propaganda. Indeed, as Adorno perceives, "The mechanism which transforms libido into the bond between leader and followers, and between followers and themselves, is that of *identification*" ("Freudian Theory" 124–25). Taking advantage of the psychological preconditioning that allows for this surrender of the self on the part of the individual and the masses, the Führer deploys his idealized ritual image as a means of subjecting the masses to his ideological imperatives. "Psychological ambivalence," Adorno believes, "helps to work a social miracle. The leader's image gratifies the follower's twofold wish to submit to authority and to be the authority himself" (127). It is this twofold ambivalence that Schuyler, too, sees as the basis of a fascistically obedient populace, and what ensures the efficacy of fascist propaganda.

This is why Schuyler stages this scene of subjection in a temple, and why the remainder of the oft-repeated "God of Love" ceremony belongs to overt propaganda: "Now followed an hour of talking from the altar. Slowly the reverend's lieutenants read propaganda charts and messages. Others showed factories, farms and powerhouses and all the far-flung enterprises presided over by Dr. Belsidus. But strangely enough the picture of that master plotter did not appear" (66). It is, of course, not strange at all that no exact image of Dr. Belsidus has managed to surface during the ceremony. Not directly a part of the Temples' canon of icons, Dr. Belsidus knows that such an iconography makes no sense without him. In this way, he is ubiquitous. He is the statue because the statue cannot be properly appraised without him; he speaks through Reverend Binks because Reverend Binks's words cannot be heard unless there is a Black Internationale run by Dr. Belsidus in which to speak them. Belsidus is every icon because he is none. By becoming visibly invisible, Belsidus as the fascist means of identification consolidates his power over the masses in the formless form of what they see when they close their eyes. He is their father, confessor, and god. They are his subjects.

If Belsidus has become a god to his subjects, he maintains the trappings of a sublunary being. Belsidus cannot be said to harbor an indifference to the flesh; in fact, he is a god who metes out his own punishment. Not beyond killing men with his own hands, Belsidus takes a particular delight in murdering white women. The first serialization begins with the narrator, Carl Slater, playing witness to Dr. Belsidus's serial murder of a white lover. When Slater questions the doctor about his moral predilections concerning such matters, Belsidus replies, "'You mean that white woman? . . . Bah! I use their women to aid in their destruction. As long as they succeed in carrying out my mission, I spare them. When they fail, I destroy them'" (11). Codes of moral conduct do not come into play for Dr. Belsidus where race functions as the determinant factor. To carry out his mission, to consolidate his plans and his ego, racism and misogyny determine Belsidus's course of action. The woman is white, subhuman, and fragments Belsidus's ego-coherence until she is eliminated. Race and gender allow him to violently clarify his situation without moral concerns or recourse to euphemism: "'Of course it's murder,' he said, smirking sardonically. 'What of it?'" (11). Murder as a matter of fact does not entail denying a form of sexual gratification. When Belsidus murders a woman, the act is premeditated and follows the logic of an intricate strategy poised to accomplish goals beyond the death of a single, or even several individuals. The killing also signifies a crime of passion. He eliminates lovers, after all. When he decides a woman has failed him, he means in bed as well as in the field. Insofar as Dr. Belsidus violently defines himself as possessing a racially pure, unified, and coherent ego, his murderous misogyny echoes that of Theweleit's protofascist members of the *Freikorps*.

As in Theweleit's psychogenetic understanding of the place of women and gender in the fascist's psyche, the feminine plays a negatively unifying role in the construction of Belsidus's black Empire. Martha Gaskin, a white woman spared death because she serves Dr. Belsidus's politico-sexual desires well, finds a home in the Black Internationale, becoming its most important and deadly terrorist. Gaskin runs the crucial European terror campaign that causes the great powers to make war on each other, thus ignoring Belsidus's forces as they consolidate power across Africa. Despite the fact that when we first meet her as she pleads with Dr. Belsidus to make personal time for her, Gaskin's work does not disappoint: "'An excellent worker,'" he exclaims when she has gone, "'but I suppose I'll have to get rid of her. You know, Slater, women work best for you when they are in love with you'" (81). A woman's role in the Black Internationale can be reduced to a word—work—but within this simple job description we find a host of duties: sexual tool, emotional comforter, and international terrorist.

Gaskin herself becomes the movement's most lethal human weapon. Having just executed a plan by which plague-ridden rats are introduced into the major cities of Europe, Gaskin refuses to leave the city despite rapidly spreading disease. The terrorists' slim chances of escaping their own carnage dwindling further, when pressed by a flunky to leave the city, Gaskin replies, "'When it gets bad, we'll leave . . . but we'll not leave until our work is done. Do you understand?'" (188). Where it concerns Dr. Henry Belsidus, a woman's work is never done. Although this work entails the sexual gratification of Dr. Belsidus, it consists primarily of mass murder and death, the final goals of Belsidus's plans for the white West. Like those of fascist Italy and Nazi Germany, the women of Belsidus's Black Empire are the objects of sexual revulsion, fear, and veneration; they expedite the birth of the new fascist man and make potent, bloody warriors.[12]

No matter the source of the violence, the pages of *Black Empire* are drenched in blood. From the murder that opens the book, to the conquest and defense of Africa, thousands upon thousands meet their ends in Schuyler's texts. It must be noted that white Africa does not succumb to Belsidus's forces by means of truce, or by unconditional surrender. The whites are massacred by a once-subjugated population converted by Belsidus and his Temples of Love into a fascist mass militia. It is "the natives," as Carl Slater calls them, who perform the task of mass murder most readily: "Reaching the Belgian Congo, they bombed Banana, Leopoldville, Stanleyville and other settlements. But it was the natives who did the most destructive work. Not only did they in a few hours destroy what the Belgians had laboriously and cruelly erected in almost fifty years of colonial exploitation, but they slaughtered white men, women and children with great ferocity. You have no idea of the blood-chilling effect of the laconic report from the head of the Black Internationale cell there which read: 'Belgian Congo belongs to us. No white person alive'" (129). The heat of battle cannot account for this slaughter; Carl Slater's natives act under orders: "They were promptly murdered, in accordance with Dr. Belsidus's orders that no prisoners were to be taken" (130). Here battlefield violence fascistically elaborates and celebrates itself. Finding its Jüngerian ontological imperative in war, Belsidus's movement is baptized on the battlefield and in the process creates a fascist black Empire across continental Africa.[13]

This thirst for white blood does not end with the "liberation" of Africa but extends into Europe as the Black Internationale wages total warfare. As mentioned before, to distract the counteroffensive of the European powers, Belsidus unleashes plague-ridden rats in the centers of every major European city, killing scores of thousands of civilians.[14] To cripple the industry of the white world, he orders not merely the destruction of every major machine-parts factory, but the deaths of the factory workers themselves. Martha Gaskin achieves this feat by creating, at the suggestion of Carl Slater, a makeshift gas chamber in a theater, killing fifteen thousand before the start of the second act of an African dance exhibition, thus merging aesthetics, fascist politics, and genocide.

Finally, Belsidus unleashes the ultimate weapon of mass destruction: the death ray that in one stroke emits an electromagnetic pulse, disabling all machinery, and fires a laser that atomizes its crippled target: "The huge nozzle waved slowly back and forth, a giant orange ray darting out on its message of death into the blue. Squadron after squadron crashed to the earth" (243). Without this phallocentric technology, the black empire's victory would have been short-lived. The role of technology in *Black Empire* cannot be overstated. Dr. Belsidus sets out on his journey of conquest with the unwavering belief that black minds function at a level superior to white minds and that black genius can accomplish anything. Of course, Belsidus is not wrong—the innovations and inventions manufactured by the finest young black minds are staggering. From death rays to hydroponics, from fax machines to hypno-robots, the catalogue of achievement compiled by the Black Internationale falls in line with the finest of pulp science fiction stories. It also adds to Schuyler's serialized fiction of black genius the celebration of technology crucial to fascist political endeavor. Belsidus echoes the claims of engineers in fascist Germany as well as Italian Futurists in stating, "It is the skilled technician, the scientist, who wins modern wars, and we are mobilizing the black scientists of the world. Our professors, our orators, our politicians have failed us. Our technicians will not" (46).[15]

With his weapons beyond the pale of imagination, a population armed and ready to wage holy war, and brutal masculinity, Dr. Henry Belsidus's power over the Black Internationale is absolute and absolutely fascist. He signifies the agent by which Schuyler can exact, in kind, his violent, revolutionary, and ultimately literary vengeance for Italian aggression in Ethiopia. The culmination of Belsidus's and Schuyler's labors comes when the Italians are butchered at the hands of the Black Internationale's air force at the end of the second serial: "The bombers wheeled, dived to within a few feet of the ground, their machine guns spitting death pellets at the frantically fleeing Italians. In a few moments the place was a shambles, a field of bloody desolation" (255). Here, in the final pages of *Black Empire*, Schuyler enacts in fiction the very moment he fantasized in his 1935 *Courier* column: fascists die under his literary muzzle; blood splatters across the page like spilt ink. Serializing his brand of Ethiopianism and African American exceptionalism in the pages of the *Courier*, Schuyler restores Menelik II to glory by transforming him into a native New Yorker and fascist Übermensch. When the smoke clears, one wonders if Schuyler's Ethiopians will be able to mark a substantive difference between Mussolini and the God of Love.

One thing is certain: Schuyler's God of Love, as well as his *Black Empire,* transforms Marcus Garvey as well into a near-future superman by negating him as inferior to the mandates of his own black fascist ideology. Dr. Belsidus's brave new black world realizes Schuyler's ideological aesthetic of black fascism by placing it within the realm of science fictive political fantasy. In so doing, Schuyler need not engage in any meaningful way with the possibility of an actual black fascist praxis. In other words, his black fascist aesthetic, because it dwells in, and is conditioned by, a fictive space, allows Schuyler to extol the virtues of black fascism without actually having to promote any form of fascism outside a literary milieu. Despite the fact that *Black Empire* was serialized in a newspaper, Schuyler did not want to make headlines, something that cannot be said for Sufi Abdul Hamid.

4 "In Turban and Gorgeous Robe"
Claude McKay, Black Fascism, and Labor

> What one discovered before proceeding very far [with reading Claude McKay's essay "Labor Steps Out in Harlem"] was that the erstwhile revolutionist was wallowing in the black fascist trough along with... the Garveyites... and the more recent distinguished converts in the infantile paralysis of "voluntary segregation."
> —George S. Schuyler, "Views and Reviews" (1937)

> Today he denounces his own brain child as black fascism.... Schuyler's inept attempt to slander me merely discredits himself.
> —Claude McKay, "McKay Says Schuyler Is Writing Nonsense" (1937)

What Schuyler identifies as McKay's "wallowing in the black fascist trough" and "voluntary segregation" was not far from what Schuyler himself proposed in the fictional world of his "brain child" *Black Empire*—a fact that did not evade McKay's keen critical mind.[1] Interestingly enough, this fact was not lost on Schuyler, either. When Schuyler's *Pittsburgh Courier* published McKay's rebuttal, the newspaper omitted McKay's discussion of Schuyler's politics. Originally appearing in the *Amsterdam News* under the title "McKay Says Schuyler Is Writing Nonsense," McKay's *Courier* text was heavily abridged and given the parodic title "Schuyler Lashes Here and There Like Mad Dog—Bites Everybody."[2] The analytical sections accusing the mad dog of practicing his own brand of fascism did not reach the *Courier*'s readership.

If the Claude McKay of the 1930s and 1940s increasingly came to believe that only a god could save us, then this would not be the mad dog's "God of Love," but instead a god of labor. McKay's turn to the Christian Church reveals a thinker seeking a transcendent solution to material problems. Even so, McKay never abandoned a deep and abiding concern for the toils and evils of this world and never ceased to write and fight for fundamental change.[3] However, McKay's agenda in the 1930s and 1940s for social transformation is radically different from the one he adopted during the early twenties while actively pursuing (all the way to Moscow) the full measure of Communist ideology and activism. After his disillusionment with Communism, far from quietly succumbing to social complacency on the way to a form of activist Catholicism, McKay outlined a program for radical change based on the apotheosis of black labor and the adoption of aspects of fascist ideology. McKay's journey from Communism to Catholicism saw him develop a belief in what he called the "group life" and how this existence relates to segregated labor unions and black labor in general. His deep admiration for, and defense of, the Harlem anti-Semite soapboxer, cultist, and labor leader, Sufi Abdul Hamid, speaks to this belief and a form of fascism that grew out of it. It was for love of the Sufi that McKay wrote "Harlem Runs Wild" (1935), his attempt to deflect blame for the 1935 riot in Harlem from Hamid to Jewish merchants. "Harlem Runs Wild" is a prelude to McKay's unfinished last novel, *Harlem Glory,* his paean to Hamid and his brand of black fascism.

The Piebald Mantle

Unlike Garvey and Schuyler, McKay had firsthand experience with life under fascist rule. He informs us in *A Long Way from Home* (1937) that he counted among the highlights of his travels his discovery of "the phenomenon of the emphasis on group life" in a given land: "Wherever I traveled in Europe and Africa I was impressed by the phenomenon of the emphasis on group life, whether the idea behind it was Communist co-operative or Fascist collective or regional autonomy" (*LWH* 349). Where McKay does not find this emphasis on group life—no matter how democratic a land he travels in—he discerns a spiritual crisis reflected in the state, the Volk, and a race. No matter the national politics, if "group life" defines a nation's Volk, McKay approves. When this "group life," or "soul," arises from a nationally or racially designated Volk, the political situation it inhabits matters little. McKay can find, without much difficulty, the redemptive aspect of Communist and fascist dictatorships, for "even the dictatorships were making concessions to the strong awakened group spirit of the peoples. . . . Labor groups and radical groups were building up their institutions and educating their children in opposition to reactionary institutions" (*LWH* 350). As a reaction against reactionary institutions, labor groups and radical groups came into being and began to flourish, which is to say that without the existence of the oppressive regime (what McKay understands as a "dictatorship"), these liberating labor and radical movements could not come into being as reactions against the reactionary. Just as Bataille theorized, and for McKay as well, extreme interdiction brings about positive radical change. Therefore, interdiction is latently positive and necessary for revolution. McKay's proof for this assertion is seen in a nation lacking a dictatorship—the African American "sadly lacks a group soul":

> But there is very little group spirit among Negroes. The American Negro group is the most advanced in the world. It possesses unique advantages for development and expansion and for assuming the world leadership of the Negro race. But it sadly lacks a group soul. And the greatest hindrance to the growth of a group soul is the wrong idea held about segregation. Negroes do not understand the difference between group segregation and group aggregation. And their leaders do not enlighten them, because they do not choose to understand. (*LWH* 350)

The concept of racial "aggregation" escapes the American Negro masses because their leaders refuse to comprehend the advantages of an anti-assimilationist position for black workers. McKay's position calls for the enlightenment of the black masses by a leader or guide, a de facto dictator (the means of identification) able to disseminate knowledge of an onto-racially determined group soul, the subject of labor. Thus, as Gramsci understood while commenting on Italian Fascism, "the worker or proletarian is not specifically characterized by his manual or instrumental work, but by performing this work in specific conditions and in specific social relations" (8). The worker performs not only his work but a social function obscured by that work. The case for segregation demands segregated unions as a means of empowering black labor and uplifting the race, which McKay sees as an undifferentiated whole and as the product of its labor. Labor's work here is not merely work but uplift through segregation and, ultimately, subjectification.

For McKay, organized, segregated labor presents a potential of such enormity for the racial-hierarchical and sociopolitical reorganization and enfranchisement of the American Negro that it takes precedence in his thinking over the specifics of political organization: "Anyway, it seems to me that if Negroes were organized as a group and as workers, whatever work they are doing (with or without whites), and were thus getting a practical education in the nature and the meaning of the labor movement, it might even be more important and worth-while than for them to become members of radical political parties" (*LWH* 353). This "practical education in the nature and the meaning of the labor movement" teaches that organized labor, racially divided, could energize the Negro's political efforts for enfranchisement to such a degree that it would obliterate and reinvent the political sphere. In McKay's thinking, the political cannot be dissociated from the labor movement. Without the labor movement to provide its contextual basis, the political, radical and otherwise, has no life of its own and cannot be conceptualized.

In every sense, however, the labor movement itself avoids conceptualization unless it has a single voice with which to articulate its practical and theoretical needs. Bearing in mind that for McKay, the transnational Negro subject lacks any and all sense of his racially coded group soul and cannot devise for himself the nature of his own nature, the great leader who shall undertake to educate the masses in the ways of the labor movement shall arise from the vanguard among blacks: African Americans. According to McKay in 1937, such a man exists only in his imagination and as "a monument of verse": "I suppose I have a poet's right to imagine a great modern Negro leader. At least I would like to celebrate him in a monument of verse" (*LWH* 354). McKay's right to imagination was exercised in his only recently published *The Cycle* with the sonnet "Sufi Abdul Hamid":

Oh how they wrapped them in a maze of lies,
To tag the name of Black Hitler upon you—
Wealthy and sinister whites whose raucous cries,
Inflame the nation with all things untrue.
The Negro papers and the Negro writers
They bought and set them at your heels like hounds,
Because you urged the Negroes to be fighters,
Even though they lose all of a hundred rounds!

Poor Negro! The white papers, lawyers, judges,
All ganged together, pushed you to your grave,
Because your name was Arab and their grudges
Foredoomed your crufixion [sic] as a knave.
Because you cried, white men, you always rob
My people, give them now a decent job! (*Complete Poems* 45)

Tagged "Black Hitler" for his allegedly virulently anti-Semitic soapbox speeches, the Sufi has been "wrapped" with "them" (presumably his speeches) in a "maze of lies." The construction of the maze has been financed by affluent whites who, sensing a threat in the Sufi to the flow of cash from Harlem to their wallets, buy off the Negro papers and intellectuals and effectively lose Hamid among the many twists and turns of their duplicity.[4] Espousals of self-determination and self-defense make up the true content of Hamid's rhetoric. Anti-Semitism never found a place in Hamid's vituperations, as was the case for all of Harlem, according to McKay. Any such charge of anti-Semitism, like the one brought against Hamid by the Jewish Minute Men in 1934, merely served conspiratorial ends. Hamid's end would come by means of a media crucifixion sentenced him by the very businessmen from whom his "Don't Buy Where You Can't Work" boycott campaign sought to compel fair labor practices. More important, the crucifixion of Hamid is one without hope of resurrection: his political and organizational demise takes with it not merely the hopes of black labor, but the political aspirations of the race as a whole in America and beyond.

Hamid's beginnings are less well defined than his end. Bishop Amiru Al-Minin Sufi Abdul Hamid was born under the shadow of an Egyptian pyramid on January 6, 1903—a fact his parole officer produced documentation attesting to at one of Hamid's many legal trials. The truth of his origins lies in obscurity. Police at the scene of his death, a plane crash on Long Island on July 31, 1938, gave his real name as Eugene Brown, of Lombard Street, Philadelphia. David Levering Lewis tracks the Sufi's birth to Lowell, Massachusetts (300). Perhaps only the effects of his deeds, and not the aliases under which he traveled, including the "Black Hitler," shed light on Hamid's shadowy birth and life. In 1930 he founded, in Harlem, the Universal Temple of Tranquility; in 1932 he led a successful jobs boycott in Chicago; also in 1932, he began boycotting

Harlem merchants; in February 1934 he, as part of a coalition of activist groups, organized and executed a successful boycott of Blumstein's department store. Effectively neutralized as a force in Harlem's labor politics by his legal woes and his deserved reputation among the African American intelligentsia as a charlatan and racketeer, Hamid turned, during the late 1930s, to his experience as a cultist. Relying on the mystical and hoping to challenge Father Divine's standing as Harlem's premier cultic figure, Hamid died attempting to reach those lofty heights.

Brought down by collusive whites and blacks, radicals and moderates, when Hamid fell, McKay's poem hints, he did not descend alone. McKay fulfils at least two aesthetic goals in his poem. He dreams Hamid the great race man into being, and he builds a monument to his own stillborn creation. Whatever insight the creation of this two-headed being gave McKay into Hamid and his movement, blindness accompanied it. This inability to see Hamid as anything other than a great race man is shown by McKay's description in *Harlem: Negro Metropolis* (1940) of a moment when American Nazis pay Hamid a friendly visit:

> It was only after the wide publicity given him as a "Harlem Hitler" that the Sufi had his first contact with American Nazis. It happened that I was at his office one day trying to get some facts for an article when two Germans or German-Americans called on him. They invited him to a meeting in Yorkville. Later he had told me that he had gone with his chief aide, Francis Minor (now president of the Harlem Labor Union) whom the Bulletin had called "Hermann Goering." "I was curious," he said "to find out what the pure blond Nordicans could have to offer to the pure black Africans when their Hitler says we are no better than monkeys. But I couldn't imagine cooperating with the Nazis any more than with the Ku Klux Klan." (*HNM* 203)

To establish that the Nazis' visit was provoked by a lie, McKay takes care to situate it after the media crucifixion had begun. McKay accepts without question that such meetings have never happened before. He also does not question that Hamid tells the truth about the content of, and his feelings about, the meeting. McKay believed that Hamid—whom McKay thought could wear the "piebald mantle" of Marcus Garvey—"couldn't imagine cooperating with the Nazis any more than with the Ku Klux Klan," even though Garvey himself, in a much publicized disaster, cooperated with the Ku Klux Klan.⁵ It could be the case that McKay is more interested in objective reporting here than defending someone he believes to have been a great labor leader. Perhaps curiosity is a good enough reason for Hamid to take such a meeting. Much could be added to this already too lengthy list of conditions under which McKay's statement is not problematic.

In any event, McKay himself at this time came under attack for being a "Potential Fascist"; he writes that, because of his support of Hamid, "I was soon regarded in Harlem as an enemy of the Communist fake Popular Front and a Potential Fascist" (*HNM* 234). Of course, the "Communist fake Popular Front" often made such seemingly outrageous charges. Nevertheless, with his staunch defense of Hamid, McKay gave them cause to doubt his sincerity. Despite claims to the contrary, McKay in fact perceived what he believed to be an acceptable level of fascist ideology in Hamid's labor politics. The reason for this acceptance can be attributed to McKay's belief that the field of political choices for the Negro, as mentioned previously, did not extend beyond Communism and fascism. McKay makes this conviction clear in *Harlem: Negro Metropolis* when he writes, "It is not to be wondered at since the Russian Revolution has revealed its true character to the world, that people, wherever they are faced with the ultimate choice of Communism or Fascism, prefer the later with its perceived principle of national or racial unity as against the internecine class war of Communism" (258). Everyone, regardless of race, faces the "ultimate choice of Communism or Fascism," and, "When predicated on labor, the decision to be reached is clear." McKay's self-imposed political task demanded that he create in poetry the great leader who would make the choice between Communism and fascism no choice at all by virtue of his perfect embodiment of the manhood of the race. An imperative of emulation would supersede an otherwise inessential political decision. The best means of identification is the work of art, and for McKay, art and politics are therefore not separate. The critical conceit that McKay's work contains artistry and that any political content to be found therein is a coincidence is based on the assumption that McKay believed himself an artist, not an activist (Helbing 51). However, this assumption does not take into consideration that McKay did not so easily separate art and politics. He believed that his art was his politics, and that the political manifests its own forms of art and means of identification.

The presence of an aesthetic as well as a political problem is evidenced in the totality of McKay's literary output. McKay's oeuvre poses the question of how, aesthetically, to imagine the political as the effect as well as the cause of a transnational black subject. We are asked to do this without falling into the vagaries and impossibilities of Garveyism, or toeing the Party line as Cyril Briggs did (for the most part) after the African Blood Brotherhood came under the Party's wing.[6] Having helped to draw this line in the first place, McKay's solution announces itself as a shift in the formal means of his artistic production, one that allows him to gather his political energies into a single space. Fiction takes precedence in McKay's creative output of the 1930s, becoming his most concrete means of representing and enacting a successful black revolution (Stephens 601–2). The group soul dwells within McKay's fiction, set there to awaken within blacks its own revolutionary consciousness. The group soul, or spirit, is thus bound to creativity and aestheticized communal being.

McKay's biographer Wayne Cooper rightly surmises, then, that "In the twenties, he turned from international communism but not from the common Negro, with whom he had always closely identified. He came to the conclusion that in Negro working people there existed an uninhibited creativity and joy in life which Europeans, including Americans, had lost. . . . He laid much emphasis on the need of Negroes to develop a group spirit" (303). This basis for Negro solidarity in fact eludes concrete grounding. The Negro spirit, the existence of which McKay posits in the closing chapters of *A Long Way from Home,* plays throughout the transnational black body politic and binds blacks at the level of exploited black labor. It reveals itself in fiction as a means of identification. The novel, then, becomes the site par excellence and modus operandi for a black group soul. Because of this, what McKay seeks to represent is not a given social reality but the idea of a better reality. Thus, McKay eschews socialist realism as the genre of the proletariat best suited to his political aims. As a mimetic textual strategy, realism would have obscured McKay's desire not merely to represent, but to give birth to, the group soul.

McKay's group soul is, of course, loyal to the interests of specific members of the group. That is, it does not ask but assumes the consent of all. For McKay, the black group soul is first and foremost masculine. Even the earned marital bliss of *Banana Bottom*'s Bita can be read as McKay's continued attempt to establish the idealism of dominant configurations of black masculinity (R. Greenberg 261). Bita continues an ongoing conversation McKay has with himself, which begins, in his fiction, with *Home to Harlem*'s Jake. As Hazel Carby understands it, "Jake's journey is not just a journey to find the right woman; it is, primarily, a journey of black masculinity in formation, a sort of *Pilgrim's Progress* in which a number of threatening embodiments of the female and the feminine have to be negotiated." Indeed, "Central to the success of the emergent black middle class in these two novels is the evolution of urban codes of black masculinity" ("Policing" 749, 747). Seemingly without any knowledge of *Harlem Glory*, Carby chooses the apt title of *Pilgrim's Progress* for the journey of and to black masculinity in McKay's fiction. Buster, the "Jake" figure in McKay's unfinished last novel, *Harlem Glory*, receives his baptismal moniker "Pilgrim's Progress" from Glory Father, a.k.a. Father Divine, on entering his new life as a "Glory Souler." The "Pilgrim's Progress" that Carby recognizes as an integral part of *Home to Harlem* and that returns at the end of McKay's career in *Harlem Glory* can be found throughout the entire body of McKay's fiction. It traces the unification of the male ego through sexual relationships. This Pilgrim's Progress sees women as means to the end of male ego coherence and fulfillment, and, on a larger scale, the realization of the group soul as a combined nationalist and masculinist ideal.[7]

In this sense, male-female relations are productive; they help to create the group soul. They are also the analogues of the means of production. As Theweleit has theorized, since fascism is "a form of reality production that is constantly present and under determinate conditions, it can, and does, become our production. The crudest examples of this are to be seen in ... male-female relations, which are also relations of production" (221). Tacitly understanding the nature of fascist production and the production of fascism, McKay genders organized labor as he insists on its segregation. Black labor unions are sites in McKay's fiction ostensibly outside of sexual relationships that offer his male protagonists opportunities to realize nationalist and masculinist impulses. The practices of interracial labor unions and "open shops," however, appear among the various forms of emasculation in McKay's fiction (McLeod 343).[8] Whereas one can readily accept the claim that McKay *believed* he saw through the facade of the "open shop" labor union, the idea that he anticipated wide acceptance of the notion that the "open shop" emasculates workers remains to be seen. The supposition that McKay bided his time advocating segregated unions while awaiting the advent of nonracist unions does not account for his pro-segregationist labor writings of the 1930s and 1940s, in particular *Harlem: Negro Metropolis* and its supplement, *Harlem Glory*. Geta LeSeur concludes, "Until his conversion to Catholicism, in the last few years of his life, the concept of a proletarian revolution was the strongest of all his temptations to desert his belief in a pure black identity" (230). That McKay did not succumb to this last temptation militates against the belief that troubling aspects of his conceptions of labor, race, and masculinity can be written off as utopian fantasy. The quest for a formative black masculine identity ontologically beholden to black labor and black community occupied McKay's writings of the 1930s and 1940s and must inform any understanding of the "group soul," or "oversoul," McKay envisions in *A Long Way from Home* (B. Griffin 48). McKay in fact disdained the assistance of white labor unions and the white liberals he associated with them, and desired the realization of this black "oversoul" as a product of black male labor and community. There exists no greater testament to this than his defense of Sufi Abdul Hamid against accusations that the soapboxer indirectly caused the 1935 Harlem riot.

The Composite Mind of the Negro

The first line of McKay's 1935 essay "Harlem Runs Wild" informs us, "Docile Harlem went on a rampage last week" (221). Incited to riot, "docile Harlem" displays an atypical violence. McKay insists that the average Harlem denizen does not aspire to be anything other than the picture of passivity in the face of economic exploitation and rampant civil and social injustices. Yet a riot erupted on March 19, 1935, one that McKay feels compelled both to condemn as foolhardy and to praise as the manifestation of an aberration in the slave mentality of collective Harlem. Insisting that Harlem rioted despite its nature, McKay ostensibly endeavors to pinpoint the exact cause of the violence. However, as "Harlem Runs Wild" unfolds, it becomes clear that McKay's actual goal in the essay is to deflect blame for the riot from Hamid. Given that Hamid's inflammatory, racist rhetoric had been viewed as in part responsible for the riot, it is incumbent on McKay first to identify the targets of the violence, and from this extrapolate the causes.

McKay does not equivocate on this point: whites were not the targets of violence. Harlem did not become embroiled in a race riot: "A few whites were jostled by colored people in the melee, but there was no manifest hostility between colored and white as such" (221).[9] Indeed, the race-neutral conditions that spawned the riot "merely served to explode the smoldering discontent of the colored people against the Harlem merchants" (222). McKay most certainly is being disingenuous here. The very idea that the riot might be considered something other than a race riot is absurd. Even if violence was not directed against whites, the riot was nevertheless a race riot. However, McKay makes the case that the Harlem explosion can be traced back to the fact that "colored people" on a global scale succumb rather easily to the slightest provocation.[10] McKay claims, "Colored people all over the world are notoriously the most excitable material, and colored Harlem is no exception The population is gullible to the extreme. And apparently the people are exploited so flagrantly because they invite and take it" (222). The accusation of colored excitability is an odd one given that McKay begins his essay with the claim that Harlem is docile. What McKay attempts to establish with this inconsistency in logic is an economic cause for the riot, while maintaining the "manhood" of the race. In effect, McKay's riot positions itself in a sophisticated theoretical model at variance with itself. His carefully wrought argument against the racial character of the violence serves only to underscore the facts that the riot rampaged through the streets of Harlem in direct response to racially determined economic conditions, or economically determined racial conditions. Either way, race plays a major role in the event.

But McKay's greatest wish for the essay is to displace blame for the riot from Hamid to another cause. Bearing this in mind, McKay's rioting mass must be gullible and easily excitable. Without these shared characteristics, the riot's participants could be said to have had a concrete purpose in mind and therefore a traceable source of malcontent. McKay offers us a vision of the riot in which "agitators" with little of value to say but much to promote by way of senseless sensationalism incite a riot. "These agitators," as McKay understands them, "are crude men, theoretically. They have little understanding of and little interest in the American labor movement, even from the most conservative trade-union angle. They address their audience mainly on the streets. Their following is not so big as the cultists and occultists. But it is far larger than that of the Communists" (222).[11] The agitators' crudity and lack of associations, accompanied by a paucity of theoretical rigor, effects an irreparable breach separating the "soapboxers" from legitimate, socially conscious, and politically effective orators. At its worst, the "spectacle" of the soapboxer would be complicit with the logic of the spectacle in general, which, according to Guy Debord, allows "the ruling order [to discourse] endlessly upon itself in an uninterrupted monologue of self-praise. The spectacle is the self-portrait of power in the age of power's totalitarian rule over the conditions of existence" (19). Trapped in an endlessly self-referential power structure that manifests in all forms of spectacle, the soapboxer cannot but use the language of the oppressor. It is precisely this belief that led Gramsci to write: "It seems to me that, for the moment, American negroes have a national and racial spirit which is negative rather than positive, one which is a product of the struggle carried on by the whites in order to isolate and depress them" (21).

Perhaps in a conscious effort to thwart this white struggle, soapboxers, Sufi Abdul Hamid among them, celebrated the Nazis' upsetting of "the international applecart." According to McKay in the *New Leader* in 1940,

> It is interesting to listen to them and to hear remarks of individuals in the crowd. While not altogether pro-Nazi, they do gloat over the Nazis upsetting the international applecart, and they are not pro-British. Many of them declare that a Nazi victory might be better for the black people. It is not because they imagine the Nazis having any tenderness for black people. But they believe that a Nazi victory would stir the blacks from their present lethargy either to live or to die. (*PoCM* 277)

Taking aim once again at what he perceives to be the inherent lethargy of blacks, McKay writes off the Nazism of street orators with a negative dialectic. Nazi victory will shock blacks out of their apathy and bring them to arms. This justification for the soapboxers' sympathy with the Nazis rings hollow when we realize that their schadenfreude over Nazi victories in Europe arises from a profound feeling of admiration for Germany and its upsetting of the "international applecart." No doubt disturbed by Nazi racial rhetoric, McKay's soapboxers exhibit pleasure over, and a seemingly bizarre identification with, the Nazi will to power. The idea that one must root for Nazi victory as a means of supporting a subsequent black revolution is absurd. But even if we take McKay at his word, Nazi anti-Semitism doesn't trouble him so long as the revolution comes.

McKay is not unaware that he, through his reading of Hamid, flirts with anti-Semitism. Although Hamid had been dead some three years by the time of this 1941 essay, to address preemptively any charge of anti-Semitic sentiment, McKay tacitly acquits his beloved and beturbaned soapboxer of the charges of anti-Semitism while rescuing Nazism for the Sufi's cause. The visionary Hamid preternaturally and prematurely tapped into the collective desire of an African American political unconscious that well suited McKay's profoundly anti-Communist beliefs of the 1930s and 1940s. Thus positioned, Hamid was able to showcase the divided mind of the Negro as it manifested its contradictions in the streets, as McKay puts it in "Harlem Runs Wild." McKay resolves the Negro mind in conflict with itself with the figure of Sufi Abdul Hamid, whose overt anti-Semitism somehow avoids the label of anti-Semitism in *Harlem: Negro Metropolis* and "Harlem Runs Wild." Whether the "unsophisticated" lot of McKay's cavemen agitators counts for anything in his mind remains in question; but it is certain that "the Sufi" commanded McKay's respect and admiration:

> One of the agitators is outstanding and picturesque. He dresses in turban and gorgeous robe. He has a bigger following than his rivals. He calls himself Sufi Abdul Hamid. His organization is the Negro Industrial and Clerical Alliance. It was the first to start picketing the stores of Harlem demanding clerical employment for colored persons. Sufi Hamid achieved a little success. (HRW 222)

Hamid can be credited with convincing Koch's department store to hire colored clerks—a victory that removed the Black Hitler from a space of relative obscurity in Harlem but still did not win him respect among its leaders: "At first his movement got scant sympathy from influential Negroes and the Harlem intelligentsia as a whole. Physically and mentally, Sufi Hamid is a different type. He does not belong" (223). Despite the Koch victory, Hamid's methods alienated him from Harlem's intelligentsia.[12] Known for bombastic speeches stuffed with anti-Semitic sentiment and powered by a black labor nationalism calling for the end of black patronage for businesses run by Jews, "spaghetti slingers," and Greeks, Hamid soon ran afoul of Jewish activist groups and eventually landed in jail. McKay's picturesque agitator,

> [i]n the midst of the campaign . . . was arrested. Some time before his arrest a committee of Jewish Minute Men had visited the mayor and complained about an anti-Semitic movement among the colored people and the activities of a black Hitler in Harlem. The *Day* and *Bulletin*, Jewish newspapers, devoted columns to the Harlem Hitler and anti-Semitism among Negroes. The articles were translated and printed in the Harlem newspapers under big headlines denouncing the black Hitler and his work. (223)

Intimating that a conspiracy of Jewish special interest groups caused the incarceration of the Sufi, McKay attempts to occlude the fact of Hamid's anti-Semitism by reducing the effort to silence him as purely economic in nature. Hamid's anti-Semitism is, however, what Horkheimer and Adorno call the "luxury of the masses." "The fact that the demonstration of economic uselessness," Horkheimer and Adorno write, "tends to increase rather than to lessen the attraction of the nationalistic panacea, points to the true nature: it does not help men but panders to their urge to destroy. . . . Anti-Semitism has proved immune to the argument of inadequate 'profitability'" (170). Struggling for economic self-determinism and so "profitability," Hamid's anti-Semitism is indicative of stock investment made by those with nothing.

Whether McKay's assessment of the situation accurately approximates the turn of events falls under the heading of speculation. It is the manner in which McKay seeks to discredit those who discredited the Sufi that commands our attention. McKay refuses to ask the question that nevertheless plays a crucial role in the essay's overall defense of the soapboxer, namely, why is Hamid being called an anti-Semite if there is no anti-Semitism in Harlem? The very fact that McKay feels he must address the charge as if unfounded tells us much about the mechanism of McKay's apology. In taking umbrage at the harassment to which the Minute Men subject the Sufi, McKay strikes a posture of denial, which has the contradictory effect of raising the suspicion that a virulently anti-Semitic Hamid pontificates on the streets of Harlem. After all, had there been no genuine bone of contention between the Minute Men and Hamid, McKay need not have attacked the Minute Men on the basis of a conspiracy theory, but on that of inaccuracy. McKay's presentation of a conspiracy theory is a rhetorical maneuver that leaves a lingering doubt as to McKay's own position vis-à-vis anti-Semitism in Harlem.

This is not to say that there was no bias, if not a conspiracy, against Hamid that mobilized the Minute Men and precipitated their accusation. As McKay relates, the case against the Black Hitler ultimately failed because of such a bias:

> On October 13 of last year Sufi Hamid was brought before the courts charged with disorderly conduct and using invective against the Jews. The witnesses against him were the chairman of the Minute Men and other persons more or less connected with the merchants. After hearing the evidence and the defense, the judge decided that the evidence was biased and discharged Sufi Hamid. (223)

Clearly, McKay believes justice has been served during the trial of Sufi Abdul Hamid. Whatever bias lead to the wrongful imprisonment of the Sufi could not withstand the judicial proceedings that heard the testimony of only high-ranking officials of the Minute Men and "other persons more or less connected with the merchants." McKay's use of the word *merchants* here reveals the underlying ideological bulwark of the essay: the belief that Jewish economic interest and power felt threatened by the Sufi's appeals to racial solidarity and black economic self-determinism. In other words, McKay, after positing that the riot did not erupt because of black-white division and hatred, tacitly cedes the cause of the riot to another brand of racial dissention. The riot was a race riot, *but between black and Jew,* not black and white.[13]

According to McKay, the Minute Men cultivated violence in Harlem when they attempted to ride the Sufi out of Harlem on a rail. Jewish-determined, penurious economic conditions in Harlem showcased by racially determined, unfair hiring practices spread the seeds of the violence. McKay's diagnosis of the cause of the riot names a disease rooted in the very pavement of Harlem: the economic dependency of the black majority on Jewish, not white, capital. Whether or not Hamid's rhetoric maintained that black Harlem's fight for economic, and so racial, self-determinism must be waged against "greedy" Jews, McKay's analysis of the situation did.[14] Through Hamid, McKay surreptitiously identifies and condemns the cause of many of Harlem's Depression-era ills at the same time as he positions the origin of the riot into a space of pure, disinterested, racially neutral economic determinism—something he must do to avoid the charge of Nazi sympathizer.[15]

McKay can thus present the Sufi as espousing black nationalist economics while at the same time disavowing any feeling of animosity toward the group he sees as holding the most economic leverage in Harlem: "He said that once when he visited a store to ask for the employment of colored clerks, the proprietor remarked, 'We are fighting Hitler in Germany.' Sufi said that he replied, 'There is no Hitler in Harlem.' He went on to say that although he was a Moslem he had never entertained any prejudices against Jews as Jews" (224). Although McKay does not make clear when this exchange took place, it is doubtful that it took place before the time of the riot. It seems more likely that McKay fabricated this story after World War II, or at least after the American military campaign against Hitler had begun. In any event, McKay's shrewd shopkeeper accuses Hamid of betraying his race. By investing his invectives with the Nazi jargon of racial authenticity, economics, and anti-Semitism, the Führer of Harlem inadvertently translates his nationalist message into a discourse that undermines black self-determinism and racial pride. This is why it is crucial for McKay to make explicit that Hamid "was opposed to Hitlerism, for he had read Hitler's book, 'Mein Kampf,' and he knew Hitler's attitude and ideas about colored peoples. Sufi Hamid said that the merchants of Harlem spread the rumor of anti-Semitism among the colored people because they did not want to face the issue of giving them a square deal" (224). Because much of his rhetoric did reflect a positive reading of *Mein Kampf*, McKay must engage at several removes with the infamous book in order to remove its stain from the otherwise unsoiled rhetoric of the Sufi.

In the end, McKay's report of Hamid and his role in the riot reads as a convoluted tale of racially coded hatred, as well as a poetic portrait of the great race leader who never was. At war with itself, McKay's essay reflects the very "composite mind of the Negro" it limns:

Of the grapevine intrigue and treachery that contributed to the debacle of the movement, who can give the facts? They are as obscure and inscrutable as the composite mind of the Negro race itself. So the masses of Harlem remain disunited and helpless, while their would-be leaders wrangle and scheme and denounce one another to the whites Each one is ambitious to wear the piebald mantle of Marcus Garvey. (224)

As a reflection of the "composite mind of the Negro race itself," the riot can be explained with recourse to Marcus Garvey. Without Garvey's successor in place, there is no way to organize the Negro's latent violence, to transform the mob into a crowd. The violence that plagued Harlem on March 19 unfolded as do the very collective thoughts of Negroes: chaotically. After subsuming himself in the mass, the Negro requires a guiding principle. In other words, to become a de-individualized, unified, and monolingual organism, the mass of Harlemites first had to become a crowd. For Elias Canetti, the crowd has purpose, as opposed to the mob or mass. It is the arbiter of the annihilation of individuality and the formative agent of group psychological agency. In the destructive crowd, Canetti believes, "the individual feels that he is transcending the limits of his own person. He has a sense of relief, for the distances are removed which used to throw him back on himself and shut him in. With the lifting of these burdens of distance he feels free" (20). This freedom, however, can only be attained by loss of the self through identification with an other. Directed violence as a means of identification engenders the crowd, or third term, the step beyond the composition of the individual mind. McKay seeks this violent directive in the place Marcus Garvey left vacant. The composite mind of the Negro requires a unifying factor in the person of a leader.

The riot sums up the fact that the Negro mind can exceed the sum of its parts. Any attempt at a unified presentation of the contradictory Negro mind fails because it will have misrecognized the essentially fragmentary nature of such a mind. What is needed to bring this mind to order is a leader, or a work of art that creates one. If one means of identification is unavailable (the leader), another can take its place (the work of art). This is precisely what McKay's unfinished novel about Harlem-based cults, *Harlem Glory: A Fragment of Aframerican Life,* sought to do.

Left and Right, Fascists and Communists, Triskists and Stillinnites

Even though *Harlem Glory* remains a fragment because McKay did not live to bring it to completion, Aframerican life in itself could never be anything but fragmentary. Without a strong identifying principle in place, the composite mind of the Negro defies the logic of totality. The "total" sociopolitical scene that Aframerican culture helps to create is afflicted with double-consciousness. This is not the double-consciousness of W. E. B. Du Bois, whose *Souls of Black Folk* (1903) posited the existence of coherent yet split African American psychological composition. For Du Bois, the Negro mind maintained, behind the veil, empowering aspects of African culture as it projected to the white world a second if not secondary face amenable to Euro-American values.[16] Whereas for Du Bois something behind the veil transcends temporal qualification, for McKay we find that the situation is quite otherwise.

McKay's "composite mind" perpetuates self-contradiction as its essential modus operandi, leaving us with a political vision, in *Harlem Glory*, refracted through two lenses. One is Communist and one is capitalist, with black fascism forming the "Third Way."[17] Communist and black fascist paradigms are created by combining the ideological positions of Father Divine (*Harlem Glory*'s Glory Savior; Communism) and Sufi Abdul Hamid (Omar in the novel; fascism). The amalgamation of the two positions is McKay's reinvention of Garveyism. For McKay, Marcus Garvey embodied the Negro mind in all its contradictions, for better and for worse, better than anyone else.

But the bond between Glory Savior and Omar goes beyond Garvey: Harlem's economic matrix links Glory Savior to Omar. The two called each other "partner" at one time, together owning and operating an employment agency: "The Glory Savior was no ordinary ignorant Negro preacher. Formerly he was Robert Byrd and once operated [with Omar] an employment agency in Harlem" (66). Unable to place customers in the Depression-ravaged market of Harlem, Byrd devises another way to make a buck: "Noticing that those who were most fervent in praying and singing were the most enthusiastic workers, he conceived the idea of harnessing religion to his Helping Hand plan of work. Upon this issue Sharpage [Omar] disagreed with Byrd. Sharpage was more intellectual than Byrd. He contended that there were too many churches and cults in Harlem and it would be better if colored folks were not so possessed with religion" (67). Sharpage does not wish for Harlemites to succumb to an illusion, and so a racket for mass manipulation and economic gain and social control. In this sense, McKay's understanding of religion does not fall far, in terms of its effects, from Freud's: organized religion is a mass deception and manipulation engendered by psychical needs.[18]

After arguing with each other over the morality of exploiting these very psychical needs, the partners break with each other on the basis of disparate conceptions of racial uplift and its relation to religion. For Byrd, there can be no advancement of colored peoples without a substantial increase in his own personal wealth, and the best way to do that is through the auspices of his own cult. On the other side of things, Sharpage, not wanting to add to the race's misery by giving the Volk yet another cult to waste their savings on, decides to forgo the thought of lining his own pockets in favor of what he deems best for the race. Whereas Sharpage feels a keen sense of racial responsibility, Byrd sees Harlem employment as a type of racket. Their combined principles of leadership form a tenet of Nazi ideology: the desire for racial purity and superiority mixed with the awareness on the part of the ruling intelligentsia that this fiction of race serves, ultimately, to eliminate class struggle and subjugate the masses to state capitalism.[19]

This fundamental difference between the two leads Byrd to the construction of a hermetically sealed society that, as a structural necessity, annihilates difference between members through various means of identification. Glory Savior seeks what Hannah Arendt calls "[t]otal domination, which strives to organize the infinite plurality and differentiation of human beings as if all humanity were just one individual, [and] is possible only if each and every person can be reduced to a never-changing identity of reactions, so that these bundles of reactions can be exchanged at random for any other" (*Origins* 438). To achieve "total domination," it is essential, then, that "Glory Savior's new society [be] based on certain laws such as: non-sex, non-mortality, non-race, non-color, collective work, collective living, collective recreation and complete faith in him as savior" (67).

Where Byrd collapses difference, Sharpage increases difference to such an extent that he nearly effaces the very image of racial purity he seeks to represent:

> It was presumed that he had been in service during the World War, probably as a sailor, and that he had remained abroad and traveled extensively. No one knew exactly how, but he knew a lot about Europe and the East....
>
> Now after a period of eclipse, Sharpage appeared on the streets of Harlem wearing a turban, a belted leather coat, boots and spurs and announcing himself as Omar, The African, founder of a new religion and a new idea of labor for the colored masses. The new religion was a philosophical form of Islam as it had been evolved in Africa, said Omar, and the new conception of labor for the colored masses was to be worked out in the Yeomen of Labor, which he had organized. (69, 70)

McKay's Sufi Abdul Hamid, Omar has ostensibly moved beyond rigid descriptions of nationhood and nationalism to embrace the black world in its entirety. He manifests a transnational ideal of black being that does not claim Africa or any other geographical location as its birthplace but instead offers a floating signifier of diaspora. As the Black Hitler of the text, Omar holds together his notion of the race with a brand of Sufism cobbled together from various sources and presented as a philosophical collage intended to unify and promote the power of black labor. Omar, then, posits an authentic black being that manifests itself in the products of black labor, much like Heidegger's *techne,* which names "not only the activities and skills of the craftsman but also . . . the arts of the mind and the fine arts. Techne belongs to bringing-forth, to poiesis; it is something poetic" (318). Techne "brings forth" the revelation of a "being" of a people as veiled; it unites human activity and productivity into the ludic expression of a people's intrinsic Being. This "jargon of authenticity" Omar speaks allows McKay to place the "piebald mantle" of Marcus Garvey around Omar's well-traveled and weatherworn shoulders to cover the backside Garvey left exposed.

This "new idea" is the fusion of a highly secular conception of Islam and anything else Omar (the Sufi) can get his hands on that somehow speaks of an original black thought without having, as in the case of

Garvey's appropriation of Christianity for the Blackman, to bend over backward to make it so. It merges with a Black Nationalist labor front into a theosophical system designed for the sole purpose of racial self-determination in Harlem. Finally, the idea conjoins the fascist charismatic leader with the people to such an extent that the personal welfare of the ruler cannot be estimated without taking into account the size of the number in each union member's bankbook. In other words, Omar cannot grow wealthy without his constituents doing likewise. He operates a system of profit that creates, according to McKay, a "new man," and a new, unrivaled sense of community: "His new idea embodied the closer unity of all colored people as a group and the intensive reconstruction of the colored community" (70).[20]

The greater part of Harlem, however, finds itself ideologically split, dividing its loyalty between Omar and Glory Savior. The distinction McKay draws between those who support Glory Savior and those who favor Omar hinges on age: "While the great mass of plain people, following the tradition of old time religion, was partial to Glory Soul [Glory Savior's movement], many of the young vanguard of workers who were caught in the toils of Depression were inclined to listen to Omar. The conservative colored leaders and the intelligentsia, while scoffing at Glory Soul and inclined to take his cult humorously in spite of its increasing numbers, were openly skeptical of and even hostile to Omar" (71). A fascistic cult of youthful vigor translates into successful political engagement. The Glory Soulers seek refuge in an illusion of social well-being, whereas Omar's Yeomen of Labor (Hamid's Negro Industrial and Clerical Alliance) transcend mystification to tackle socioeconomic reality head-on. In doing so, they overcome whatever obstacles white (or Jewish) capital places in their way. What McKay calls for, then, amounts to a religion of labor that would include a fascistic cult of youth. He envisions the apotheosis of black labor in itself and as engendered by the fascist leader who gives back what he takes and in so doing manufactures the purified, young black body and soul.[21]

Thus, Omar insists, "We colored folks need glorious bodies and not glorious souls. This is the age of the New Deal and a new society is forming" (71). Naming the Volk as the object of his work, Omar hopes to make manifest the young black body in its ideal form. He understands the working black body as the ultimate expression of blackness in general. There can be no inherent blackness that does not work. Blackness works itself into blackness. Lukács sees class consciousness as becoming self-aware through a historical-material dialectic taking place in and between embattled "classes" that, in capitalism, "constitute [the] immediately given historical reality" (58). Similarly, "race" for McKay is the absolute subject coming to knowledge of itself through racial struggle and the understanding of the individuals who make up the "races" as concrete, discrete historical subjects. Defined as labor as well as the apotheosis of labor, black being encapsulates the very essence of the black race as the subject of history.

Labor, then, forms the communal bond between the black masses worldwide. This does not mean, however, that the McKay of the late 1930s and up until the time of his death found his way back to Communism, or that *Harlem Glory* presents a Marxist alternative to the Stalinist Soviet Union and what McKay saw as an anemic Communist Party in the United States antagonistic to African America's unique economic interests. The two social movements of *Harlem Glory*, the Glory Soulers and the Yeomen of Labor, cannot be dissociated from one another: "Yet the two movements of Glory Soul and of Omar respectively were like a two-faced mirror reflecting the strange unfathomed mind of the colored minority" (72). Echoing his sentiments concerning the unique composition of the colored mind, McKay insists that one cannot construct a reading of *Harlem Glory* based on the separation of the Glory Soulers from the Yeomen. Instead, the antipathy Glory Savior and Omar have for one another must be understood as a general self-loathing and contradiction within the African American community as a whole. The very Volk that Glory Savior and Omar each seek to create cannot be imagined as anything but a "composite image" of the combined visions of the two fascistic leaders. This is why the Glory Soulers greet each other "with the salute, now universally called Fascist" (96). Although McKay uses Glory Savior to parody Father Divine and the Communists, every aspect of McKay's text itself functions in a dual and contradictory fashion in portraying the overall fascist nature of the composite Negro mind, even when that nature appears to favor Communism.

McKay, then, offers us a political vision that exceeds the obvious categorical political markers indicating a choice between a naïve representation of Communism (Glory Savior) and an equally simplistic understanding of fascism (Omar). Because McKay clearly favors Omar and his Yeoman, when we consider the two movements and their leaders as one, *Harlem Glory* yields a highly nuanced and differentiated presentation of the pros and cons of the adoption of aspects of fascist ideology for African America. McKay unites fascist and Communist ideologies while removing all rhetoric of interracial cooperation to give a necessarily fragmented example of black fascism. For McKay's vision of black fascism to crystallize, he must insist on a racially informed nationalist stance as the indefatigable heart of Omar's labor movement and the source of the animosity between the Yeomen and their Socialist and Communist contemporaries. *Harlem Glory* becomes pragmatic on the streets of Harlem along the "Third Way" and in the midst of the bitter conflict between the various labor movements and the enmity the Yeomen have for the Socialists and Communists.

The Yeomen's bone of contention with Socialists and Communists is not only over the issue of interracial cooperation but also over what they see as the logical consequences of working with whites and Jews. They detest what they perceive as the subservience of blacks to leaders irrevocably alienated from black concerns. Through his heroic Yeomen, McKay fears that so-called white radical organizations will force Harlem blacks and Negro intellectuals to advance the cause of whites at home and in places other than black urban centers. In effect, blacks would become the political parrots and puppets of the Left: "Also antagonistic were the colored Socialist and Communist organizers, who unceasingly parroted the slogan: 'Black and White Workers Must Unite!' and who constantly agitated against the idea of colored workers organizing an independent union" (91). The organization of an "independent union" along racial lines would divest white radicals of their black foot soldiers and in the process raise an army whose interests ultimately fell on the side of the fence opposite the Socialists and Communists. The Yeomen, in other words, can be nothing but inimical to any form of interracial cooperation in the realm of labor, political or otherwise.[22]

This is precisely why McKay believes Negro intellectuals censured Hamid's movement—they feared the loss of the white support that McKay identifies as the source of their power. In *Harlem Glory* and Harlem, the "whites, liberals and radicals" buttressing the platforms of leadership occupied by Negro intellectuals consider Omar/Hamid to be dangerous because within his doctrine of race first they recognize Nazism: "They [Negro intellectuals] had the support of an important group of whites, liberals and radicals, who, frightened by the racist theories of Nazi Germany, were swinging to the other extreme of denying the existence of biological and geographical sub-divisions of the human species, even to maintaining that there was no such things as race" (92).[23] These radicals have gone too far by "maintaining that there was no such things as race." Their fear clouds their judgment and causes them to issue preposterous statements denying the validity of an essential difference between the races. McKay depends on essential racial difference to push his program of racial uplift through all-black labor unions. Without difference, the recognition of black identity as determined across national *and class* borders cannot be expressed as labor.

Nothing, for McKay, determines the changing, incalculable needs of the black worker except a given manifestation of black labor in a given time and place. But this manifestation can only come into being guided by what Gramsci called "organic intellectuals." Black labor must produce, in Gramscian terms, organic intellectuals, without whom bourgeois Negro intellectuals do not have the experience to speak for black labor's needs.[24] This is why Omar asserts, without the faintest hint of irony, "The colored radicals are so constipated with statistics they can't function to help Harlem" (93), and, "The colored radicals are full of confusion from living black and thinking white, I'd like to take a baseball bat and beat their backsides" (93). Perhaps "beating their backsides" would loosen them up and make them regular. In any event, Omar reduces the problem of the Negro intelligentsia to a bodily function and a physical confrontation. Their problem, in other words, can be found in the gap they create between body and mind.

This conflict of interests in Harlem on the issues of white and Jewish support creates a schism in the black mind, dividing the right brain from the left. In conversation with his old friend Madame Audace (probably McKay's caricature of Louise Thompson), whose recent, successful trip to Moscow has left no doubt as to where her political sympathies lie, Buster (Pilgrim's Progress) explains Harlem's political situation:

> "They're divided over here, too, even in Harlem," said Buster. They're always arguing Left and Right, Fascists and Communists, Triskists and Stillinnites, however you pronounce them, colored folks are agitated about everything in the world but themselves.... Colored folks are agitated about Hitler and Mussolini and everything in the world these days excepting themselves. (97)

Political agitation on the streets of Harlem encompasses every possible political position available during the 1930s. The deep divisions to be found in Harlem's political life separate so many political programs, and so confusedly, that by the time Buster finishes his analysis of Harlem's political climate, we are left with an apparent political relativism. Buster does not distinguish between "Triskists and Stillinnites, however you pronounce them." The distinction Buster makes is not political, but phonetic. Buster's poor pronunciation (he has no problem with Hitler and Mussolini) underscores the fact that, in Harlem, these names have been appropriated to suit particular political needs. Most important, if Harlemites argue over everything including "Left and Right, Fascists and Communists," then McKay's Buster identifies a pro-fascist attitude in black Harlem advocated at least by agitating "colored folks."

The appropriation of the ideological basis of various radical political points of view in Depression-era Harlem thus cannot be understood from within the bifurcated black political mind as a simple matter of Communism and socialism pitted against each other and against black bourgeois indifference or conservatism. Likewise, black political thought in the 1930s evades the reductive, schematic understanding of an interracial Popular Front battling white fascism. We must instead, as McKay makes clear, widen the political playing field when approaching black political allegiances and sympathies during the Great Depression and recognize the strain of black fascism running through Harlem. McKay felt the black fascist strain of thought to be fairly obvious; after all, he was accused of harboring it.[25]

Although McKay denied any affiliation with a fascist program, he nevertheless leaves ample ambiguity in *Harlem Glory* about the desirability of fascist political agitation for blacks. This ambiguity arises in McKay's text, and his anti-Communist, pro-Hamid writings in general, as an effect of his overall negation of Communist, interracial political struggle in favor of an all-black, anti-Semitic labor movement. McKay does not so much propose an overt form of black fascism as he intimates its positive value in his outspoken animosity toward what he perceives to be Jewish-controlled Communism and Socialism. Thus, McKay's insistence in "Harlem Runs Wild" that the riot had nothing to do with racial antagonisms betrays a wider condemnation of Jews as the bankers holding almost all of Harlem's monetary and intellectual capital. When McKay attacks Communists and Socialists, he also rails against Jewish intellectuals, whom he sees as manipulating the very capital they purport to be interested in helping black Harlem wrest control of. McKay circumscribes, then, a vicious circle, the outline of which becomes visible only when we comprehend the unwritten positive moment of his negation of Communism.[26]

The rallying power of Madame Audace's statement—"Hitler and Mussolini are a danger to colored people everywhere" (97)—loses its thrust when McKay's omniscient narrator goes on to describe her as a dupe of the Communist Party:

> Since those days she had made a pilgrimage to Soviet Russia. She was one of the many of the intelligentsia class who had been influenced by the conversion to Orthodox Communism of the leading French writer, Andre Gide, who visited Soviet Russia and became a foremost apologist to the Bolshevik regime. Madame Audace visited Soviet Russia, saw what she was shown and returned to Paris a confirmed "fellow-traveler" in the Soviet way of life, seizing every occasion to promote the interest of the Soviet system. (98)

Influenced by the Soviet "apologist" Gide, Madame Audace, "a confirmed 'fellow traveler,'" promotes, during this "opportunity" before Glory Savior, "the interest of the Soviet system." In effect, she positions Communism and the Popular Front as the only alternatives to the dangerous fascist leaders.[27] Parroting the Party line, Audace's warning falls on deaf ears because it comes from Moscow, and so ultimately does not—because it could not—have the specific interests of blacks in mind. What sounds like race consciousness on the surface reveals itself to be nothing other than the empty self-aggrandizement of the CP. Madame Audace, then, stands in for the anemic Negro intelligentsia McKay complains so bitterly of throughout *Harlem Glory* and most of his writings of the 1930s and 1940s. She satisfies the novel's self-imposed requirement to portray the relationship between black and red as one inimical to black self-determination and economic and racial uplift.

The role assigned Audace, however, demands that she portray more than the black Communist flunky shouting down bourgeois nationalism and promoting subservience to the Comintern. She also points to the positive moment of what on the surface appears to be an overwhelmingly negative analysis of black politics in Harlem during the Depression. If she speaks for black Harlem's financially privileged intelligentsia, then she does so from two vantage points. The first is from that of someone with the perspective of a feminized political engagement ill-suited to the positively represented, masculinist ideology of Omar, the African. The second is of someone who backs down out of fear from Nazi racist ideology, which McKay finds to be a potent ideological basis for a race-based incorporation of politics and labor subsumed under the heading of "the Volk." In other words, McKay refuses to shrink from the possibility of appropriating Nazi racist ideology for the advancement of Negro concerns.

One such concern is the necessity of segregated labor unions. Even as Omar denies his overt advocacy for the creation of segregated unions and for segregation in general, he views segregation as the essential means through which to achieve black self-awareness and power. He explains himself to a crowd from a soapbox: "But they say I'm advocating segregation. . . . I am not advocating segregation, but black folk cannot run away from themselves. Black folk, where will you run to? The white folks don't want you. They'll use you for this thing or that thing and turn you loose again" (94). This call to arms, seemingly clear-cut in intention, actually addresses two separate but equal topics at the same time. It suggests on the one hand that the question of whether the Negro should segregate himself from members of other races revolves around the gravitational center of the Negro's essential being. The true condition of the Negro never escapes racial determination and therefore entails a primary and primal state of segregation that cannot be surmounted. On the other hand, McKay's Omar believes that race can be transcended momentarily as a service to interracial cooperation, but that, without hope of deviation, the conclusion to such cooperation will always be the same: black disenfranchisement. Thus, the Negro finds himself determined positively, spiritually, and materially through segregation.

In this way, McKay merges two seemingly disparate approaches to the identification and evaluation of the primary mechanism of historical progression: one spiritual, the other material. The collapse of the spiritual and material in segregation transforms proletarian labor into the foundation or essential base of the ontology of blackness. McKay does this by disrupting a theological-mythological narrative of black racial exceptionalism by lacing it with details that contradict a purely spiritual determination of blackness, suggesting instead the material basis for any conception and development of black being.²⁸ The genius of Omar, then, reveals itself not simply as the apotheosis of labor but also as a contrived spiritual, or religious, practice centered on the saleable personal labor of the black proletariat. There is therefore no contradiction or ambiguity of logic when Omar, the materialist, asserts, "If we black folk must have a religion, I bring you a new religion. I bring you Islam" (82–83), and on another occasion: "My religion is the new religion of labor. Tell your preachers to mind their own business" (92). Recognizing that "black folk must have a religion," Omar offers the attainment of a beautiful soul by the construction of a body made beautiful through labor. Omar's cult of the body positions him close to Nazi ideology. In McKay's text, Omar merely substitutes the physical perfection, the apex of beauty, of the Aryan form with that of the working black body.²⁹

Translating Hamid's Nazism into Omar's, McKay posits Omar as a necessary counterbalance and complement to Glory Savior's Communistic cult. Instead of having "Colored folks . . . collected in Glory Homes like the Communists in Russia" (82), Omar brings them to the street:

> On a Lenox Avenue corner he came upon a huge crowd, dominated by Omar, The African. Black Omar, powerfully tall and stout, was arrayed in Russian boots and American spurs, a Chinese blue cape with Moroccan red lining, an English officer's belt, with his head crowned by an Arabian white turban. Buster stopped to listen, for Omar was denouncing the Glory Soulers. . . . The crowd was excited, tense, like soldiers waiting for the signal to go into action. (80–81; 82)

Positioning his "soldiers" along the sidewalks of Harlem, "Black Omar" addresses the troops. He wears as usual a jigsaw puzzle of national costumes, yet he maintains, and even promotes, a sense of an essential black being through this transnational self-presentation. Staggering in implication, Omar's mix of international dress and nationalist rhetoric displayed before what amount to militarized masses in the labor wars suggests not so much international cooperation between the races and nations as a racial exceptionalism that every nation will recognize by force. Omar's embrace of racial and national difference signifies a record of future militaristic achievement. His turban and gorgeous robe in combination with "an English officer's belt" connect Omar's call for black self-determination with black conquest. Indeed, Omar fascistically imbues his soldiers with a conscious sense of the militaristic nature of their calling, commissioning his dues-paying followers with martial titles in order to enhance his movement with fascist pomp and circumstance. It is a lesson Omar has learned well from the example of Marcus Garvey. Thus, Omar represents what Deleuze and Guattari called the two major types of social investment, segregative and nomadic: "first, a paranoiac fascisizing (fascisant) type or pole. . . . And second, a schizorevolutionary type or pole that follows the *lines of escape* of desire." The line of escape is to become other, to say, according to Deleuze and Guattari, "I am not your kind, I belong eternally to the inferior race, I am a beast, a black. . . . What matters is to break through the wall, even if one has to become like John Brown, George Jackson" (277). Or Marcus Garvey.

In fact, Omar's movement functions both as the repository of the remnants of the failed Garveyite movement and that which naturally supersedes Garveyism.[30] Omar has re-stitched Garvey's "piebald mantle" and transformed it into a transnational Technicolor dream coat. Thus Buster's friend Opal, whom he knows from the carefree days of the Renaissance in the 1920s, tells a familiar tale within Omar's ranks of how he and many others like him ended up Yeomen: "Opal was a stocky West Indian brown man, who came to the United States when he was a lad on a banana boat. He had been a member of the Universal-Negro-Back-To-Africa movement. When that movement failed, he drifted unattached to any organization" (84).

As the successor of the Garveyite movement, Omar's Yeoman extends a lineage that embraces any and all previous Black Nationalist labor movements and stretches back to the beginning of time. Contained within it is the eternal, essential element of McKay's ontology of black labor, and the mythological basis for black racial superiority. This eternal kernel of black greatness comes outfitted in the fashion of the day. Omar's "BUY WHERE YOU CAN WORK" movement—as opposed to Hamid's "Don't Buy Where You Can't Work" movement—comes replete with uniforms and various and sundry fascistic, fetishistic symbols of rank. The accoutrements of military discipline assure Harlem that Omar is no con artist:

> "Well, it's not a racket," said Opal, "I'm the commander of Omar's Yeomen." There were epaulets on his shoulder-straps.

"Any money in it?" Buster asked.

"Not much, but I believe in it, for it's a part of the labor movement." (83)

Where there are epaulets on shoulder straps, there can be no doubt. Militaristic pomp and circumstance condition faith in the movement, diffracting skepticism as to Omar's financial intentions. If there's no money in the movement, then its means and ends must be righteous. Not driven by greed, Omar's faith is created and enhanced by masculinist, martial qualities that guide his movement's existence, not greed. When Omar holds up a young boy to his soldiers as the promise of his labor movement, he exhorts, "Look at his intelligent face! Look carefully, my friends. That face is a man's face, a real man's face in a boy's body" (82). Representing youthful black labor's essential, purposeful, and beautiful masculinity, the boy embodies the promise of a return to racial grace and the creation of a self-determined, black economic empire free of Jewish influence.[31] Youthful black laborers are the vanguard as well as the avant-garde. But unless the black masses adopt Omar's universal religion providing the ontological basis of black labor's superiority and unity, the racial "group soul" will be atomized, and the narrative thread of Omar's mythical Nazi mantle will be forever rent.

McKay attempts to enact this fusion of vanguard and avant-garde with *Harlem Glory* itself. To remain forever a fragment, forever rent, *Harlem Glory* accepts the implications of its own fascist position by remaining firmly in the world. Taking place in an easily recognizable 1930s Harlem, McKay marches his formidable soldier and spiritual leader, his Sufi, through a fictive terrain mundane and fantastic: mundane because of its all-too-familiar functions and foibles; fantastic because it places in the world an improbable black fascism and makes it inevitable. Dressing himself in Marcus Garvey's piebald mantle, the one tried on but rejected by Schuyler's Dr. Belsidus, McKay's Omar is an aesthetic solution to black leadership and fascism. McKay sings his ideal leader, his African American L'Ouverture, his black Moses, into the material world, just as he said he would do.

5 His Rod of Power
Zora Neale Hurston, Black Fascism, and Culture

> Jethro, an Ethiopian, gave instructions to his son-in-law, Moses, in establishing government. Exodus 18:22–24. Thus, Moses was not ashamed to be instructed by a black man.
> —Prince Hall, "A Charge Delivered to the African Lodge, June 24, 1795, at Menotomy, MA" (1797)

> Many a brave hero fell, but history, faithful to her trust, will transcribe [Denmark Vesey's] name on the same monument with Moses, Hampden, Tell, Bruce and Wallace, Toussaint L'Ouverture, Lafayette and Washington.
> —Henry Highland Garnet, "An Address to the Slaves of the United States of America" (1843)

> Why should we be discouraged because somebody laughs at us today? Who to tell what tomorrow will bring forth? Did they not laugh at Moses, Christ and Mohammed? Was there not a Carthage, Greece and Rome? We see and have changes every day, so pray, work, be steadfast and be not dismayed.
> —Marcus Garvey, "African Fundamentalism" (1924)

According to Zora Neale Hurston, Toussaint L'Ouverture's phallic power is as a manifestation of the god Damballah. The chain of divine signification does not end there. Damballah's existence as a snake marks merely an alternative form of his life as Moses's rod of power. However, in Hurston's retelling of the life of Moses, *Moses, Man of the Mountain,* the titular character is not the only character in the text to wield such a rod. Hurston's Pharaoh establishes his new rule of law by penetrating the Hebrew womb with his "rod of state," which is intent on genocide:

> Pharaoh had entered the bedrooms of Israel. The birthing beds of the Hebrews were matters of state. The Hebrew womb had fallen under

the heel of Pharaoh. A ruler great in his newness and new in his greatness had arisen in Egypt and he had said, "*This is law. Hebrew boys shall not be born.* All offenders against this law shall suffer death by drowning." (1; emphasis added)

So ends the first paragraph of *Moses, Man of the Mountain*, establishing the novel as a meditation on the nature of the authoritarian state and of absolute political power. "Hardly less than Machiavelli in *The Prince*," Blyden Jackson observed in his 1984 Introduction to *Moses*, "she discusses power—the kind of power, political in its nature, which is the prime object of concern for the Florentine in his famous treatise on statesmanship" ("*Moses*" 52). Yet is it Machiavellian political power Hurston discusses, or, in 1939, Hitlerian? Indeed, Hurston's Machiavellian turn serves to orient her analysis of absolute political power not toward Florence, but Berlin. *Moses*'s Pharaoh presents Hurston's examination of the ideological content invested in the creation of the fascist state along the lines of the *Führerprinzip* (*Führer* principle, or principle of the male, charismatic, authoritarian guide or leader) at work in National Socialist Germany, and the role that ultranationalism plays as a religious faith in supporting fascist political power. Through not only the figure of Pharaoh, but of Moses himself, Hurston critiques the ideological premises of National Socialism while at the same time conceding the value of generic European fascism for a program of African American uplift via black cultural nationalism. The black cultural nationalism Hurston advocates with her appropriation of the Mosaic myth is achieved along lines similar to the creation of the fascist authoritarian state.

Killing Me Softly with His Snake

Dust Tracks on a Road (1942) finds Hurston speculating as to the viability and desirability of race purity:

There will have to be something harder to get across than an ocean to keep East and West from meeting. But maybe Old Maker will have a remedy. Maybe even He has given up. Perhaps in a moment of discouragement He turned the job over to Adolph Hitler and went on about His business of making more beetles. (*DT* 192)

Hurston asserts that maintaining racial purity cannot be done. This does not mean, however, that she denies an originary state of racial purity, but that the vicissitudes of sexual license prohibit a lasting lineage of racial integrity without compromise. The joke targets Hitler as a would-be god who knows no better than to believe that human sexuality can be contained and directed, and that racial purity, obliterated by the very instinct Hitler denies free reign, can still be found.

Thus Hurston tacitly assumes in her autobiography that the sexual admixture of race brings with it a corruption and then reformulation of culture, which, in itself, carries an obsolete but traceable kernel of racial purity, a genetic matrix housing vestigial elements capable of being reactivated. Informing her anthropological work, she carried this assumption with her to Haiti: "All over Haiti it is well established that Damballah is identified as Moses, whose symbol was the serpent. This worship of Moses recalls the hard-to-explain fact that wherever the Negro is found, there are traditional tales of Moses and his supernatural powers that are not in the Bible; nor can they be found in any written life of Moses. The rod of Moses is said to have been a subtle serpent and hence came his great powers" (*Tell My Horse* 116). Recalling that Toussaint is the human expression of Damballah, Hurston understands Haitian history as something divine. She weds material history (Toussaint) with myth (Damballah), and then turns the screw once more. Moses becomes, for Hurston, the overdetermined signifier of historical black revolution and mythical black essence; Moses is Damballah, who is Toussaint. Where Hurston writes of Moses, she tacitly references Haiti history and mythology.

As he appears in Haiti as a mythological and cultural nexus of racial identity and certification, Moses cannot function as a measure of racial purity. Instead, he signifies a hybrid iconographic genealogy that manifests itself as the locus of a new pantheon apart from the Voodoo or Christian churches. A collage of Voodoo, Christianity, and Judaism, the image of Moses surpasses the sum of its cultural parts. For Hurston, culture, like blood, makes no claim to a functional racial purity, but carries within it an all but forgotten originary instance of its constitutive, undifferentiated elements. Moses, as a cultural artifact, assembles within him the specific people he represents at the moment of his appearance. He embodies the signifier (understanding "race" here to be a product of a hybrid, yet unified culture) par excellence that marks the racial integrity of a Volk. To the extent that Moses inhabits a protean body of mythological discourse, he displays the ability to suit himself to the needs of a people by conditioning them as their most effective, powerful leader and, more important, their undeniably masculine redeemer. Moses represents the beliefs, values, and communal bond of a racially coded Volk while creating the very aspects of a people he represents.

In this respect, Moses presents an absolutely singular (yet hybrid) cultural figure. He takes the place of an originary event that demands continued racial purity by raising miscegenation to the apex of cultural production. As an absolutely singular creative force, Moses gives birth to a racially coded and culturally bound nation informed by the magic of his inevitably masculine rod of power. He kills whatever divisiveness may have existed within the Volk in its material existence and destroys contradictions in its philosophical constitution. Thus, in Hurston's short story and rehearsal for *Moses*, "The Fire and the Cloud" (1934), we find a Moses near death who has constructed his own tomb, mistaken by a talking lizard to be Moses's love nest:

> From the top of a low bush near the left foot of Moses the lizard studied the work. "It is good. But you have been a long time in the building of your nest. Your female must be near death from retaining her eggs."
> "No Fecund female awaits this labor."
> "A man alone!"
> "A man alone." (*CS* 117)

"A man alone" has no need of a "fecund female." His sex exercises in his solitary use of his rod of power, which he draws out as a measure for how far he has been "drawn-out" by the practice of nation-building:

> "How do you say that you are alone if of your kind such hosts of multitudes be at hand?"
> "I am that I am and so I am alone. I am Moses, The-drawn-out. It is given me to call God by his power-compelling names. I bear his rod. The blind and the mute have companionship, but I am a leader." (*CS* 118)

Moses transmits his legacy not by blood but by the transferal of masculinist power. "A man alone" nevertheless keeps the company of another man, to whom he gives his rod of power at the moment of his death so that the nation may be born: "'But wait, O Moses!' the lizard squeaked after him. 'You have left your rod behind.' 'Oh, Joshua will pick it up,' he called back and strode on (*CS* 121).

Sovereignty passes between men without women, men with no other love than the state. The rule of law that defines the race is not passed from one ruler to the next by blood lineage but by the cultural inheritance of sovereign masculinity. Blood plays no part in Hurston's thinking on racial purity. She construes it instead as a cultural bond between people that constructs a Volk. This bond unites discrete racial and cultural entities into a hybrid formation that nevertheless transcends its status as a hybrid to become a protean purity without origin. Racial unity is achieved via the homosocial rather than the hetero- or homosexual. Moses, in other words, bequeaths his rod as a means of maintaining racial purity found not in the blood, but in "pure" cultural products—an insight to which Hitler, according to Hurston, remains blind.

Hurston's interest in fascist dictators went beyond speculation as to what Hitler could and could not see. Her *Tell My Horse* glorifies the Vincent regime and showcases a fascination with fascist authoritarian rule. In the book, Hurston understands the Haitian political mind as simply desiring monarchical leadership. Haitian "democracy," which does not follow "the American concept," is reduced to the people's choosing, in corrupt elections, who is to rule them like a king (*TMH* 75). With Hurston's untroubled appraisal of the Haitian political conscious in mind, Gilroy reads her "extraordinary enthusiasm" for a Haitian colonel, as well as her assumption that the officer arouses the same type of excitement in his men, as a flirtation with fascism. "The combination of his bodily perfection and a firm political hand . . . is not," Gilroy suggests, "of course, enough to damn him as a fascist, but the resonance is a strong one, and it is significant that Hurston also articulates a contempt for the moribund political system that, in her view, fetters Haitian progress" (*Against Race* 234–35). Hurston's excitement over the colonel is not, of course, enough to damn her as a fascist, but it does implicate her in a fascist fantasy. What she finds attractive is not *any* man in uniform, but one who embodies the promise of a strong masculine, militaristic, authoritarian hand setting to the task of transforming a "moribund political system" into the mechanism of Haitian progress.[1] Following the chain of divine signifiers, Hurston's Moses grows out of this enthusiasm for the promise presented by the quasi-fascistic image of the colonel, and of the Vincent regime. She supports this image elsewhere in *Tell My Horse* when she speculates:

> Of course Haiti is not now and never has been a democracy according to the American concept. It is an elected monarchy. The President of Haiti is really a king with a palace, with a reign limited to a term of years. The term republic is used very loosely in the case. There is no concept of the rule of the majority in Haiti. The majority, being unable to read and to write, have not the least idea of what is being done in their name. Haitian class consciousness and the universal acceptance of the divine right of the crust of the upper crust is a direct denial of the concept of democracy. (75)

Haitians are congenitally incapable of democracy. What they require is a strongman. Hurston's passion for Haiti is bound to her desire for dictatorship. She did not feel this passion for U.S.-based Black Nationalist political programs, especially the Garveyite movement, despite the fact that Marcus Mosiah Garvey shared with Hurston an attraction to fascism.

Aside from Hurston's and Garvey's shared affinity for fascism, in *Moses* there is no understanding of the new nation in terms of a biological conception of race, and therefore there is no positive evaluation of the Garveyite movement. The black cultural nationalism Hurston describes in the novel disavows that of Garveyism, which is, biologically speaking, race-specific. We recall that for Garvey, the biology of race eluded the extreme limit and originary moment of the idea "racial purity," an idea Hurston found worthy of scathing sarcasm. Tony Martin reminds us that Hurston "benefited from early exposure in the *Negro World;*" but he is quick and correct to note that Hurston's essay "The Emperor Effaces Himself" (1928; unpublished) was a "scurrilous" attack on Garvey. "As the article progressed," Martin relates, "the satire became more vicious. Hurston accused Garvey of fraud and poked fun at his very reasonable campaign to have African peoples portray God in their own color" (*Literary Garveyism* 76). Reasonably or not, Hurston took issue with Garvey for his color-based program of uplift for reasons beyond her desire to ingratiate herself with Carl Van Vechten and others. In opposition to Garvey, Hurston does not consider race to be first but instead places culture disembodied from a biological imperative in the lead position. Hurston, gainsaying the primacy of the natural science of race, submits to the notion of cultural production as productive of the race.

Indeed, Hurston's turn toward fascism is the turn away from Garveyism (whether or not it deployed some fascist strategies) as the ideological basis of African American nationhood understood first and foremost as the construction of heredity and not heritage. Instead of a biological mysticism at the center of nationalist sentiment, Hurston's *Moses* offers a radicalization of commonplace readings of the Harlem Renaissance's cultural aesthetic of an authentic African American being that permits racial détente. The negation of the *primacy* of biological determinism as the measure of racial faculty thus presents in *Moses* a readable text through which intra- and interracial understanding is mediated by the apotheosis of culture.

Although it can be said that Hurston turns to a conservative civil rights politics later in life, the fascist underpinnings of the apotheosis of culture found in *Moses* by no means support a conservative political program.[2] Generic fascism, to echo Zeev Sternhell, is neither right, left, nor centrist; it is a radical revolutionary politics that borrows from across the political spectrum and denies traditional political categorization. It is a misreading of the radical revolutionary nature of the novel's political orientation that has led critics to view *Moses* as "flawed" because, if seen through the prism of a conservative, centrist, or liberal politics, the various threads Hurston seeks to weave into a single textual tapestry interrupt each other without reconciliation. Instead of enhancing the strength of a unified thematic line stretching throughout the novel, the overdetermination of Hurston's images (Moses included) breaks the narrative totality into sequestered vignettes that relate to each other by the sole virtue of the authority of the Mosaic myth itself.

Yet this is not so much a "flaw" as a method of textual production through which Hurston enables herself to layer an already overdetermined myth with what appears on the surface to be incompatible political situations—those of African Americans, Jews under National Socialism, and generic European fascism itself. The Mosaic myth lets

Hurston transcend the specific historical situations of oppressed and oppressor while maintaining a folkloric understanding of the historical specificity that grants her leave to combine them. With the Mosaic myth, Hurston empties history of its specific content only to reappropriate it for the sake of a comparative analysis of the plight of the Jews in Europe in the face of National Socialism and of African Americans in the Jim Crow South—and for the viability of ideological premises of fascism for African American leadership. The shadow of Nazism, in other words, extends far enough to darken the pages of *Moses*.

"The shadow of Nazism," Deborah McDowell asserts, "is cast from the beginning of *Moses, Man of the Mountain*, which opens on the process of marking Hebrew male babies for extinction" (xv).[3] This does not mean to imply that *Moses* consciously predestines the Holocaust, or that the situation of European Jews in 1939 mirrors that of African Americans during the same year, but that National Socialism's rhetoric of "blood-and-soil" provided Hurston with a general framework with which to examine race relations in the United States. Barbara Johnson points out that "[a]t a time when Hitler had cornered the market on blood-and-soil nationalism, it is not surprising to find Hurston questioning the grounding of nationhood on racial identity" (21), to which I would simply add that it is not surprising to find Hurston mediating her discussion on the grounding of nationhood with an implicit examination of the general premises of National Socialist authoritarian rule and racial origins. The fact that Hurston's Moses cannot be said with certainty to be Hebrew does not discount a reading of black cultural nationalism in the text, but instead reinforces it. Johnson believes that "Hurston's Egyptian Moses stands for the culturally dead father or mother: Africa, the source of the repressed tradition carried to the Americas by the slaves" (20). The figure of Moses, in other words, possesses a long history of interpretation and revision within the African American folk tradition such that Moses represents a past, a history, a tradition, and a nation as an emblem of freedom from bondage and racial oppression. Moses is the cultural locus for a traumatized and disparate people.[4]

In Hurston's hands, the signifier Moses goes a step beyond folk tradition and, as Maria Diedrich understands it, "radically transcends the mere folk-in-literature approach . . . it is Hurston's courageous endeavor to aesthetically re-create and document the complex theological, philosophical, and political potentials inherent in the Moses interpretation as it had developed in black folk religion since slavery times" (177). That Hurston allows for a strong reading in favor of Moses's racial heritage as Egyptian and not Hebrew echoes her belief that, as Johnson puts it, "[t]here are no 'pure' races, no unmixed origins, and this may be another reason for the choice both Freud and Hurston make to turn Moses into an Egyptian" (24).[5] McDowell concurs with Johnson: "Hurston is not so much intent on establishing the patriarch's origins beyond dispute, but rather on casting doubts about Moses' 'pure' origins and, by extension, on the very idea of 'racial purity'" (xiv). In challenging "the very idea of 'racial purity,'" Hurston, following her Columbia University mentor Franz Boas, removes it to the realm of biological mysticism while at the same time stipulating that any belief in the supremacy of one race over another on the grounds of biological determinism necessarily finds its validity in a kind of religious fervor, or blind faith.[6] Indeed, McDowell tells us that "[t]he novel identifies concerns with racial origins—and perhaps origins more generally—as the genesis of many of the world's evils. Hurston could not have chosen a timelier year in which to launch these concerns" (xiii).

The deeply encoded nature of the meditation on National Socialism and American racism presented in *Moses,* however, might lead one to believe that the book's appearance in 1939 was more than "timely," a belief that, if not lost on Hurston's contemporaries, caused them to view the work as something less than it was, as "light," and inconsequential. Alain Locke, in a 1940 review of *Moses* for *Opportunity,* insisted that Hurston's *Moses* is "caricature instead of portraiture. Gay anecdotes there are aplenty, but somehow black Moses is neither reverent nor epic, two things . . . that any Moses, Hebrew, Negroid, or Nordic, ought to be" (7). In his 1941 essay "Recent Negro Fiction," Ralph Ellison proclaimed that "for Negro fiction [*Moses*] did nothing." Hurston herself doubted, for different reasons, the book's ultimate success, admitting, "I have the feeling of disappointment about it. I don't think that I achieved all that I set out to do. I thought that in this book I would achieve my ideal, it seems that I have not yet reached it" (R. Morris 308).[7]

But perhaps the book's ambiguous merit lies in the very double move that makes it a work of intense power as well as a comical romp through the Bible. Christine Levecq argues that "By juxtaposing not only two different historical and cultural contexts but also two different social classes, Hurston creates a socially, politically, and culturally charged heteroglossia" (437). Yet Levecq's Bakhtinian analysis identifies only "two different historical and cultural contexts," when clearly there are at least four. The first two, understood by Levecq, consist of African American history and culture, and those of German Jews. As we have seen, the third and fourth are present from the opening lines of the novel: namely, National Socialism itself, and, abstracting it to the limits as Hurston herself does in the novel, generic European fascism. Still, Hurston's *Moses* does not attempt to analyze rigorously National Socialism but instead engages in a "heteroglossia" of European fascisms, including National Socialism as the dominant textual referent *because* of its virulent racism. That Hurston was able to intertwine at least these three historical and cultural contexts speaks to the novel's intensity and success, but it also underscores the difficulty she had in combining different social contexts within a single work that attempts to create a unified narrative field. Where one cultural context begins, the other does not so much end as become effaced by its successor. With this in mind, my reading of *Moses* is divided into two parts, the first dealing with how Hurston understands National Socialist ideology as a racial "blind faith" displaced to the state as the engendering agent of the charismatic, authoritarian ruler; the second identifying fascist rhetoric in the novel's black cultural nationalism.

Rameses, the God

"The province of Goshen was living under the New Egypt and the New Egyptian and they were made to know it in many ways. The sign of the new order towered over places of preference. It shadowed over work, and fear was given body and wings" (1–2). In the "New Egypt" and Rameses' brutal rod of state, Hurston presents the *Führerprinzip* as one of the political manifestations of the ideological myth of national rebirth as the recapturing of the nonrational being of the nation by means of masculine vitality and health. The "New Egyptian," characterized by a concept of racial contamination, personifies Egypt's return to racial purity. For Hurston, fascist rhetorical power relies on the insistence that the alien, the cultural and racial outsider, compromises the health of the nation, and that the nation becomes effeminate and corrupted by its inclusion of a people living outside of its manifest destiny. Indeed, the "Hebrews had already been driven out of their well-built homes and shoved further back in Goshen" (2). "Hebrews were disarmed and prevented from becoming citizens of Egypt, they found out that they were aliens, and from one decree to the next they sank lower and lower" (2). So harsh were Pharaoh's new laws that "Hebrew women shuddered with terror at the indifference of their wombs to the Egyptian law" (1).

The subjugation and subsequent surgical removal of this cancer will in turn revitalize the diseased body of the nation. Rameses' recent rise to power, an allusion to Hitler's 1933 seizure of power and the ascendance of fascism as the dominant political ideology in Europe, is played out along cultural lines as the demonization of the cultural other as an inherently corrupt race. Rameses, "[a] ruler great in his newness and new in his greatness" legitimates his new, great power through the murder of firstborn Hebrew males. Rameses distinguishes himself as the new ruler of Egypt by forcing the Hebrews out of Egyptian society, invading the Hebrew bedrooms, and violating the Hebrew women. His actions, mandates of the state, are reflections of his sovereign power and desire to become an entity distinct from the traditional representation of the sun god on earth, figuring him instead as a serial rapist and killer. He is ruler beyond the law because he has the authority to create not only the law, but its legitimating originary moment.[8]

In exercising his execrable absolute authority over the Hebrews this new ruler takes on the countenances of father and murderer of all newborn male Hebrews. The "rod of state," the ornamental articulation of the sun god's power, forces its entrance into the Hebrew womb with the goal of preventing the conception of male offspring. The law refutes the claim to life of the newborn Hebrew males with a preemptive strike. To insist that male children shall not be *born* is tantamount to insisting that Hebrew males shall not be conceived—an impossible stricture to obey. Thus, Pharaoh manifests his power as the impossibility of the law.[9] The ability to render the womb incapable of producing a male child dictates that Pharaoh's power extend itself beyond the womb with the ability to render the inevitable impossible.

The excuse Rameses uses to justify the institution of the impossible as law is history itself, in that Pharaoh reconfigures history to portray the Hebrews as both the cause of Egypt's previous sufferings and the reason why Egypt cannot fully recover:

> All that he [Rameses] had required of them was that they work and build him a few cities [and monuments] here and there to pay back in a small way for all the great benefits they had received in their long residence in Egypt and also to give back some of the wealth they had so ruthlessly raped from the helpless body of Egypt when she was in no position to defend herself. . . . His piercing eyes and all-hearing ears had discovered a well-organized plot to swindle Egypt out of her just amount of work out of them, by slowing up their work—a most reprehensible and low-down trick worthy of Hyksos and Hebrews! But he had a remedy for this. (19–20)

The Hebrew is diseased with the plague of criminality and so his existence within the body of the authoritarian state corrupts the law. Indeed, Rameses decries the Hebrews as rapists, insisting that they "give back some of the wealth they had so ruthlessly raped from the helpless body of Egypt when she was in no position to defend herself." As Hurston names the character of National Socialism's demonization of the Jews, she also alludes to the economic and cultural crises Germany faced after defeat in World War I and the Allies' imposition of crippling war reparations. For Rameses, national economic failure and humiliation sanctions the oppression of the Hebrews and provides him with a rallying point for extreme nationalist sentiment and the denunciation of a perceived cancer within the body politic of the nation.

Hurston thus presents the National Socialist doctrine of the state as an organic vessel superior in nature to other national-cultural bodies through the figures of Rameses and his authoritarian Egypt.[10] She also asserts that if the rhetorical thrust of national rebirth in fascist ideology is to retain its potency, the illness plaguing the national body is necessary for the nation's rebirth into health.[11] That there is an illness—the Hebrews—posits that the body of the nation is sick, and that it has been ill during the decades preceding Rameses' ascension to power. It signifies that this time before Rameses, identified politically and culturally, is indeed a *history* of national weakness and decadence, and that the body can be healed by recapturing a time before the history of illness, a time steeped in myth and pregnant with the true destiny of the nation.[12]

The elimination, or sacrifice, of the cultural other will accomplish this regeneration of the previously degenerate nation, because the perceived cause and symptom of the illness has been removed.[13]

The extermination of newborn Hebrew males punishes a crime other than that of the "impossible" living presence of the victims. In the eyes of Rameses, criminal activity, indeed treason and rape, exemplifies the Hebrews' racial character and enacts itself in the unavoidable conception of male children, committing a moral offense against a sacred order. Male children are conceived against the will of the gods and the state, and so perform the impossible negation of divine law. The infant male indicts Pharaoh's power over the Hebrew womb as impotent, diminishing his rod of state as nothing other than a showpiece. By law, Pharaoh engenders gender. The crime of the male child is committed at the moment of conception. In other words, the crime is not that male children exist, but that they are conceived in the first place. This crime amounts to an act of treason, an undermining of the sexual prowess of Pharaoh, insofar as his violent sexuality expresses itself as the desire for absolute political authority. To insult Pharaoh's performance in Hebrew beds, then, is to soften his rod of state. By birthing boys, Hebrew mothers eclipse the power of the sun. This insult denies the authority of Ra and blackens of the eye of Horus, the "golden god! Lord of both horizons. The weaver of the beginning of things" (3).

At "the beginning of things," the beginning of history, Hurston identifies fascist political authority as bound to a single-minded mythological self-understanding of a people, causing national identity to be created by, and subsumed within, the progressive unfolding of history as Nazi myth.[14] The crucial moment of this mytho-historiography (one of Hurston's means of identification) is that of Egypt's freedom from bondage, its divine deliverance from Hebrew evil. "Here they were," Pharaoh tells us in a moment of indirect speech, "Hebrews, who had come down into Egypt as the allies and aides of those oppressors of the Egyptian people, and as such had trampled on the proud breast of Egyptian liberty for more than three hundred years. But the *gods* had used the magnificent courage of the *real* Egyptians to finally conquer and expel those sheep-herding interlopers whom the Hebrews had aided in every way they could to deprive the *real* Egyptians of their homes and their liberties" (Hurston 19; emphasis added). Capable of seeking out and marshalling Egyptian courage, the gods have ordained

Egypt's historical turn to glory. The gods endow the Egyptian Volk with a sacred communal tie—the defeat of the Hyksos and Hebrews—to be realized in the working of the state as a teleological movement toward a superior destiny. It is a new Egypt and therefore a new national destiny. Hurston presents the authority of the fascist charismatic leader as irreproachable because to question his authority would place the questioner outside the existing theological, cultural, and racial order of the nation and thus identify the questioner as antagonistic to the sacred destiny of the nation. To challenge the authority of the charismatic leader on any level labels the party issuing the challenge an enemy of the state. As Hurston presents it, the fascist state requires a sacred, mythologized history as the ideological condition of its absolute authority. This mytho-historiography expresses itself in nationalism as a religious principle. The charismatic leader exerts his power through the force of the gods; he descends out of the clouds bringing the glory of his triumph of the will.[15]

With this great victory, Hurston establishes Pharaoh's desire for absolute sovereignty as a myth of an absolute political authority granted to him by Horus at the beginning of things. Horus weaves the tapestry of history by representing the origin as a nascent form of historical unfolding. This origin gives rise to the narrative of the Ra's chosen people. Pharaoh's divine authority rests on the determination, at the beginning and by means of an act of originary, divine violence, that Pharaohs are the keeper of the origin.[16] The origin exists within Pharaohs, for Pharaohs are the divine presence of Ra on earth. In other words, a Pharaoh cannot be for himself, but for the sun god. In this way, Pharaohs, including Rameses, guarantee the continuity of a history stretching back to an originary moment bathed in the "authentic" light of the "true" god. Pharaohs are historical truth, and as such, the laws they create and uphold justify themselves in history as Nazi myth.

The mantle of Pharaoh thus exists eternally, secure at the beginning of things, even though the man representing the eternal entity "Pharaoh" finds himself exposed to death. Pharaoh by right possesses two bodies, in the same sense as Kantorowicz's two bodies of the king in medieval political theology. One of the Pharaoh's two bodies is immortal and has as its supreme characteristic, outside its immortality, a direct relation to the laws of the godhead; the other body is perishable and serves as a slave to the legislative will of the people. Thus, Hurston's

Amram can describe Rameses as a "flesh and blood man, just like you and me." Yet the Hebrews, before a meeting with Rameses called to air their grievances, are also given to understand "what a blessing it was for Pharaoh to not only let them [the Hebrews] see his sacred body, he was actually going to let them listen to his voice. He was going to speak to them, using his sacred voice and lips" (19). As a result of this divine body and bureaucratic will, any new Pharaoh is an old Pharaoh. The power of the Pharaoh contains the rule of law as understood as the will of the sun god from the beginning of things. The righteousness of these laws is established before their inception. Any new law created by a Pharaoh predates its own establishment because all Egyptian law is already included in the beginning of things. The very possibility of law precedes any one Pharaoh. Because the law exists before the office of the Pharaoh, the "new" law is an impossible law. It is this impossibility of law that Rameses uses against the Hebrews to distinguish himself from the office of Pharaoh, reinventing himself as "Rameses the god." As such, he exists prior and superior to the gods worshipped by his people and so embodies the "new," true destiny of Egypt.

In Rameses, the "incarnation of the sun-god" that "intensified [Egyptian] nationalism," Hurston figures the fascist rhetoric of an essential being and destiny of the nation as over and against other nations. This being dwells temporally in advance of the period of decadence, of racial infection within the body of the Volk. As Hurston understands it, the inscription of history into myth performed by the fascist state drains history of its content and invests it with the Nazi myth of a people unified in the person of the charismatic leader. As the religious, authoritarian principle of the fascist state, the charismatic leader acts as the means of identification, as a touchstone for a unified national body born of myth. The rewriting of history thus allows for the creation of a legal apparatus that has the moral authority to perform any task so long as the task falls within the best interests of the nation, which it always does. The law is infused with an aestheticized political content such that the creation and enforcement of the law perform aesthetic acts; they exist, as actions, for themselves.[17] Hurston asserts with *Moses, Man of the Mountain,* that, in creating laws that call for the enslavement and mass slaughter of a disenfranchised "minority" population living within the national body, the charismatic leader heightens the sense of communal unity of a nation and reaffirms the rhetoric of the destiny of the people that endows the *Führerprinzip* with a religious character in the first place. Exactly as Benjamin believed, this aestheticization of legal and political power establishes along cultural and racial lines violence for the sake of the state, which, in this case, is violence for its own sake. This conception of political violence removes the new charismatic leader from historical and legal precedence and posits the authority of his power on a state of exception.[18]

If Rameses is to set himself apart as a Pharaoh, only in the state of exception can he create new laws, for by law, one Pharaoh is indistinguishable from another unless this logic of succession succumbs to a radical interruption. To establish a new law is actually to resurrect an old law, insofar as the law pertains to the Egyptians as *the* people of the sun. Rameses escapes this double bind by expressing his absolute sovereignty over a non-Egyptian people. The origin from which Pharaoh derives this power acts as the articulation of the *new* ontological basis for the Egyptians as a people, effectively providing Pharaoh with his state of exception and so the opportunity to create the truly new law. Furthermore, for Rameses to create laws for a people who are not bound by the ontological assumptions of the beginning, but nonetheless recognize Pharaoh's divine authority, would be to create *new* laws for Egypt and so unify Pharaoh's two bodies as simply "Rameses."

This political theodicy investigated by Hurston stipulates a condition in which all legal authority concedes even the illusion of autonomy in favor of a rule of law guaranteed in its moral efficacy solely by the authoritarian ruler. The very process by which the fascist dictator undermines the rule of law with the goal of rewriting its parameters within those of a mytho-historiography conducive to a revision of the ontological status of a nation is addressed by Amram when, in conversation with Caleb, he intuits Pharaoh's motivation:

> "You all talk like somebody else made these laws and Pharaoh don't know nothing about 'em. He makes 'em his own self and he's glad when we come tell him they hurt. Why, that's a whole lot of pleasure to him, to be making up laws all the time and to have a crowd like us around handy to pass all his mean ones on. Why, he's got a law about everything under the sun! Next thing you know he'll be saying cats can't have kittens. He figures that it makes a big man out of him

to be passing and passing laws and rules. He thinks that makes him look more like a king. Long time ago he done passed all the laws that could do anybody good. So now he sits up and studies up laws to do hurt and harm, and we're the only folks in Egypt he got the nerve to put 'em on. He aims to keep us down so he'll always have somebody to wipe his feet on. He brags that him and the Egyptian nation is eating high on the hog now." (5)

The laws Amram speaks of are those that condemn Hebrews to death or brutal slavery. The assumption Amram advances denies that someone other than Rameses designed the laws used to oppress Hebrews. Amram is not wrong in his assumption; the law, in existence from the originary moment of the Egyptian peoples both as its own possibility and impossibility, sanctifies a priori the slaughter of newly born Hebrew males. But the divine phallus of Rameses insists that no male Hebrew children shall be conceived. Pharaoh dictates the conditions that bind Hebrews to slavery and murder, but Rameses writes the law that forbids the conception of males. The fascist rule of law that Hurston treats in *Moses* is positioned before the very moment that inculcates the previous system of law into the body politic of the "chosen" people. The usurped rule of law does not exist before its origin; it does not account for the lawless terrain situated before its own mythological constitution. The empty space before the origin of the previous rule of law contains the negative realm invaded by the Führer to lay claim to a divine authority centered on his individual character. Because Hurston's Hitler/Pharaoh has staked his claim to the divine with Hebrew blood, Amram is correct in his censure of the cruelty of the *new* Pharaoh and not that of the eternal Pharaoh

Caleb and Amram continue and lodge the complaint that Hebrews have no space in which to worship and so are unable to sacrifice:

"And look what he done done! Passed a law we can't go in the temples no more. He says their gods ain't our gods."

"Like what other gods do we know anything about. It gives you a real empty feeling not to have no gods anymore. If we can't go to the temples in Thebes and Memphis and Luxor, we could build us one in Goshen and sacrifice, Amram. Maybe if we do that they might help us to get our rights back again." (5–6)

Sacrifice here takes on the quality of a political task; it falls in line with the logic that identifies the act of sacrifice as the offering of a gift to the godhead.[19] This gift will in turn secure the favor of the godhead for the sacrificer-community within a political economy that circulates around divine authority. If sacrifice "might help us to get our rights back," then Hebrews decry the loss of a political tool while being fundamentally aware that this very tool is being used against them. In the case of the drowning of Hebrew boys, the god for whom lives are taken is a secular god. Rameses' legal project is one designed to force Hebrews, with their freedom and their lives, to build a dynasty based not on the glory of the gods but on the political acumen of a man.

For Rameses to achieve his political goals absolutely, it is essential that he expel all Hebrews from Egyptian religion, for Rameses can only create the truly new law if Hebrews are exiled from Egyptian religion and thus from Egypt itself in an ontological sense. Indeed, Rameses cannot make a new law if the new law in question pertains to Egyptian subjects who accept him as the son of the sun god. This is so because every law—past, present, and future—is contained within the origin of the law as the ontological precondition of the Egyptian people. If Hebrews are allowed to practice Egyptian religion through their own volition, they can only recognize the authority of the Pharaoh and not that of Rameses, regardless of their physical oppression. This realization, as well as the notion of building in his image a new Egypt through Hebrew labor (Rameses, via Hebrew labor, has already erected the new city "Rameses"), is the fruit of Rameses' long hours of legal study. Every law has already been passed; new legal statutes can only be written in the blood of the racialized other. But for this writing to take place, the racialized other must be racially homogenous with the ideal racial type of the fascist state, and also radically other than this ideal.[20] In Hurston's analysis of National Socialist racial doctrine, race is delineated first and foremost by religion. The victimization of the racialized other must therefore at once promulgate the new mythology of the state and the dictator, and at the same time be denied access to a positive valuation within the scheme of this biological mysticism.

The reason Rameses is able to extend his rod of state, denuded of divine authority, into the Hebrew womb is not finally because of the crime of "rape" he believes the Hebrews to have committed against Egypt. It is instead owing to the fact that Hebrews are classified under the law as partial Egyptians by virtue of the racialized gods they once worshipped but are now denied. The worship of Egyptian gods places Hebrews in the same theological-ontological context as the "authentic" Egyptians, where Rameses has power over Hebrews as the conduit of the sun god's power insofar as the Egyptian rule of law has divine value for the people for whom it was crafted.[21] In Hurston's estimation, this power endows the authoritarian state with the ability to expunge the racialized other *by any means necessary* from the ontological condition that defines the National Socialist state, allowing the Führer to create new laws for a victimized people who, robbed of their being, are not human. Hence, the status of Hebrews in Hurston's text is paradoxically that of the hybrid. They are not Egyptians because they were Egyptians. But this past title of "Egyptian" was, for Hebrews, always provisional at best. It was only a matter of time until "the dishonesty and general wickedness of the Hebrews had reached the gods in their remote retreats and the gods had cried out for cleansing. The gods had announced emphatically that they would visit no altars that Hebrews were allowed to approach. Hebrews must not approach a single temple in Egypt. Neither must they build temples to Egyptian gods in Goshen. The gods were forbidden the boundaries of Goshen" (20–21).

The great distance between man and the gods in their remote retreats contains a temporal component. It was simply a matter of *time* before the gods recognized the inherent dishonesty and wickedness of Hebrews. In other words, the perception holds sway in the new mythology that a period of racial assimilation existed and infected the body politic with a degenerative cultural disorder until the time of the divine recognition of the ontological condition of the racialized other as essentially against the rule of law of the fascist state. To be "essentially" Egyptian indicates that one acts in accordance with the laws of the Egyptian gods because of an ontological inheritance displayed by faith in and conformity to the law. Once the Hebrew ruse is uncovered, the gods are "forbidden the boundaries of Goshen." The question arises of who has the power to forbid the gods anything. Through the sacrifice of the racialized other, the man above the gods has created new laws to which even the gods are beholden. Rameses, through the sacrifice of the Hebrews to himself, consolidates his political power as the framework of an entirely new fascist nation.

With a High Hand

It is this originary framework that will be challenged and co-opted by Hurston's Moses as she shifts the parameters of her meditation on the fascist authoritarian state to the realm of black cultural nationalism. Indeed, moments before Moses is "called" by Yahweh, he sits "up on the mountain passing nations through his mind" (125), in effect unwittingly preparing himself to accept Yahweh's command, "'Go down into Egypt, Moses, and lead my people to the place I have provided for them. I AM WHAT I AM'" (127).

By obeying Yahweh and championing the cause of Hebrews, Moses becomes the nexus of interpretive models for the text, containing within his figure not only the manifestation of a general program for the emancipation of oppressed minorities within an authoritarian society but also the identification of the specific location of an African American revolutionary identification with newly emancipated Haiti. Within this context, however, Hurston can only formulate a very general plan for the empowerment of African Americans vis-à-vis Haiti; and indeed she offers no advice to the European Jew beyond a schematic representation of the construction of nationhood and cultural self-reliance. Yet both Hurston's critique of fascist power and her model of Haitian-based black cultural nationalism maintain as a necessary structural element the demonization and murder of the racialized other. Of course, for Hurston the two models of nationalism and the creation of the nation differ in that the fascist state depends upon a demonization of the *biologically* racialized other. In following Boas and placing an emphasis on the cultural nature of race, her black cultural nationalism upholds a doctrine of exclusivity only insofar as this principle of exclusion hinges on the acceptance of a religious faith as the basis of African American cultural authenticity. Whereas Hurston's Rameses forbade the Hebrews' worship of Egyptian gods, the worship of the god of Moses is open to all who accept the Hebrew faith, which in Hurston's retelling is overdetermined as Voodoo. With her retooling of the Mosaic myth, Hurston maintains with her mentor Franz Boas that race is a cultural phenomenon, and that the "quality" of a race is determined by its cultural products. Where Hurston breaks with Boas is at the point of her essentialization of a culturally inclusive conception of race.

Beyond cosmetic details thought by both Boas and Hurston to possess an illusory permanence, Hurston believed the "race" itself is subject, through racial amalgamation, to physical evolution over time.[22] Racial identity can retain a measure of divisive permanence within a permeable yet ultimately historically stable notion of culture. However, an eternal epistemological guarantor outside of the realm of biology is still required by such a concept of race. A jargon of authenticity is still a jargon of authenticity, be it based on biological "fact" or theological and cultural mandates. That said, it is thus important to identify the manner in which Hurston presents the event leading directly to the Hebrew exodus. This event confounds the means of African American cultural and political emancipation with Pharaoh's gruesome oppression of the Hebrews. Moses's brutal masculinity is nearly identical to Pharaoh's.

Moses performs acts of extreme violence because he believes that Yahweh

> "has got to prove himself before them all to make folks believe. They have heard of God by ear but they don't know ... So what would be a better chance to show his powers than for Pharaoh to refuse and for me to beat him down with my powers? That's what I am to do. I don't want his consent, really. It would spoil everything I planned. I mean to whip his head to the ground and then lead out with a high hand." (146–47)

Betraying a hint of pleasure at the prospect of whipping Pharaoh's head to the ground, Moses insists that he must defeat Pharaoh to instill in the Hebrews faith in Yahweh. He does so through the spectacle of violence, and repeatedly, for Moses does not have in mind a single battle, but a series of violent humiliations to be visited upon Pharaoh and Egypt. The decisive wonder, the act that brings Pharaoh to his knees, entails doing unto Egypt as Egypt has done unto Goshen. Moses commits the mass slaughter of Egyptian children:

> Darkness balanced up on midnight looking both ways for day. Then the great cry arose in Egypt. They cried and died in Egypt. It was the great cry that had issued first from the throat of Israel years before and spread to the rim bones of the world and come back again. And now it poured through the mouth of the Egyptian nation ... Pharaoh looked upon his first-born and wept. (178)

"Darkness" defeats the sun god. Moses, practicing eye-for-an-eye justice and then some, visits upon Egypt the plague of murder and does so knowing, indeed intending, for this spectacle to be watched. Playing out his program for Hebrew emancipation through actions designed for visual pleasure, Moses conflates politics with aesthetics, aesthetics with violence. Through extreme violence, "Goshen" becomes "Israel." Moses thus surpasses the ultranationalist violence of the oppressor with one based on a de-racialized religious faith combined with a racialized cultural determinism, as opposed to biological mysticism.

In so doing, Moses implicates Hurston's text in the very fascist model she critiques, with the understanding that the fascism she instills and criticizes in Pharaoh has a virulent racial component common to National Socialism. For this is also the moment that Israel becomes racially exclusive; though Hurston notes that Hebrews themselves are composed of disparate racial elements, Moses, after the Exodus, asserts that racial amalgamation, the mixing of nations, "tak[ing] up too many habits from nations they come in contact with," should be avoided. For Hurston, Boas's doctrine of racial amalgamation loses its validity once Hebrews leave Egypt.[23]

Where Boas perceived a fluid understanding of racial development hindered only by racism, Hurston essentializes race along cultural lines. This entails replacing a violent mythology of the nation with an equally violent folklore of and for the Volk. The extreme violence employed by Moses to achieve the cultural goal of racial and political empowerment takes on the quality of violence for the sake of violence, in that Moses could simply raise his right hand and free the slaves.[24] Instead, the means Moses employs to deliver his people, and the rhetoric with which he does this, falls within the parameters of fascist political theology that begins and ends with the primacy of blood sacrifice.

This is why the essential activity of the Egyptian gods in Hurston's text is to take the sun as their signified meaning, their ontological basis, consigning them to veneration committed in bad faith. To communicate with the gods of Egypt via the "triple-formed messenger of men to the gods" is to receive false information from this messenger insofar as the being-in-darkness of the "true" origin of the authentic nation (God) is not considered.[25] Henri Hubert's and Marcel Mauss's tripartite mechanism of sacrifice, within an inauthentic understanding of national foundations, only goes so far. Hubert and Mauss speculated that there are three characters involved in sacrifice: the god, the victim, and the one who sacrifices. If one of the sides of the sacrificial triangle is insufficient to the ceremony, all sides are corrupted. For Hurston, the unity of the nation rests on ideological and cultural assumptions and not on an authentic mode of national being. Failed sacrifice lacks the power to establish a rapport with the God essential to authentic nationhood. The crisis of failed sacrifice creates a faulty picture of the nothingness from which civil law gains its divine aspect. This is so because, until the time of Moses, there has never been a victim adequate to the task of communicating with the one true God.[26]

It takes a Moses, the cultural signifier par excellence linking African America and Haiti, to speak with and for the nameless God of the darkness, to free African Americans from the yoke of an oppressive, ideological understanding of African American history.[27] Because sacrifice does not go far enough, the Jim Crow South and white America in general can exploit sacrifice as a means through which to surmount the American democratic ideology of equality among men and create the essential, racially exclusive image of an "American" disencumbered of inherent contradictions.[28] The victim delivers this new, coherent totality, and so Hebrews in Hurston's text deliver the message from Pharaoh to Rameses. Paradoxically, Egyptians as sacrificial victims convey the request from Moses *to God*.

In their respective quests for nationhood, both Pharaoh and Moses seek to interrupt and then rewrite history through acts of fascistic sacrificial violence. Pharaoh maintains absolute political power (and bequeaths it to his son, Suten-Rech Ta-Phar) with an act of sexual violence against Hebrew women, insuring the eventual death of a "really old story" (history), the "truth" (myth) contained in the Book of Thoth. It is the Book of Thoth as Nazi myth that Moses will recuperate as the absolute truth of history. Moses first hears of the book in the recollections of Mentu, his childhood servant and mentor. The book exists, at first, in the form of an oral record, a distinctly "Hebrew" method of mnemonic transfer. Of the book, Mentu tells Moses:

> "To tell you the truth, I don't know anything about it. All I know is what I have heard. It was told by the father of the father of my father to the father of my father and the father of my father has told it to me."
>
> "It is a really old story then."

"Sure. And the cry of it is that there is a book which Thoth himself wrote with his own hand which, if you read it, will bring you to the gods. When you read only two pages of this book you will enchant the heavens, the earth, the abyss, the mountain, and the sea. You will know what the birds of the air and the creeping things are saying. You will know the secrets of the deep because the power is there to bring them to you. And when you read the second page, you can go into the world of ghosts and come back to the shape you were on earth. You will see the sun shining in the sky, with all the gods, and the full moon." (53)

Hurston here aligns the African American oral tradition with the "truth" and monuments, with a *revision* of history. The history of the truth is entrusted to male progenitors, identifying the truth-in-memory as belonging to the masculine. Unwritten history, the "true" history, is recorded by males; whereas the feminine, as in fascist ideology, acts as a medium between the perpetuation of "true" history and the constitutive, inauthentic mnemonic trace designed for the purposes of designating "human nature." Hence, the masculine quality so important for what amounts to the recuperation of national identity, as defined racially but as a function of culture is a priori mediated by the feminine. Intent on building a nation, another phallus finds its way into the Hebrew womb.

Aside from allowing Moses to assert the superiority of masculine authority via the feminine as vessel, the Book of Thoth in Hurston's novel is the Center itself insofar as the book is a tool with which men communicate with the eternal. The book is a *written* sacrifice; it performs the same function as the event of blood sacrifice but does so at a deeper, more profound level. Sacrifice as writing takes priority over bloodletting, for the book presents the reader with an avenue to the knowledge of darkness, or God. It imparts to the reader the possibility of knowing the unknowable, of experiencing the knowledge withheld from the ceremonies of Egyptian sacrifice and Rameses' slaughter of the Hebrews. God whispers the laws of nature in the pages of the book, gifting the reader with the possibility that Law itself is preordained by the God among gods. The book relates intimate knowledge of the power of Ra by allowing mortal eyes to look on the sun and perceive that there is a divine darkness beyond it.

The task that the Book of Thoth performs in Hurston's text consists of identifying this blind spot in American democratic ideology within which the truth of a forgotten history, that of African Americans, can make itself known. This truth is not a rewritten falsification of an immediate African cultural presence in African America but an intuitive understanding of the cultural link between culturally rich Africa and African America via Haiti. It is another Nazi myth.

The word of God in this myth is also the unwritten word, or aporia, in the comparison between the legitimacy described in the Book of Thoth and that of Rameses' fascist regime. The book serves to recode history, to invest it with a Nazi mythology and cultural logic, a new chosen people. It is because of this that Moses must have the book.

> "Where is this book, I ask you, Mentu? I mean to read it."
> "The cry of it is that it is in the middle of the river at Koptos, in an iron box; in the iron box is a bronze box; in the bronze box is a sycamore box; in the sycamore box is an ivory and ebony box and in the ebony box is a silver box; in the silver box is a golden box and in that is the book. And there is a deathless snake by the box to guard it. That is all that they told me so I don't know anymore." (54)

Moses will wrestle with this snake, Damballah, and the snake will be overcome. In appropriating Damballah, Moses gains the right to a new rod of state, one infinitely more powerful than that of Pharaoh. Moses measures this rod against Pharaoh's in a violent, aestheticized spectacle played out in and for the Egyptian and Hebrew publics. The contest is a protracted political event that eventually sees the slaughter of hundreds of Egyptians. In essence, this battle reverses the roles of Hebrews and Egyptians in the ceremony of blood sacrifice as Moses, the sine qua non of the *Führerprinzip,* unleashes his plagues for the purpose of creating a new nation. In so doing he sets African American culture free.

The basis of Moses's new nation will be a religious principle more powerful than the one upon which Pharaoh established his fascist state. Indeed, as the charismatic leader, Moses demands submission to his right hand not only from the Egyptians but from Hebrews as well Both Miriam and Aaron lose their lives—in moments eerily suggestive of political assassination—for questioning Moses's authority (265, 275). And because the "Voice had said [to Moses] to take a nation across the

Jordan" (260), the Hebrews' enforced forty years in the desert see a time not only of hunger and warfare but of the consolidation of a nation *through* hunger and warfare. "The years went on doing their slow drag over Israel and left it fat and strong. When Joshua marched out against a people he won" (267). Joshua's military prowess cannot obscure the fact that he takes his orders from Moses, the greatest general both Egypt and Israel ever produced, one who literally defeated enemies single-handedly. For the new yet struggling nation, war gives character, solidifies community, and awakens in the blood the historical mission. Indeed, the Promised Land itself must be invaded and conquered.

Moses thus forms his fascist state on the basis of a political theology centered on the charismatic leader; the principle of cultural reinvigoration through a glorification of the masculine and the relegation of the feminine to the roles of incubator of the new man and woman warrior in the service of the nation; racial and cultural exclusivity; a valorization of warfare as the site of a nation's revelation to itself of its manifest destiny; a credo of violence for its own sake, which in turn informs the aestheticization of politics; and a rigorous foreign policy of aggression and isolationism.[29] In *Moses, Man of the Mountain*, sacrifice as a spectacle for kindling and ideologically buttressing ultranationalist sentiment sets itself the task of building nations by destroying others. It is a weapon Moses exploits in greatest measure, and one that is fascist to the core.

In fact, it is Hurston's desire to present a "core," or ideological kernel, that in part motivates her decision to retell the biblical tale. The truth-value of black fascism lies not merely in biblical exegesis but in the black vernacular tradition's veneration of Moses itself. This is to say, that where Schuyler and McKay construct black fascist fantasies and, ultimately, impossibilities, Hurston lays the historical and epistemological-mythical groundwork for a possible black fascist program. Stripped of specifics, Hurston offers ideological impetus and mythical force to the very idea of black fascism. The idea itself, though hinted at in Hurston, does not receive the full articulation of its politico-ontological imperative until Richard Wright's 1953 novel, *The Outsider*.

6 Richard Wright's Jealous Rebels
Black Fascism and Philosophy

> Wright was an excellent writer of horror stories of the Edgar Allan Poe or King Kong order, but the white critics were practically destroying him when they tried to hoist him up as a Negro leader and say that Bigger Thomas was a symbol of the Negro race.
> —Claude McKay to Ivie Jackman (July 15, 1944)

> [Richard Wright] has had a roll in the hay with the existentialism of Sartre, and apparently he liked it.
> —Arna Bontemps, Review of Richard Wright's *The Outsider* (1953)

If McKay puts Nazi mythology to work, then Hurston's *Moses, Man of the Mountain* and Richard Wright's *The Outsider* (1953) work out a new Nazi mythology. In this sense, Wright's scathing review of *Their Eyes Were Watching God* (1937) and Hurston's immediate and equally opprobrious rejoinder condemning Wright's *Uncle Tom's Children* (1937) as a violent, masculinist view of African American life mark a methodological, not ideological, divide between the two. The irreconcilability of the Wright-Hurston debate is questionable in the light of Hurston's *Moses*, which is every bit as violent and masculinist as anything Wright ever wrote. This fact, coupled with Hurston's and Wright's shared preoccupation with the positive aspects of a possible form of fascism developed by blacks bridges this divide. As William J. Maxwell has observed, "During the 1930s, both Hurston and Wright harnessed folk ideology to provide a symbolic countermeasure to a Great Migration that threatened to empty the population and cultural power of the black belt" (157). An aspect of this "harmonic convergence" between Hurston and Wright resonates with fascism as well.

Wright began his consideration of "folk ideology" and fascism in the 1930s, presenting his findings in the novel *The Outsider*. Written after World War II and the Holocaust, *The Outsider* does not claim to valorize black fascism but instead presents itself as an existentialist work.

Yet Wright's novel, understood and accepted as an existentialist work by almost every critic to approach it, in essence goes beyond existentialism. It finds totalitarianism, driven by the Nietzschean will to power, to be nothing less than the very ontological basis of sovereignty in Western political theory. For Cross Damon, the novel's murderous protagonist, there exists no overriding existential indifference in the face of an indifferent universe. Through his unquenchable desire for recognition and his countless heinous acts of violence, he tests the boundaries of political power in theory and wrests from absurd existence what I call the fascist absolute.

Indeed, the violence of Wright's protagonist is so extreme that it can be said that Cross Damon never met a man he didn't kill. Having cut a swath of seemingly senseless destruction through the streets of Chicago, Damon, the ex–postal worker presumed dead but living from beyond the grave under an alias and the occupation of "student," travels to New York. There, in the name of self-preservation and political theory, the killing continues. Ultimately, what lies at the bottom of his bloodlust can be identified as an insatiable desire for power. Damon displays in the moment of the kill a greed that arises from a distorted perception of both Communism and fascism, one that conflates the two and which Damon subsequently identifies as his own uniquely American hunger. Wright characterizes Damon as the ideologically unadorned heart of both fascism and Communism, as the political will to power of the totalitarian dictator bereft of subjects, political party, and parliamentary procedure. As a fully matured and academically trained Bigger Thomas, Wright's Damon represents the possibility for African American radical political action and empowerment beyond Communism and fascism. Not Wright's escape from the realty of black life in America to French Existentialism, Damon instead signifies the irreducible totalitarian essence of blacks in America. Wright's conflation of existentialism, fascism, and Communism, played out through Damon's narrow conception of both totalitarian ideologies, undercuts his critique of totalitarian ideology, and instead justifies it.

How Bigger Was Really Born

In "How 'Bigger' Was Born" (1940), Wright understands African American politics as the demand that African America choose between Communism and fascism.¹ This political mandate allows for no other alternative to its two choices and sees no inherent contradiction in the logic that states that an African American can be a fascist. Wright justifies his observations as the products of objective scientific inquiry and not as the heated emotions of a writer who, at the time the essay was written, still found himself deeply invested in the Popular Front: "When the Nazis spoke of the necessity of a highly ritualized and symbolized life, I could hear Bigger Thomas on Chicago's South Side saying: 'Man, what we need is a leader like Marcus Garvey. We need a nation, a flag, an army of our own. We colored folks ought to organize into groups and have generals, captains, lieutenants, and so forth. We ought to take Africa and have a national home'" ("Bigger" 445) ²

Garvey offers the model of the black fascist, who, according to one of the myriad Biggers, stands for militarization under the authoritarian leadership of a single man fighting for a nation and all that it signifies. Africa must be colonized for its own good and the good of the race. Bigger Thomas not only can be a fascist: the "nationalist implications" of his life practically demand his transformation into one. For the Wright of the late 1930s and opening years of the 1940s, Communism presented the only organizational and ideological structure capable of preventing this metamorphosis from taking place.³ It remained to the writer to capture the nationalist impulse in Bigger Thomas and redirect it into that which transcends nationalism.⁴

Wright visualized a crucial section of the draft of his 1937 essay "Blueprint for Negro Writing" as precisely this mechanism for the conversion of nationalist sentiment into class consciousness: "Negro writers must accept the nationalist implications of their lives, not in order to encourage them, but in order to change and transcend them. They must accept the concept of nationalism because, in order to transcend it, they must *possess* and *understand* it. And a nationalist spirit in Negro writing means a nationalism carrying the highest possible pitch of social consciousness" ("Blueprint" 1381). In accepting the "nationalist implications of their lives," Negro writers also accept those of the life of Bigger Thomas. In doing so, they become ("*possess*") the nationalist and fascistic subject to show the way beyond nationalism and fascism. For Wright, fascism in African America could not be avoided—it had to be surmounted. This explains why, "for purposes of creative expression . . . the Negro writer must realize within the area of his own personal experience those impulses which, when prefigured in terms of broad social movements, constitutes the stuff of nationalism" ("Blueprint" 1384). This personal experience transcends the very class structure it seeks to destroy. Wright has not identified how "the stuff on nationalism" permeates the body of diverse individual writers and, consequently, the deviations and divergences between the individuals who make up the political playing field that Wright tacitly claims exists as a coherent, black whole.[5] Wright combines rural and urban proletarians to create the Volk, and so also the subject of Black Nationalism and, potentially, black fascism. He has the authority to do this because as a writer whose personal experiences have the ability to speak for the black whole if rendered in the right way, Wright's autobiography can claim a universal status.

Thus, when Wright clarifies why "the humble" generate the defining limits of the Volk in the preface to *12 Million Black Voices* (1941), "It is not . . . to celebrate or exalt the plight of the humble folk who swim in the depths that I select the conditions of their lives as examples of normality, but rather to seize upon that which is qualitative and abiding in Negro experience, to place within full and constant view the collective humanity whose triumphs and defeats are shared by the majority, whose gains in security mark an advance in the level of consciousness attained by the broad masses in their costly and torturous upstream journey" (xx). The "qualitative and abiding in Negro experience" is in fact precisely what Wright insists he does not exalt, namely, the "plight of the humble folk." There can be no doubt that Wright considers a member of the talented tenth representative of the "abiding" Negro experience only insofar as the experience, alien to his or her manifest résumé as a Negro, nevertheless informs it as paper to the ink printed on it. A bourgeois Negro is one who is out of touch with, but not wholly alienated from, the "abiding" experience of his or her race. Wright believes he writes for all Negroes and not just Bigger Thomas when he declares, "Whether he'll follow some gaudy, hysterical leader who'll promise rashly to fill the void in him, or whether he'll come to an understanding with the millions of his kindred fellow workers under trade-union or revolutionary guidance depends upon the future drift of events in America" ("Bigger" 447). It "depends on the future drift of events in America" as well as the effectiveness of Negro writers in delving into themselves and excavating universal class consciousness. It also depends on the "drift" of events outside America, as the Bigger Thomas of

Native Son makes clear: "He liked to hear of how Japan was conquering China; of how Hitler was running the Jews to the ground; of how Mussolini was invading Spain. He was not concerned with whether these acts were right or wrong; they simply appealed to him as possible avenues of escape. He felt that some day there would be a black man who would whip the black people into a tight band and together they would act and end fear and shame" (*Native Son* 115). World events and the machinations of foreign leaders and powers have the ability to frame otherwise unbounded and ambiguous desires. They put into focus ill-conceived longings and confused domestic upheavals; they decide the inevitable, protracted, and violent contest between Communism and fascism for the hearts and minds of African Americans.

This desire to know an object by experiencing it firsthand informs much of Wright's travel writing of the 1950s, in particular *Pagan Spain* (1957). Shortly after arriving in fascist Spain, Wright lets his desire attach itself to what we may call "Franco's Big Book of Fascism" instead of paying attention to the young woman with whom he appears to be out on a date. Before convincing the woman to give him the book, Wright "picked up her book and rapidly leafed through the pages, seeking clues; I saw the volume dealt with the aims and principles of the Franco regime and was in the simple form of questions and answers—a political catechism for the Spanish masses. Suddenly, desperately, I wanted that book" (*Pagan Spain* 17). "Seeking clues" to what? Whatever mystery he wishes to solve, he feels a desperate desire to do so. The book, the object of his desire, substitutes for something else, for the solution to the mystery that is intimately bound to the Franco regime, Falange, and fascism. This quest for fascism unfolds in Wright's body of work most explicitly in *The Outsider,* a text he wrote in "exile" in France, where he struggled "at the side of Sartre" against "various forms of concealed fascism," or so we discover in an interview with the author:

> All French progressives are happy to have you among us, and we are happy to see that you are at the side of Sartre and his friends in the struggle which counterpoises freedom through socialism to various forms of concealed fascism. Have you any definite plans?
>
> I am a foreigner here and my collaboration with Sartre is limited to certain special fields. I cannot be a member of the RDR since it is not fitting for me to take part in questions of internal French politics.

> But I am in complete agreement with the RDR as far as its views on international questions are concerned. (Kinnamon and Fabre 131)

Fascism only partially concealed solves the riddle whose answer runs through *Pagan Spain* and has a posteriori dire consequences for Bigger Thomas. What remains to be seen, and what Sartre and his existentialist superfriends aim to discover, denotes what Wright perceives as the essence of the totalitarian personality. Wright pursues this personality in *The Outsider* but without abandoning his commitment to fighting for the race.

Sleeping with Sartre

The notion that its author had abandoned not only his commitment to fighting racial injustice but also the very reality of his racial designation was the overriding concern of *The Outsider*'s critics when it appeared in 1953.[6] Richard Wright's novel is ostensibly about an embittered and domestically embattled Chicago intellectual and postal clerk who, mistaken for dead after a train accident, moves to New York to start a new life—but not without killing several people along the way to and at his destination. The reasons for the bloodshed do not encompass a long list: Cross Damon kills to hide his identity and because of what he perceives as personal affronts sustained on the level of political ideology. This does not mean, however, that Damon actively engages in political agitation or has much concern for the social world in which he finds himself. Wright's critics attack precisely this point, underscoring an almost unanimous belief at the time of *The Outsider*'s publication that Wright's antihero sidesteps a direct confrontation with racial injustice in the United States in order to represent existentialist man as he survives the violent contradictions and complexities of the twentieth century. As one reviewer put it, "*The Outsider* has a Negro for its hero; but it is not primarily his plight as a Negro, but as a thinking, questioning man in the perplexing twentieth century that concerns Mr. Wright" (Prescott 193). Another reviewer echoes the same sentiment: "The leading character is, to be sure, a Negro, but his principal problems have nothing to do with his race. They are pre-eminently the problems of the human being as such, for this is, so far as I can recall, one of the first consciously existentialist novels to be written by an American" (Hicks 198).

The thought running through both the high praise and the withering criticism that Wright's novel received is that the book had little or nothing to do with Negro life. This assumption attempts to limit the extent to which the African American can provide an archetype for the representation of the whole of humanity, insisting that the problems of the Negro have virtually no general qualities but instead collectively unfold as an absolute historico-material singularity. If Wright writes an outsider character that, because of his very status as socially alienated from the black whole, embodies the whole of the (Western) human condition, then the underlying assumption of *The Outsider*'s defenders and detractors is that "the Negro" cannot alone embody the full scope of the human. The Negro summons individual and communal powers that are, *in essence,* totally alien to the Western tradition. In the pages of *The Outsider,* the book's detractors charged, Wright sleeps with the enemy. Arna Bontemps summed up this attitude best when he wrote in his review of *The Outsider:* "[Wright] has had a roll in the hay with the existentialism of Sartre, and apparently he liked it" (208).

Bontemps' rather famous barb aimed at Wright's apparently homosexual, miscegenous intellectual practices is exemplary of the critical opinions offered by much of the literary intelligentsia concerned with *The Outsider.* Wright has gone white, and from the wrong side of the color line he has sent us a massive, far-too-often incoherent and ultimately socially inconsequential tome apropos of something other than Negro life as it is lived.[7]

Reading the unwieldy and frustrating novel caused experiences of social displacement and intellectual vertigo so severe that the question of *The Outsider*'s status as possibly a joke became the main line of critical interrogation. As Roi Ottley put it: "I suspect Wright is mocking us with a ghastly joke. His main character, Cross Damon, was driven by no discernible motives—racial, political, or religious—even though the author would have us believe he is a rational person. Actually, he is not a Negro, but what Wright describes as the 'psychological man'" ("New Monster" 205).

In other words, the faint, continual sound one hears emanating from the pages of *The Outsider* can only be the dying laughter of Richard Wright as he prepares us for the realization that his novel offers nothing other than its own nothingness, its own absurdity. This suspicion unintentionally captures at least one aspect of Wright's novel. As an exercise in existentialism, Wright's roll in the hay with Sartre has produced a gargantuan novel about the essential absurdity of "being and nothingness." The laugh one perceives may very well be the same one haunting Camus' nameless protagonist in *The Fall*. Seemingly a betrayal of *Native Son*'s desire to create paths to meaningful social action beginning in the work of literature, Wright's joke resonates with an understanding of existentialism as a philosophy of negation and nihilism, and so a system of belief inimical to social activism.

Nothing, however, conditions us for the nature of the related but far more insidious betrayal that Lorraine Hansberry accuses Wright's *The Outsider* of perpetrating: "*The Outsider* is a story of sheer violence, death and disgusting spectacle, written by a man who has seemingly come to despise humanity.... Cross Damon is someone you will never meet on the Southside of Chicago or in Harlem.... As a propaganda piece for the enemies of the Negro people, of working people and of peace, *The Outsider* has already been saluted with a full page spread of praise by the *New York Times Sunday Book Supplement* (3-22-53)" (Hansberry 220). Hansberry condemns Wright for committing at least two crimes in *The Outsider:* Wright has executed his work in bad taste, and the novel sleeps with the enemy. In other words, Wright has become a tool for the espousal of anti-black sentiment; his work aligns against his own race and is disgusting in any artistic sense. In effect, Wright's exile has turned him into a race traitor whose first act of treason unleashed Cross Damon against Bigger Thomas, allowing him to stab Bigger in the back.

Pitting these two against each other is hard not to do. Indeed, one cannot avoid comparing *The Outsider* with Wright's most famous novel. *The Outsider* marks Wright's first novel since 1940's *Native Son*. Both novels follow the same basic narrative strategies: Cross Damon, like Bigger Thomas, finds himself embroiled in unhappy domestic circumstances, at odds with his overbearing mother, and put upon by women he cares nothing about; and, as a result of frustration and impotence in the face of white oppression, perpetrates multiple homicides. Murder in both novels represents severe inter- and intraracial social alienation (Rugoff 196). Bigger Thomas hulks alone and blindly through Wright's 1940 novel, becoming the inverted echo of the subsequent Cross Damon, who is the fruition of Wright's efforts to create an existentialist hero existing solely as a response to American social conditions. Thus,

Native Son stands in the light of *The Outsider* as the nucleus for the later novel's inception and development, and showcases French existentialist thought avant la lettre.

This means that Wright's intellectual interests did not change after his roll in the hay with Sartre. They simply found a systematic expression for what lurked, like Bigger Thomas in comparison to Cross Damon, intellectually malformed in its shadow. The antagonistic American racial scene is the basis for Wright's *black* existentialism. This reading of Wright as a progenitor of black existentialism transforms Wright from the "race traitor" identified by his contemporaries into a philosophically astute and socio-theoretically honest writer with an abiding and profound interest in Negro folk life.[8] Wright does not write propaganda for anti-black forces but instead captures, as early as *Native Son,* the philosophical essence of African American social, historical, and individual existence. *Native Son* is an unfinished attempt to formulate what could be described as an African American existentialism that completes itself with *The Outsider,* which moves from a space of artistic and political failure to a realm of higher philosophical perception and debate, as well as to a political integrity Wright himself could not match when he tried to be a Communist (Turner 311).[9]

The artistic rite of passage Wright undergoes to transcend Communism is also his abandonment of socialist realism as a mode of artistic expression. *The Outsider* is something other than an exercise in realism: it is part fantasy, part essay, part pulp fiction, part sociology, and part philosophical treatise. It is, in terms of its formal presentation, a hybrid, unallied with any particular mode of textual production (Singh 359). As such, the book escapes easy generic categorization, defying the very conventions it relies on to present itself to its public.

In this sense, Wright and Damon undertake and execute a quest for identity at the combined levels of content and form. The protean character of the text's open formal structure signifies Damon's moral attitude. Both function in and as negation, canceling the totality toward which each strives in favor of a fragmentary existence held together by intense fear and dread. Again, what Bigger Thomas cannot do as a matter of intellectual constitution, Cross Damon accomplishes as the negative plenitude of Bigger's undeveloped potential (Adell 381). As a "man" who, following Kierkegaard, experiences his being as the ontic development of ontologically a priori fear and dread, Damon takes the philosophical basis of African American social existence to its inevitable conclusion. Existentialism does not offer Wright fertile terrain in which to plant the seed of a potential philosophical analysis of African American life. Rather, fear and dread, emotions Wright takes as the precondition for an existentialist understanding of being-in- (and for) the world, already denote the essential determinations of blackness in America.[10] Wright, then, finds in racism both the theoretical exemplar and practical functioning of American society and the general outline of existence as such. *The Outsider* posits that the absurdity of American racism and racism in general perfectly captures the absurdity of existence (Tate 392). African American social reality encapsulates de facto the general and essential theoretical principles of French existentialism. Sartre has not seduced Wright—Wright has taken Sartre.

If American racism best describes, as existential example, existentialism in theory, then the fact of Damon's blackness cannot be dissociated and dismissed from Wright's text. The critical appraisals of *The Outsider* that seek either to restore Damon to a socially determined and active mode of blackness or to discard his status as a "black man" in favor of "existentialist man" contend that the text presents us with an either/or—a choice Wright does not offer. The fact that Damon is a black man means that he is an existentialist man. Wright's complex and finely (if unrealistically) wrought Cross Damon defies simple categorization, including one that determines his "plight" as "real." This is because Damon embodies a primarily philosophical representation of African American existential social existence, as opposed to being a general example of a sociohistorically specific and realistic representation of being-in-the-world (Hakutani 366).

Damon's very real—as well as philosophical—status as radically outside the multiplicity of communities and agencies that make up social existence situates him within a sphere of absolute alienation. He can not participate in the political life of African Americans, accrue spiritual or material wealth, or experience human emotions unconditioned by fear and dread. But the situation Damon finds himself in does not place him outside all forms of human society (Coles 59). The social and the human, as conceptual existentials, do not correspond exactly to one another in Wright's novel; they are in combat, each the other's negative moment. In *The Outsider*, to be radically individual means to be human, all too human. There is no "human community" as such, unless this phrase designates a community of one. "Community" in *The Outsider* designates a social construction alienated from the human or the natural. Struggling for an internally coherent identity, Damon is, as Chidi Maduka perceives, "a controversial revolutionary character whose fight for self-identity leads to his committing ghastly murders" (61). The product of social alienation, this 'fight for self-identity" excludes the human as a solution to the struggle, residing outside the self, existing alienated from itself. As such, it is revolutionary. Damon's "ghastly murders" perpetrate offenses against an order alienated from the human, which Wright takes to be not an essence but a choice. His "revolutionary" acts give priority to human existence over the socially alienated concept of essence, establishing an existentialist ontology that Wright sees as essentially black.

The Demon and the Cross

There is no contradiction in Wright's logic. The concept of "blackness," however defined, is only valid here insofar as it manifests the primacy of the existential choice of the human and as it is thought of with regard to the social and historical forces that shape it.[11] Wright believes these forces shape a human destiny linked with various manifestations of a single, inevitable totalitarian politics. What Wright describes as ideology attaches itself to the human in becoming the social. However, the human itself is contingent on sociohistorical circumstances and so a product of and standard-bearer for the twentieth century, and cannot be dissociated from totalitarianism. For Wright, in the twentieth century totalitarianism marks the existential condition of the human. Communism and fascism name the political ideologies best suited to the ontic conditions of the human and thus to the materiality of the political and social. If the social conditions of African Americans posit a variant of existentialism as their philosophical basis, then the existential condition of the human in the twentieth century, manifested in Communist and fascist ideology, is also that of African America. Wright's fear and dread expressed in *The Outsider* is not only that there is a possibility that African America will take on the characteristics of a totalitarian state (if the black nation were to achieve statehood), but also that the human condition as totalitarian is "essentially" that of the African American.[12]

Such an assertion relies on attention to fine shades of difference. Under suspicion of murder and undergoing District Attorney Houston's philosophically challenging yet otherwise accommodating third degree, Damon decides that he does, in fact, hate fascists more than Communists.

> "You don't like Communists, do you?"
> "No."
> "Which do you hate more? Communists or Fascists?"
> "Well, I'm afraid I hate the Fascists more, sir."
> "Why?"
> "Well, they've more real support. Of course, this is a debatable question. Maybe I feel like that because I'm a Negro and Fascists are dead against us."
> "If you had the opportunity to send two of them to their graves in one blow, would you do it?"
> Cross looked at Houston and laughed.
> "Would *you*?" he countered. (518)

Damon's hatred of fascists is not without ambivalence. The justification for privileging the fascists in Damon's private hierarchy of hate boils down to a matter of numbers: the greater mass of people lend support to fascism, ergo fascism presents the greater evil and must be combated with greater ferocity. Priority is not given to the expected line of reasoning when Damon decides against the fascists, for Damon does not overly concern himself with the fascists' program of white supremacy and the annihilation of so-called inferior races. The racial politics of fascism as Wright delineates them in *The Outsider* occupy a subsidiary place in Cross Damon's analysis in which totalitarian ideology amounts to the greater evil. As Damon answers Houston's question with the only answer he could possibly give without coming across to Houston as either stupid or insane, he undoes the expected affirmation with a carefully inscribed mark of uncertainty. Damon insists that he cannot insist that the fascists *must be* for him cause for the greater concern. It can only be said for certain that *perhaps* Damon feels as he does because he is a Negro and the fascists are dead set against him.

Satisfied with Damon's response, Houston does not register the fact that Damon feels fear in addition to a certain degree of ambivalence arising from his uncertainty as to which totalitarian ideology can be said to be worse. When Damon replies to Houston's loaded question, "I'm afraid I hate the Fascists more, sir," it is not with hatred of fascism (Cross more than embraces the potency and righteousness of his negativity) but loathing of having to decide the question at all. Damon's fear speaks to his anxiety over the irreducibility of the two radically separate political positions.[13] In fact, in *The Outsider* fascism and Communism are twins:

> "And these two men, what are their backgrounds?" Houston asked at last.
> "That's a damned strange thing, Mr. D.A.," Farrel said. "Gilbert Blount was a member of the Central Committee of the Communist Party of the United States—"
> "You're kidding," Houston protested with wide eyes.
> "No, sir," Farrel insisted. "It's a fact—"
> "And who's the other one?"
> "His twin. A Fascist, they say—." (354)

By the very figure of legal authority, the difference between the fascist and the Communist is effaced. If Houston, and by extension Houston's men, cannot mark a substantive separation between Gil Blount and Herndon, then there exists within the ideological framework of Wright's text virtually no satisfactory difference between the psychological aspects of the two political programs in question.[14] Emphasis must be placed on Wright's concern for the psychological and philosophical as they relate to manifestations of totalitarian politics. *The Outsider* presents no other causal indication from which to proceed when seeking to delimit the unique qualities of each of its respective political frames.[15] If we can discern any distinction between fascism and Communism, on the one hand, and Cross Damon's still-to-be-determined political program, on the other, then it would be one of political inversion. Cross's crimes themselves speak for him where he cannot articulate his own difference. His feats of extreme violence and personal and political liberation display themselves, draped in bloody red, as the mirror images of the totalitarian twins fascism and Communism.

Characterizing Damon's crimes, Houston, Wright's voice of pure reason, insists, "But this is a kind of inverted pro-communist and pro-Nazi propaganda. They've so distorted these men that no one could ever recognize their psychological types" (436–37). It is, above all else, a question of psychology. This is a necessary move for Wright to make if one of his objectives is to represent not simply a nascent dictatorial black fascist mentality but the primacy of such a psychological disposition within the black male. Disposed to an almost congenital condition of latent fascism, this psyche would escape any easy classification, including the twin descriptions of fascism and Communism present in the book. This would result in a categorical placement of the violent criminal in his own group. He would be spiritually akin to a fascist and a Communist (they are, psychologically and philosophically speaking, the same thing), while remaining on the outside, siphoning his personal justification from an identification with, and reaction against, his ideological soul mates.[16] As Houston points out, "such a killer could not be either a Communist or a Fascist, could he? . . . [H]e'd have to be somebody psychologically akin to either Blount or Herndon and yet somehow outside of them. I can't see either a Communist or a Fascist acting in that way" (374, 375).

The difference, then, between fascists and Communists, in one corner, and Cross Damon, African American Übermensch, in the other, can be seen at the level of praxis. Psychologically, the three parties (and Cross is his own party) submit to no difference between them. But in terms of signification within the realm of the physical and social, circumstance creates different results for each of Wright's ideologues. Social reality does not distort psychological disposition so much as create it and then provide different, specific outlets for its manifestation. In other words, Cross cannot be labeled a fascist, not because he evades such a label categorically, but because the social conditions under which he lives preclude his self-realization in the form of a fascist as such. Because he is a Negro and fascism does not escape the confining definition of virulent racism, Damon cannot with any authority become a fascist. Becoming fascist is not within his racial prerogatives. There exists, however, a clause within his psychological contract that allows him to partake in the very essence of fascism and Communism. Wright's omniscient narrator tells us, "The essence of the Party was open lawlessness and it could smell lawlessness in others even when it could not identity it correctly" (470). Clearly, Cross Damon shares in this essence—he is, after all, nothing if not lawless. But the claims for the lawless men do not stop just outside the extreme limit of the law. Exceeding the rule of law is merely a starting point for the unfolding of what amounts to the fascist man's true essence.[17]

Musing on the subject, Houston speculates: "I wonder if such men have any value? Might not they be the real lawgivers. . . . Maybe. . . . Who knows?" (380). Men of power—communists, fascists, Cross Damon—break the law only to establish the new law. The moment the crime is completed signifies the moment the rule of law loses its justification and can therefore no longer delimit the differences between Damon and his totalitarian counterparts. By taking the law into his own hands, Damon, like Hurston's Moses and Pharaoh, creates the law. The effect of this is to cause a disruption within the logic of the will to power that permeates Wright's text and ultimately decides who can be recognized as what on the totalitarian ideological food chain. Although the rule of law, as Carl Schmitt believed, functions as a generality, the general can only be understood by that which falls outside of it—the radically singular, or state of exception.[18] Damon's ability to give law comes when he suspends the law, creating a state of exception through extreme violence. Violent crime creates a new political order in which Damon can be identified as fascist if he so chooses. This is not to say that Damon becomes fascist at the moment of his crime but that he can be identified as such by the denizens of his social climate. Such identification remains a legal matter. Who or what decides who or what can be called fascist, and how we determine what can ultimately be described as an epistemological value to political classifications, are the questions that Wright's Damon begs and answers with ultraviolence.[19]

What matters here, then, is what kind of man you are. Character, as determined and developed by social circumstance, decides one's political affiliations. Herndon can be called a fascist because of where he comes from, not who he is. Where Wright does mark substantive differences between political ideologies, they appear at the point of grotesque regional caricature. Gil Blount, Wright's urban communist cowboy, breaks down Herndon for us and in so doing describes not simply the man but the method by which Wright's text displays ideological differences:

> "Now, let me tell you the kind of man this Herndon is. I mentioned last night that he was a Fascist. He is. I'm not understating it. Herndon began his life as a Texas oil man and he made piles of money.

He has the old-fashioned American racist notions, all of them, right up to the hilt, including the so-called biological inferiority of the Negro. He even claims that he has found a philosophical basis and justification of his racial hatred. Understand? He hates not only Negroes, Jews, Chinese, but all non-Anglo-Saxons. . . . And he is smart enough to give you a mile of specious arguments, gotten out of crackpot books, for his anti-Semitism, anti-Negroism, etc. All of his arguments boil down to this: God made him and his kind to rule over the lower breeds. And God was so kind and thoughtful as to arrange that he be paid handsomely for it." (264–65)

Declarative statements do the work for us: if Blount says he's a fascist, then fascist Herndon must be. Throughout the book, however—or in least that small portion of it through which Herndon remains breathing—the representative fascist character displays no characteristics of the fascist aside from a virulent racism, which, having nothing uniquely fascist about it, could in fact could be part of several different ideological arsenals. The only pieces of evidence Blount produces to prove Herndon's fascism are that Herndon is from Texas and a successful entrepreneur. Herndon is a fascist because of regional background and material success.[20]

Of the exhibits brought into evidence in the mock trial that determines Herndon to be a fascist, not a single one of them rises above the level of the circumstantial. Being a successful, virulently racist capitalist landlord does not make one a fascist. However, throughout the course of Wright's text, neither Blount nor anyone else will ever offer a deeper analysis of the distinctive nature of fascism, what defines a fascist, and how Herndon qua fascist functions in *The Outsider*.[21] Down to choosing a fascist's name for his character—Herndon recalls Angelo Herndon, the famous black Communist—Wright intentionally distorts his presentation of the psychological nature of fascism to recast it as essentially identical to Communism.[22] "Herndon, the fascist beast" (313), becomes Blount, the Communist animal. Neither is to be outdone by Damon, the Jealous Monster. For what Damon feels amounts to an irreducible jealousy of the power the fascists and Communists wield.[23] As Damon indirectly muses, "Was it such a bad world after all? The only trouble was that he and his kind were restlessly envious of the priests, the churches, the Communists, the Fascists, the men of power. . . . That was it" (555).

"He and his kind" tell us what we need to know: they brook no difference between totalitarian ideologies aside from relative political positions performed for the sake of power. This is not power marked by the specificity of its manifestations but power absolute and indifferent to political programs. When Damon looks upon Blount, Herndon, and his other victims before the kill, what he sees does not corrupt his sense of right and wrong, thus allowing him to perform heinous acts of violence and bringing his essential being into focus. Damon births, at the moment of confrontation and death, his own subjective, fascist agency as outsider and overlord. He kills for love of power, and murderous violence is the only power afforded him. For Damon, each murder increases the capital with which he exercises absolute, yet virtual, totalitarian will to power.[24]

How Damon kills is as important as whom he kills. Damon must have his weapon of choice. "He's worried about the gun, Cross thought. Otherwise, I've acted in a way to make him trust me, to make him feel that he is the boss; but my having a gun makes him feel that I might have a will of my own" (265). His gun provides him with the means to reveal himself not only to himself but also to the universe. When he is exercising lethal violence, Damon's perception alters to such an extent that a vision of the universe offers itself to him: "The universe seemed to be rushing at him with all the concreteness of its totality. He was anchored once again in life, in the flow of things; the world glowed with an interest so sharp that it made his body ache" (304). This is not a hallucination without physical consequences. Damon's body aches under the strain of the revelation and subsequent engagement with the world. The totalitarian universe can be experienced only at the moment when the violent act most thoroughly compromises that totality. The disruption of human unity, murder satisfies Damon's individual hunger for an impersonal, naturalistic understanding of "universal" responsibility. The taking of life reinscribes Damon, not in a human continuum, but instead in a natural order of impersonal continuity and freedom.[25] The existentialist hero taking absolute responsibility surrenders culpability and reestablishes for himself the convincing illusion of brotherhood, namely, a form of "communism" attained by totalitarian means for the purposes of achieving totalitarian ends.

Within this totalitarian frame, Damon is *essentially* lawless; he does not recognize an authority beyond the law he creates while committing murder.²⁶ Damon is his own sovereign; as such, he fills the void Wright sees as indicative of the twentieth century: "What these sincere people do not realize is that Communism and Fascism are but the political expressions of the Twentieth Century's atheistic way of life, and that the future will reveal many, many more of these absolutistic systems whose brutality and rigor will make the present-day systems seem like summer outings" (491). Damon is nothing if not brutal and rigorous. As such, he signifies what stands next in the line of political expression characterized by "absolutistic systems." He awaits the coming of his masses; he awaits his own apotheosis.

Offering a theological-psychological profile of the Communist-fascist double murderer, and so dabbling in self-analysis and self-apotheosis, Damon concludes, "That [such a man] is an atheist goes without saying, but he'd be something more than an atheist. He'd be something like a pagan, but a pagan who feels no need to worship. . . . And, by the nature of things, such a man sooner or later is bound to appear" (426–27). The inevitable pagan returns eternally, taking his proper place at the zenith of the totalitarian dictator pyramid totally devoid of a sense of inferiority. This pagan amounts to little more than an animal; yet the pagan-animal does submit to an intellectual rigor that escapes blind brutality. It knows that it knows no boundaries, that its lust for destruction, its carnage in the name of competition, exceeds all manifest systems of law. The pagan-animal possesses an awareness of its status as both animal and pagan disencumbered of any genealogy of morals. All rituals performed by such a man will have been founded and sanctioned by him alone, and they will apply only to him. This Übermensch has no true congregation because he takes part in no "absolutistic system" aside from the one he creates. He obeys only the laws he gives, never those he receives. He is, in effect, a god.²⁷

The matter then resolves to a single fact of the will as it operates in the world and on the world's representations. What Damon ultimately concerns himself with is the question of divine right or sovereignty: "Had not Houston admitted that maybe some men had the right to become lawgivers? Was there not, maybe, in Houston's heart the capacity to respect some forms of forceful crime? Had not men respected the crimes of Napoleon, Stalin, Mussolini, and Hitler?" (411)²⁸ Although Wright goes to great philosophical lengths to establish the fact that dictatorial power depends on fear as its final arbiter, the need to respect the dictator serves as a measure of a man's latent or emergent ferocity of ambition. It also gives to the aura of the dictator an additional recourse for the justification of whatever means he chooses to meet whatever ends. The list of names that Wright produces is an all-star catalogue of Antichrists. However, by his own logic, Damon's name should be added to the list, if for no other reason then that he shares the same essence of being with the Antichrists.[29] Devoid of congregation and striving to become his own god to himself, the man who shares in this essence exceeds the boundaries of the human: "Lucky is the man who can share his neighbor's religion! Damned is the man who must invent his own god! Shun that man, for he is a part of the vast cosmos; he is akin to it and he can no more know himself than he can know the world of which he is in some mysterious way a part.... Blessed is the artificial man, the determined man, the social man" (483).

No longer human, but identified with the impersonal, inhuman forces of the cosmos, the mystery of the incomprehensible world can only be solved once we understand that *world* has no relation to nature but signifies instead the manufactured world, the artificial world to which belongs the "artificial man." This man, the one-dimensional man, forms the product of his multifaceted, dynamic, yet ultimately artificial social relations. The subject-position here claimed by Marcusian one-dimensional being succumbs to its inner logic of social and individual alienation.[30] The collective and the subjective merge as the ineffaceable same. Authentic life thus reveals itself to be that which marks its difference not within a relational field of finite, human sociocultural systems but as the inhuman, amoral sphere of absolute difference and of an absolutistic, asocial system. The very difference Damon seeks to perform and have recognized does not reveal unique individuality within a finite set of possible subject-positions but instead absolute otherness, "outsiderness" as akin to the divine. This position, however, can only be ascertained without differential quality and quantity. Damon inhabits the same essential space as Mussolini, Hitler, and Stalin—their respective differences can only be calculated in and by the sociocultural circumstances within which they manifest an otherwise uniform being.

What Damon rebels against is a frame of sociocultural reference that does not allow for his becoming dictator. His crimes speak to this jealousy and need; they are the vehicles by which he seeks to reach a point where the self effaces itself and casts itself anew: "His was a passion to recast, re-forge himself anew, and he was certain that Gil and Hilton had once in their lives felt what he was now feeling, that his reaching out for another pitch of consciousness had haunted them just as it now plagued him. But they had resolved their tangled emotions in the rigid disciplines of Communist politics" (255).[31]

The intensity of one's engagement with radical politics depends on the extent to which one can claim to be a victim of confused, powerful emotions. As in the case of Cross Damon, the men who suffer from an excess of emotion and a plenitude of consciousness cannot but succumb to a rigid doctrinal structure in which all expenditure falls under the watchful eye of an absolute dictator. As a means of controlling a seemingly uncontrollable subjective imbalance, Damon and his ilk withdraw from themselves and into various systems of totalitarian belief and practice. They seek to master the given system to which they cathect their nearly bankrupt emotional investments. This is the reason why "Men like Hilton did not spend their days scheming how to get hold of dollars; they worked at organizing and exploiting the raw stuff of human emotions. In their being close to the common impulses of men, in their cynical acceptance of the cupidity of the human heart, in their frank recognition of the outlandish passions they were akin to priests" (327).

The currency that the Damons of the world traffic in exceeds a spiritual value, to the point where it meets the spirit and becomes one with it. Contrary to the two-dimensional, dime-store pulp anticapitalist rhetoric Wright inserts into the mouths of his communist supporters and antagonists, Hilton, Blount, Herndon, and Damon not only seek wealth but hunger for the same form of wealth across negligible ideological differences. Like McKay's Glory Savior and Omar in *Harlem Glory,* Communists, fascists, and Damon in *The Outsider* all aspire to control spiritual capital—economic advantage offering but one way to achieve political hegemony. Even manifest ideological differences between Communism and fascism in Wright's text—the distribution of wealth, power, and so forth—thus obtain insofar as they form the basis of a collective self-delusion projected against a smoke screen created by men with no motivating force other than raw power.[32] Damon thus eliminates the possibility of motive in his crimes: "'Don't impute motive to me,' Cross insisted. 'Am I condemning you and men like you for what you've done? You did what you did because you had to! Anybody who launches himself on the road to naked power is caught in a trap.... You use idealistic words as your smoke-screen, but behind the screen you rule.... It's a question of *power!*'" (477).[33]

This is perhaps what is so hard for DA Houston to understand when attempting to ascertain the nature of the criminal he seeks: the crimes have no motive. But lack of motive underscores the presence of something far more telling. It reveals a language within language, a doublespeak that refuses to say anything. If indeed a meaning can be extracted from the various manifestoes, speeches, and essays in Wright's text, such a meaning signifies only the ever-expanding, amorphous, unbound movement of raw power. Damon seems to understand his own nature when he says, "How far wrong were most people in their appraisal of dictators! It was power, not just the exercise of bureaucratic control, but personal power to be wielded directly upon the lives and bodies of others" (267). Self-reflexive power is created, disseminated, and maintained by various forms of coercion.[34] Indeed, "each day millions of southern Negroes obeyed southern whites; millions of South African natives obeyed the white powers above them; millions of Germans had obeyed Hitler; and in most cases these millions had been given some fantastic excuse to justify the command of obedience The Nazis tried to win the loyalty of their subjects by conferring upon them ornate titles, non-economic rewards of various sorts, and by devising schemes of sport and joy. But the only motive that Hilton held out to Bob was *fear*" (261). Reducing the very sociocultural circumstances he had credited with creating discernable difference within manifest political positions, Wright's Damon annihilates the very productive mechanism that had spared *The Outsider* as text from the same accusation of normative totalization it imputes to absolutistic systems. Geography, national and cultural specificity, and historical accuracy disappear under the weight of Damon's (and Wright's) analysis of the reason why the Germans obeyed the Nazis and Negroes in the American South submit to whites; fear is the sole arbiter of power.[35] Despite recognizing the pomp and circumstance with which the Nazis sought to control the masses, Wright still hammers Jim Crowism, Nazism, and Communism into the same generic mould. All three ideological positions enact their respective illusions of power in the same exact way. There is for Damon only one determining factor above and beyond power, one generative quality that structures belief in a way akin to raw fear, but with a measure of authenticity in an otherwise artificial world, and that is race. Disillusioned and debased by the Communist Party, Damon's friend Bob falls back on the one thing he believes will always be there: "'I'm gonna stick to my own people,' he said heavily, his eyes glistening. He has run from one master to another: race" (259). Race is every bit the totalitarian ideology that are fascism and Communism.

That said, Wright does not see blacks joining European and Euro-American fascist parties and organizations. He sees instead the possible creation of black fascist political organs and institutions. What allows for the existence of black fascism lies at the heart of totalitarian ideologies themselves. Fascism shares its essence—the desire for power over the bodies and spirits of the masses—with an array of political ideologies otherwise at variance with each other and with a seemingly apolitical, biologically mystified conception of race. Fascism, like Communism and the soul of the criminal, has its generative moment in the racial heart of a single man willing to do whatever it takes to exert his will. Where lawlessness forges its own laws, both a dictator and a subjugated, racialized Volk come into existence, regardless of the specificity of the given political slogan under which the dictator wrests control of a population.[36] According to Wright, revolutionary force necessarily implements the same oppressive system that inspired revolutionary action in the first place. Black fascism must come to pass because the essence of the political and social oppression under which blacks suffer shares the same racial essence with fascism. Race here is not a matter of biology but similar biography in terms of general suffering and fear. African Americans can become fascists because just as with German and Italians, their suffering and fear demand it; the specificity of the suffering and fear is inessential.

This does not mean, however, that Wright empties history of its content. Indeed, the essence of fascism and all totalitarian systems of governance gathers all of modern history around it as the gravitational center of the racialized modern, western world. Historical and cultural differences collapse at the origin of totalitarianism. When Damon's thoughts wander to the question of the coherence of modern western history, they thus lead him to a hypothesis: "Perhaps he was staring right now at the focal point of modern history: if you fought men who tried to conquer you in terms of total power you too had to use total power and in the end you became what you tried to defeat" (328).

Wright's logic is quite clear: in defeating an absolutistic system, one creates what one defeated; one must fight fire with fire. As that which surmounts white supremacy, black liberation necessarily entails black supremacy. The system that acts as the vehicle for black racial supremacy will always be fascistic because it participates in fascism's essence, totalitarianism. In essence, Communism is fascism, fascism Communism. Herndon can be called a fascist because he is a white supremacist, just as he is, via Angelo Herndon, a Communist. Sharing in the same totalitarian essence, in Wright's text these positions are all the same. The form taken by black supremacy—the engine not only for black fascism, but black Communism and black totalitarianism in general—will be determined by the given sociocultural circumstances that foster and make manifest the successful revolution. The instantiation of such a system will be led by the individual qua god who is "somebody psychologically akin to either Blount or Herndon and yet somehow outside of them" (375).[37] He is a man capable of killing both Blount and Herndon; he acts on ideological grounds but obeys the dictates of his own jealous desire; he kills at will on the basis of a set of ideas outside the letter of Communism and fascism, despite sharing in their essence. Once again, Houston sums up such a man:

> "But, in order to kill the two of them on ideological grounds, this killer would have the support of a *third* set of ideas...."
> "And what is that *third* set of ideas?" Cross asked.
> "That no ideas are necessary to justify his acts," Houston stated without hesitation....
> "Two questions I'd like to ask," Cross interposed. "First, why would he partake of their lawlessness? And why do you think that Communist and Fascist ideas are alike?"
> "When did I mention *ideas*?" Houston asked scornfully. "Ideas are just so much froth on a mug of beer, my dear boy. Men are inventing ideas every day to justify for themselves and others their actions and needs. What makes these *three* men akin is the identity of the impulse in their hearts—." (376, 377)

What separates Cross Damon from Communists and fascists is his honesty; he does not presume to misrepresent his essential being with the camouflage of ideas. Unlike the Communist and the fascist, Damon moves through the world of Wright's text ideologically unadorned. He heralds his own messianic coming as the man with no other knowledge to boast of than that of the expert use of power in the service of totalitarian rule. The coming that Dictator Damon's very presence promises will thus be bereft of ideas and naked in its presumptions and ambition. The Communists and the fascists fail at precisely this juncture. By the very nature of their ideas, they fail to synthesize a recognizable, credible, sustainable ideology of power because they refuse to confess to their own essential, shared political being. In other words, Damon moves through the text denuded of ideology, as opposed to the Communist and fascist characters, who display a false doctrinal logic while promulgating a mystified socio-scientific objectivity.[38] Although Damon lacks the mass following of a dictator, he satisfies himself with the knowledge that to be in possession of a congregation poses no essential problem to his belief in his own divinity and in no way troubles his claim to a place in the canon of the twentieth century's most lethal rulers.

Without a set of objective ideas binding him to a process of self-annihilation, Damon retains the ability to walk through *The Outsider* as an outsider, as the absolute negation of the political. He becomes and remains a "complete god," or totalitarian dictator. Depending on the masses to recognize him as a "complete god" would de-totalize his conceptual reality as it concretizes whichever set of ideas he uses to perform his own apotheosis. The one true "little god" does not require the recognition of the other to claim divinity, only the other's death. Damon therefore finds satisfaction in his status as a "little god": "This spy would not be a complete god, of course; being a complete god would be reserved for the distant dictator. But being a little god was better than being no god at all" (453). Indeed, not only is being a "little god" better than being no god at all, but it's better than being a complete god beholden to the masses—to a party and so a set of ideas—for the definition and limits of his completeness and finitude.

Because of his structurally unlimited divinity, Damon, in debate with the head dialectician of the U.S. Communist Party, need not make claims to race or political party: "Today many sociologists say that the American Negro, having been stripped of his African tribal culture, has not had time to become completely adjusted to our mores, that the life of the family of the Western World has not had time to sink in, etc.

But with you, you are adjusted and more.... You've grown up and gone beyond our rituals" (562).

Without any attempt to explain how Damon "jes grew" beyond the rigid confines of the sociologists' dream of the American Negro, Wright proceeds to exclude race from any calculation of the cause of Damon's crimes. Race here matters only insofar as it plays an ostensible role in the construction of the specificity of the totalitarian personality in historicity. This is why Wright's Damon, in an exchange with Houston late in the book, can claim to have at least the potential to belong to a fascist political organization:

> "Were you *ever* a member of the Communist party?"
> "No. And I've never been a Fascist either."
> "I know that—"
> "How *could* you know that?" Cross asked.
> Houston blinked, pulled down the corners of his mouth.
> "You're a Negro—"
> "Negroes can be Fascists too," Cross told him.
> "Are you a Fascist then?"
> "No."
> "The Fascist angle is not important; they wouldn't take you in anyhow," Houston said with a tinge of satisfaction.
> "Fundamentally, Fascism has nothing to do with race," Cross told him.
> "Are you bragging about that?"
> "I'm stating facts to you, sir." (514)

For all of his philosophical posturing, Houston cannot see past race and so wanders through *The Outsider* as the blind man. He refuses to see Damon even at the moment he perceives Wright's superhuman murderer with the most clarity. Thus, Wright's Damon acts the part of Invisible Man in a play billed as a tragedy but which is instead a farce.

It is precisely because Houston cannot identify the man standing in front of him that Damon not only gets away with his crimes for so long but must commit them in the first place. When Damon makes the case for the possibility that he could be a fascist, he reminds Houston of the historical fact of Nazism as *one* racial manifestation of fascism.

"Fundamentally, Fascism has nothing to do with race," accurately describes its essential (fundamental) state. How fascism develops is shaped, in part, by race and racism. In other words, an African American can carry the essence of fascism within him. How a particular variant of fascism develops out of this totalitarian essence is racially determined. In insisting that he could be a fascist, Damon shows how important it is not to foreclose on the possibility of fascism manifesting itself in any sector of society. Houston's blindness to Damon's potential fascism on some level allows it to come into being.

In rejecting any reading of himself as victim and by becoming a victimizer, Damon asserts his own essential being as that of a Jealous Rebel, and so is in essence no different than a fascist or a Communist dictator. This does not mean that Damon either permits himself or wants to brag about his status as a potential Hitler or Mussolini, but that his vision is strong enough to see beyond cosmetic difference into the essential sameness of absolutist political positions. Damon understands those who share this second sight as men who perceive the failings of their leaders as aporias at the heart of a given political theology:

> "They see the countless mistakes that are being made by the men who rule and they think that they could do a more honest, a much cleaner job, a more efficient job. For simplicity's sake, let's call them Jealous Rebels. . . .
>
> "In order to test themselves, to make life a meaningful game, those Jealous Rebels proceed to organize political parties, communist parties, Nazi parties, fascist parties, all kinds of parties—"
>
> "No!" Blimin roared. "You cannot equate or confound Communism with Fascism! They are *different*!"
>
> "I admit they are different," Cross conceded. "But the degree of the difference is not worth arguing about. Fascists operate from a narrow, limited basis; they preach nationality, race, soil, blood, folk-feeling and other rot to capture men's hearts. What makes one man a Fascist and another a Communist might be found in the degree in which they are integrated with their culture. The more alienated a man is, the more he'd lean toward Communism." (487, 488)[39]

The Communist Party's intellectual strongman, Blimin fails to perceive that alienation determines one's political position. Alienation here announces the loss of belief; it describes the belief in a world devoid of meaning. Because Damon believes in nothing (this, we know; as he tells his love interest Eva, "You see, Eva, I don't *believe* in anything." [532]), he belongs to no political party and is alienated absolutely. Paradoxically, it is the Communist who experiences the higher level of alienation, while the fascist submerges himself in an ocean of "folk-feeling." The Communist emerges as the man most cut off from society, whereas the fascist betrays a communistic sensibility. Damon lingers in the margins of either political system. Always beginning from this position of marginality, Damon and his "Jealous Rebels" can insert themselves and operate effectively within any political system. Their manifest motivation amounts to little more than petty jealousy.

Desire thus moves the Jealous Rebel. Desire accommodates all absolutistic systems, and lawless desire relents only at the limit of the impossible as it creates its own conditions of possibility. If Damon knows "that the only difference between him and Hilton was that his demonism was not buttressed by ideas, a goal" (389), then he also comes to realize, if only instinctually, that what binds him to Hilton, Blount, and Herndon is desire. He wants them because he wishes to be them. What is at stake, and why he must kill them, has nothing to do with political ideology as such but with the desire to be recognized. This is why Damon can speak of the "fundamental" nature of fascism. There exists but a single essence to be shared by the various political and personal interests doing battle across the pages of *The Outsider*. It remains to the most cunning and lethal character to claim the title of absolute fascist master.

Thus, it is not political ideology but a vague vitalism that serves as the center of *The Outsider*, giving the book its coherence and ideological thrust.[40] When called on to articulate verbally the various codes and performative acts of the vitalism he practices, Damon can only invoke Christ: "Oh, Christ, I can't explain it! You have to feel it! You have to *live* it! It has to be in your blood before it can become real to you" (532). Whatever this is that flows in his blood and becomes real only when he kills, it separates him from the human. It opens him up to the experience of his own divinity. Violence performs divinity as the act or acts of an inhuman Jealous Rebel taking hold of and shaping the natural world. As a Jealous Rebel, Damon is at once the protagonist of a cautionary tale and an outlaw to be admired and emulated. The outlaw Damon opens up not merely the possibility of black fascism but also its desirability. To satisfy his desire, Damon does not roll in the hay with Sartre, but with Hitler.

Given the logic of *The Outsider*, however, it is wrong to give priority to Hitler. After all, it could just as easily have been the case that Damon seduced Hitler, in that, for Wright, fascism exists as an essence to be manifested in specific historical-material circumstances that are independent of race. Race is not first, fascism is. Thus, Wright's Damon gives credence to the Marcus Garvey assumption with which I began this book, namely, that "We were the first fascists." Having stripped black fascism of everything but its ideological kernel, Wright reveals a continuum of political being that transcends racial designation and national specificity. While Hurston provided the cultural basis for black fascist activism, Wright gives us its ontological core. The retrograde, yet teleological movement of black fascism culminates with Wright as it dissolves into idealist conjecture. *The Outsider's* black fascism signifies the existence of a political being disencumbered of social reality, of the very ontic existentialism of which Wright was accused. In this sense, Wright's novel is more fantasy than Schuyler's, and for this reason, far more dangerous.

Conclusion
Historical Black Fascism, Black Arts, and Beyond

In *White Man, Listen!* (1957) Wright inveighs against the titular enemy:

> Your world of culture clashed with the culture-worlds of colored mankind, and the ensuing destruction of traditional beliefs among a billion and a half of black, brown, and yellow men has set off a tide of social, cultural, political, and economic revolution that grips the world today. That revolution is assuming many forms, absolutistic, communistic, fascistic, theocratistic etc.—all marked by unrest, violence, and an astounding emotional thrashing about as men seek new objects about which they can center their loyalties. (*WML* 22–23)

Today's world is gripped by revolution, the causes of which Wright identifies as the "destruction of traditional beliefs" among nonwhites. A catastrophic collision of cultures has resulted in a myriad of revolutionary responses to white imperialism. Wright sees the struggle for culture as primary, ending with Western victory and the utter destabilization of the non-Western world. Not yet concluded, the perilous dissolution of non-Western traditional beliefs presumably erodes traditional political practices among the peoples Wright champions. The result of the loss of culture and tradition is the annihilation of stable political life, which then descends into Western forms of radicalism. Fascism is among the revolutionary ideologies Wright lists as active in countries outside of Europe and the United States: bred and now under control in the West, the fascist revolution spreads like a plague across the non-Western world. What allows the rapid movement of fascism from Europe and the United States into lands seemingly without hosts is the need among "black, brown, and yellow men" to identify with something in the wake of the loss of all cultural value. With non-Western systems in ruins because of Western intervention and violence, radical Western political movements are co-opted by their victims. The inhuman nature of these ideologies, Communism among them, lies in their instrumental nature, which is for Wright both the attraction to them, and their potency for self-destruction.

As he explains in *Black Power* (1954), it was the seductive quality of instrumentalization that lured Wright to Communism in the first place: "Yet, as an American Negro whose life is governed by racial codes written into law, I state clearly that my abandonment of Communism does not automatically place me in a position of endorsing and supporting all the policies, political and economic, of the non-Communist world. Indeed, it was the inhuman nature of many of those policies, racial and otherwise, that led me to take up the instrumentality of Communism in the first place" (*BP* xxxvi). Wright wishes to be absolutely clear: he has abandoned Communism, not in favor of fascism or other forms of absolutism and totalitarianism, but because he sees himself as a humanist. The "inhuman nature" and "instrumentality" of Communism alerted him to the presence of these qualities in the revolutions he observes. Again, Wright conflates Communism with all forms of radicalism, leaving only the choice of an ambiguous humanism qua political praxis.

The forms of fascism Wright condemns as inhuman were not, after the Second World War, manifestations of *historical* fascism. Historical fascism, or "classical fascism," names the various European fascisms present during the interwar period. "Neofascism" describes postwar variations on the themes of historical fascism. This is to say, when Wright writes about fascism in a non-Western, postwar context, he is not describing interwar Nazism, or Italian Fascism, but something if not new, then at least other. It is not merely the shift in terrain that redefines fascism as either historical, or neo. The very conditions for the existence of fascism in the postwar environment, whether in Africa or Europe, no longer prevailed. As Wolin rightly surmises, "Although neofascism bears important ideological affinities with the fascisms of yesteryear, it is extremely unlikely to attain power or to exercise a destabilizing effect analogous to that of historical fascism. In this respect it is important to understand that historical fascism was a phenomenon highly specific to the interwar period. It was very much a response to a series of crises—extreme political instability, economic catastrophe, and the Bolshevik threat—that emerged on the European scene following World War I" (49).

One reason for the false juxtaposition of historical fascism with neofascism is that the sheer horror of the Holocaust tends to reduce popular perceptions of fascism to anti-Semitism, racism, and genocide. As Bambery says, "Today the grotesque images of the dead and dying of Auschwitz are etched onto most people's minds. Little wonder, then, that fascism is often seen as a form of madness which sweeps whole nations before it. But it is more than that; it has a perverse logic of its own" (296). Unable to comprehend the thing itself in its unique, perverse logic, popular interrogation has thus far dismissed fascism as a form of insanity. As "madness," fascism, here conflated with the Holocaust, cannot be understood; the magnitude of its horror defies all logic. The terms of Bambery's analysis may not be the best or most precise, but his general point is valid. Fascism in the popular imagination is all too often simplified to the very slogans used by neofascism and so taken for something it either wasn't, or was in only a single incarnation.

The danger of oversimplification is so great that even a cultural critic as brilliant and incisive as James Baldwin falls prey to it. In his *The Fire Next Time* (1962), Baldwin compares the Nation of Islam's militant support of racial separatism with Nazi racial ideology and genocide. Linking the two via the American Nazi party, Baldwin writes:

> In any case, during a recent Muslim rally, George Lincoln Rockwell, the chief of the American Nazi party, made a point of contributing about twenty dollars to the cause, and he and Malcolm X decided that, racially speaking, anyway, they were in complete agreement. The glorification of one race and the consequent debasement of another—or others—always has been and always will be a recipe for murder. There is no way around this. If one is permitted to treat any group of people with special disfavor because of their race or the color of their skin, there is no limit to what one will force them to endure, and, since the entire race has been mysteriously indicted, no reason not to attempt to destroy it root and branch. This is precisely what the Nazis attempted. Their only originality lay in the means they used. (82–83)

Without pointing the finger directly, Baldwin condemns Muslim racism; he vilifies it as the intention to commit genocide. Whether Baldwin is right is not my concern here. At issue are the terms Baldwin uses to construct his argument. If the Nation of Islam's racist practices can only lead to genocide, then, as Rockwell's contribution and agreement with Malcolm X demonstrate, the Nation of Islam is in league not only with the American Nazis but with Hitler and the National Socialists after the fact. In effect, Baldwin reduces fascism to Nazism, and Nazism to virulent racism. After having emptied Nazism of its contents to the exclusion of virulent racism, every ideology of racial separatism becomes a latent form of Nazism and inevitable genocide. The Nation of Islam may have much more in common with the neofascists, but under the conditions of Baldwin's analysis, ideological congruencies cannot be recognized because his argument is overdetermined by the rhetorically powerful but historically and politically inaccurate invocation of historical fascism. Segregation and virulent racism are not tantamount to Nazism, and members of the American Nazi party are not pre-1945 German National Socialists. Historical, national, cultural, political, and ideological specificities have been overlooked in favor of a highly dubious hyperbolic homology. However, Malcolm X is not labeling himself a fascist as Marcus Garvey did and could; Elijah Muhammad does not write well-wrought fictions of a black fascist state as Schuyler and Hurston did and could; and the Nation of Islam did not valorize leaders who dubbed themselves "Black Hitler," and "the Führer of Harlem," as McKay did and could. The collation of historical fascism with neofascism cannot be done solely on the basis of virulent racism and requires a much deeper knowledge of the specifics of both neofascism and historical fascism.

Another part of the confusion over historical fascism and neofascism stems from what Wolin calls neofascism's "affinities with the fascisms of yesteryear." In some cases claiming more than a lineage, neofascism presents itself as an anachronistic survivor of a historically dead movement. "To be sure," Prowe asserts, "the most radical fringes of the rightists still glorify and sometimes adopt fascist slogans and myths because this gives them a dramatic presence and a sense of power far beyond that they could otherwise achieve. But related as they may be spiritually to inter-war fascism, the new movements represent a new era and are fighting new and different battles in Western Europe. In the words of Richard Stöss, 'Grandpa's fascism is dead'" (Prowe 320). Regardless of the state of Grandpa's fascism, the fascisms of the postwar period are not identical to their progenitors. Following Hegel's dictum that the reproduction of historically specific revolutions and moments of radical political upheaval manufactures farce, interwar fascism as tragedy has absolutely no shelf life after 1945 *an sich*. Therefore, the fascisms of the latter half of the twentieth century on to today have to be understood both within a generic framework of fascism and as new phenomena.

In his endeavor to do so, Laqueur states:

> The new fascism can gather strength only if it adjusts to the changed conditions. The cult of the Führer and the Duce has gone out of fashion, and similar leaders have not appeared on the scene. The impact of the media (propaganda) is as strong as ever... A new *telekratie* has emerged that can work miracles for at least a little while. Although the appeal of nationalism is still strong, in Europe it is a defensive rather than an aggressive force; war seems to be ruled out. And the extreme Right does not have a monopoly on nationalism; in a country like Greece, the Left and the Right are equally nationalistic. (93)

As Laqueur adumbrates the various historical differences between the interwar crises that led to the rise of fascism and the postwar stabilization and which make the reappearance of historical fascism very unlikely, he also divests neofascism of any strong ideological affinity with its predecessor. As a result of shifting historical paradigms, neofascism is not a diluted version of historical fascism but an almost entirely different solution. Neofascism possesses neither the extreme nationalism of fascism (it replaces it with a rhetoric of the "defense of Europe") nor its sharply defined line between left and right. And while neofascism's media resources, and thus propaganda, are much more powerful than those of historical fascism, for all of this telekratic might, neofascism has no charismatic leader, no Hitler or Mussolini. The rhetoric of war is also missing from neofascism: "Having realized that military aggression and conquest are no longer feasible, neofascism has opted for the defense of Europe" (Laqueur 93). In the face of devastating experience and a field that is without immediate enemies, neofascism has no war to make, and therefore cannot effectively deploy one of the cornerstones of interwar fascist ideology. Historical fascism's main political foe is also unavailable to neofascism: "The new fascism opposes Communism, but

Communism has ceased to be a threat" (Laqueur 94). Even the status of religion vis-à-vis the state in neofascist ideology becomes more ambiguous than it was for fascism before 1945: "There is no neofascist party line with regard to religion" (Lacquer 95).

Historical fascism's diffusion allows neofascism to invest in interwar fascist ideology without the historical precedents to fully embody fascism's ghostly afterlife. The infusion of neofascism into postwar political and cultural life allows some of its critics to identify it where it is not, or to misrecognize intentionally its apparition as a means of attacking a different target. One such mode of misrecognition is the conflation of racism with fascism. (Again, this is not to say that fascism is not racist but that it is not equivalent to racism.) Amiri Baraka committed this error in a December 24, 1974, *New York Times* interview, when he, in a seemingly abrupt move, turned away from Black Nationalism: "It is a narrow nationalism that says the white man is the enemy . . . Nationalism, so-called, when it says 'all non-blacks are our enemies,' is sickness or criminality, in fact, a form of fascism" ("Baraka Abandons 'Racism'"). Baraka indirectly defines "narrow nationalism" as racial exclusion, such that this form of nationalism is primarily defined by racism. Under these terms, the nation is in its essence a racial entity and therefore cannot maintain integrity if its racial core is polluted. This perverse mode of nationalism is also "a form of fascism"; it is fascist nationalism, or racist fascism. Although Baraka is here shrewd enough to offer an array of fascisms, of which sick nationalism is but one, the understanding giving his statement rhetorical force is that racism equals fascism. Baraka, then, offers no other conception of fascism aside from noting that fascism takes other forms which may be equally as racist as that of the Black Nationalism he rejects.

In 1964's "The Revolutionary Theater," Baraka goes so far as to reject the words *fascist* and *fascism* as anachronistic:

> The liberal white man's objection to the theatre of the revolution (if he is "hip" enough) will be on aesthetic grounds. Most white Western artists do not need to be "political," since usually, whether they know it or not, they are in complete sympathy with the most repressive social forces in the world today. There are more junior birdmen fascists running around the West today disguised as Artists than there are disguised as fascists. (But then, that word, Fascist, and with

it, Fascism, has been made obsolete by the word America, and Americanism. The American Artist usually turns out to be just a super-Bourgeois, because, finally, all he has to show for his sojourn through the world is "better taste" than the Bourgeois . . . many times not even that. (1901)

Placing his discourse on artists and fascism firmly in the present ("running around the West *today*"), Baraka distinguishes between historical fascism and neofascism with regard to culture. Art has become more fascist than fascism, which is to say, the artist has a greater claim to the legacy of historical fascism than a fascist. This distinction speaks to the perception of a fundamental shift in the parameters of the very definition of fascism, which was presumably in the past a politics that manifested itself in art, as opposed to today, when art expresses itself politically. The assertion that the artist stakes the greater claim to fascism's piebald mantle gives Baraka license to redefine fascism as an aesthetic movement, however disguised, that is in fact not fascism per se but the American as such. By placing the definition of fascism within the realm of the aesthetic, Baraka fascistically empties fascism of its historical content and then reinvests the term with the target of his critique, namely racist aesthetic praxis in the United States. "The American Artist" is actually the neofascist, a term defined not by contemporary neofascism or even historical fascism, but by American racism and bourgeois culture. Fascism is not fascism; it is Americanism, which is fascism. Baraka defaces the meaning of fascism to such an extent that the term becomes meaningless. Begging the question of whether the words *fascist* and *fascism* have meaning today, he proceeds to answer his own provocation in the negative. Thus his use of the terms has no conceptual weight; it functions as forceful rhetoric without content. Baraka uses antifascist rhetoric as empty slogan precisely as a fascist might use the rhetoric of negation. The apparent difference comes when Baraka announces the fact that the force of his statement is illusory. The American artist is a fascist because he is American, and the term *fascism* is in any event meaningless today. But despite the negation of the negation, the effect of Baraka's use of fascism is and remains palpable. His double negation serves only to reinforce the idea that the American artist does not need to masquerade as a fascist; that the fascists who pretend to be fascists have in fact misunderstood the nature of postwar fascism.

If the "American" is actually a fascist aesthetic, then Baraka must perforce either define Black Arts as wholly un-American or as an even more diluted form of fascism. For a movement like that of the Black Arts, or postwar African American expressive culture in general, the availability of historical fascist discourse is the same as it is to Euro-American culture. The Black Arts movement and some of Baraka's work could by extension only be as fascist as was possible given the cultural-historical moment. This is not to say that the Black Arts and Black Power movements were not neofascist but that to make this determination would require a completely different set of presuppositions about the nature of neofascism in its relation to the aesthetic. Although this kind of analysis lies outside the scope of this book, I will outline the basis for a preliminary investigation, beginning with an attempt at defining the Black aesthetic.

"The Black Arts movement," David Lionel Smith says,

> had several points of origin, and its genesis cannot properly be traced to any one of them. It must be understood, rather, as emanating from various local responses to a general development within American culture of the 1960s. The politics of that decade provide one central element in the origins of this movement: the civil rights movement and its radical heir, Black Power; the collapse of the McCarthyite suppression of the American left and the emergence of a New Left critique of American society and its institutions; and the reaction against imperialism, provoked especially by American, Soviet, and French incursions in Cuba, the Caribbean, Africa, and Southeast Asia. (253)

The origins of the Black Arts movement are threefold: the civil rights movement, the rise of the New Left, and anti-imperialist sentiment. Whereas analogues could be found in African American culture to the crises that gave rise to fascism in interwar Europe, the material forces of the postwar period shaping neofascism are not translatable for Black Arts writers. In other words, to shout fascistic slogans, or in the contemporary context of hip-hop, to write fascistic lyrics, does not a fascist make. If Black Arts writers engaged at times in fascistic rhetoric, including anti-Semitism, it was without programmatic intent. Unlike the writers examined in this book, Black Arts writers did not create in their works carefully wrought fascist ideological systems. The goals of the

Black Aesthetic did not include black fascism, and aside from shouting some eerily familiar slogans, the goals were also not to produce a fantasy, or an aesthetic, of black fascism.

Mitchell sums up the basic goal of the Black Arts movement: "Broadly speaking, critics associated with the Black Aesthetic movement . . . advocated that literature become an instrument of separatism and a means of disengaging African Americans from Western culture" (11). The Black Arts seek to remove blacks from the context of Western culture. To achieve this, radical *cultural* separation is required. Therefore, the ostensible purpose of Black Arts is to reeducate and remove blacks from the cultural planes of American and Western existence and inscribe them into a radically different cultural order. To achieve these ends, Black Arts artists sought, as Joyce remarks, to set themselves to the task of "addressing a black audience with the goal of spiritual awakening and sharpening political consciousness" (112). Through the work of art, the black audience arises from a cultural slumber to become politically aware. Culture and politics are here separated not by the nature of the aesthetic but by its praxis. The aesthetic itself is inextricable from the political. What matters is artistic production. The work itself has no aesthetic autonomy, existing outside of itself in its cultural and political effects.

If the ultimate goal of the Black Arts was to awaken awareness of a radically non-Western cultural-political milieu into which blacks could enter and feel completed, then the work of black art needed to contain within it a non-Western component that could be translated into the speech of Westernized black audiences. What this suggests is in fact an autonomous element in the work, namely, a black essence that can speak to all blacks at all times and revive the same cultural heritage despite Westernization. The tacit understanding of this essence produces, as David Lionel Smith realizes, extreme difficulties in defining the Black Aesthetic: "The difficulties these writers experienced in defining the Black Aesthetic exemplify a dilemma that writers of the movement never resolved, one which, I argue, could not be resolved. The concept of 'blackness' was—and is—inherently overburdened with essentialist, ahistorical entailments" (95). Blackness itself makes defining "black art" problematic. Because of the intensive, praxis-oriented aims of the Black Arts, the introduction of a purely theoretical, ahistorical element to their discourse had a negating effect along definitional lines. This is not to say that the Black Arts could not raise political consciousness or help to produce an alternative cultural space determined for blacks, but that it cannot do so absolutely. Thus, as Lorenzo Thomas describes, "young black writers in New York shared a sense of revelation that was to become the basis of the Black Arts Movement. Their concern was, basically, for a re-turning of a purely African sensibility and a style that organically developed from that feeling and stance" (56). However, this sense of revelation could not be made manifest in the very political landscape these young black artists sought to alter; "the purely African sensibility" did not exist. Any creation of such a sensibility would always already be artificial, impure, and implicated in non-black arts. Analyses of the Black Arts movement would then have to be situated within a much wider, more accurate interracial framework. Describing the cultural scene of the American 1960s and its influence over Black Arts writers, Smethurst attempts this when he maintains that "by the late 1960s a new conception of an avant-garde found its way into American culture. This was a paradoxical conception of the avant-garde that has roots in actually existing and close-to-home popular culture and is in some senses genuinely popular, while retaining a counter-cultural, alternative stance" ("Pat Your Foot" 262). The aesthetic and political engagements of the Black Arts movement were collaborative, and as such, undermining with regard to essentialist goals.

Black Arts critics, however, did not present the artistic production of the Black Arts movement as aesthetically and politically collaborative with Western culture. Instead, they viewed the work of black art as a single silo in a race war. It is because of this militaristic understanding of cultural production that Gayle can write in "The Black Aesthetic," "The dimensions of the black artist's war against the society are highly visible" (1872). However, the aggression of the work of black art does not occur in a war of annihilation, but a revolutionary war. As Hoyt Fuller has stressed, "The black revolt is as palpable in letters as it is in the streets, and if it has not yet made its impact upon the Literary Establishment, then the nature of the revolt itself is the reason. For the break between black writers and the 'literary mainstream' is, perhaps of necessity, cleaner and more decisive than the noisier and more dramatic break between the black militants and traditional political and institutional structures" (1810). The revolution cannot be successful if it is limited to the streets; hearts and minds must be won in addition to political institutions. This is why the revolt is "as palpable in letters as it is in the streets." Black Arts help to determine the fate of the revolution, and are in themselves revolutionary. According to Malauna Karenga, the black work of art is revolutionary by virtue of three simple characteristics: "Black art, irregardless of any technical requirements, must have three basic characteristics which make it revolutionary. In brief, it must be functional, collective, and committing" (1974). Not for itself, the work of black art performs a political function; it is both propaganda and pedagogy. As such, it is shared, or "collective," and politically "committing." The function of the black work of art is to engage and unify the black masses in a single purpose: the separation of blacks from the American (fascism). As Gayle outlines, "The Black Aesthetic, then, as conceived by this writer, is a corrective—a means of helping black people out of the polluted mainstream of Americanism, and offering logical, reasoned arguments as to why he should not desire to join the ranks of Norman Mailer or William Styron" (1876). Why the "black people" would want "to join the ranks of Norman Mailer or William Styron" can only be answered if it is understood that the artist guides the desires of the people (otherwise, who would care about Mailer and Styron?). The position of the black artist in Black Arts theory is that of Führer as the means of identification. However, there is in this thought no cult of personality aside from that of the work of art itself. The work of art, or the icon, does not stand in for a person, as in, for example, Schuyler's "Temples of Love"; it allows the people to enter its ideological world without the third-party mediation of a dictator.

The Black Arts movement, then, in intention, execution, and historical predicament, looks very different from both historical fascism and neofascism. However, one point of contact between the Black Arts and neofascism is anti-Semitism. The economics of anti-Semitism are in the Black Arts at the fore and, as in neofascism, unadorned with the rhetoric of religious and racial purity. The Jew poses an economic threat to African America; he does not primarily pose the threat of miscegenation or the loss of traditional African American religious practices. Because of its economic basis, black anti-Semitism was particularly acute among the black lower classes and working classes: "Among lower- and working-class blacks, then, *Jew* becomes what Stephen Henderson in *Understanding the New Black Poetry* calls a 'mascon word': a word that, like a sponge, absorbs the animus, bare intuition, disappointment, stereotypes, and rank feelings of American racial economics" (Gates and McKay 1805). "Jew," then, is a word among blacks much like "Fascism": both are empty signifiers that attach themselves to convenient targets of social and economic disgruntlement. This "mascon word" is invested with a negative content in order to express discontentment directed against the other. In the case of the "Jew," the specificity of economic oppression transcends racism based primarily on perceived racial and religious differences. The Jew is singled out not because he is Jewish, but because he owns many businesses in urban black America: "Since Jews, who own many businesses in the black urban ghetto, are white, they become catalytic not only for the release of black contempt, but also for that minority warfare welcomed by Anglo-America" (Gates and McKay 1805). Jewishness is not a factor; Jews are seen as white. Just as fascism is not fascism but something else, anti-Semitism is not anti-Semitism but anti-white racism. Yet even in this instance, black anti-Semitism (anti-white racism) is not identified as a form of either anti-Semitism or anti-white racism: "For the Black Arts movement, the Jew—like the Negro leader or the Negro jock of Baraka's *Black Art*—is simply one of the immediate, tangible, white forces of black life. Like the sycophantic and disgusting Negro leader, the Jew must be removed from occupancy if the space of a black good life is to be achieved" (Gates and McKay 1805). Just as blacks despise greed-driven, destructive black leaders, they hate the Jewish store owners in their neighborhoods. The tacit argument that underlies this discussion of anti-Semitism in the Black Arts, found in *The Norton Anthology of African American Literature,* is that all forms of black hate are actually substitutions for the same thing, namely, economic disenfranchisement. Although this reading of black anti-Semitism is far too generous and exonerating, the valid points are that anti-Semitism does exist in African America, and that the circumstances of its occurrence are unique to African Americans. That is not to say that black anti-Semitism a priori is not fascist anti-Semitism, but that, as in the cases of historical fascism and neofascism, it cannot be the sole index of black fascism. If we are to speak of black fascism, or black literary fascism, in the postwar context, then we must speak of black neofascism. To do so requires an entirely different historical-cultural model than found in this book. In part, the purpose of *Black Fascisms* was to establish that there is a need for further work in this area.

Notes

Introduction

1. My understanding of the black radical tradition is derived largely from Cedric J. Robinson's *Black Marxism*. See also Kelley, *Race Rebels;* and Bogues, *Black Heretics, Black Prophets*.

2. Gilroy, "Black Fascism."

1. Black Literary Fascism

1. The lyrics are quoted in H. C. Brearley, "The Negro's New Belligerency" 343.

2. Claude McKay, "Negroes Are Anti-Nazi, but Fight Anglo-US Discrimination."

3. See "Harlem's Hitler Brought to Court."

4. As did, according to Kelley, fighting against fascism in Spain. See Robin D. G. Kelley, *Race Rebels*.

5. For work on black Zion, see Chireau and Deutsch, *Black Zion*, and Brooks and Saillant, "*Face Zion Forward*."

6. See Anderson's *Imagined Communities*.

7. "If secession was not everywhere a feature of Ethiopianism," P. Olisanwuche Esedebe says in *Pan-Africanism*, "at least two factors were. One was the determination to save cherished indigenous values from the destructive influences of foreign missions. The other was the principle of 'Africa for the Africans' in opposition to European interference. For these reasons it seems justifiable to use the term in the wider Pan-African sense" (23). Although the specific context of even this wider sense still seems to be Africa proper, Esedebe excludes from his definition of "Pan-African" a global meaning and so preserves the idea of Ethiopia in the continent-wide, yet strict sense.

8. An example of African American exceptionalism with regard to Ethiopia and Africa as a whole is Pauline E. Hopkins's *Of One Blood* (serialized in the *Colored American Magazine*, 1902–3). The novel is about an African American

sovereign and Christian redeemer of Ethiopia, and, as Kevin K. Gaines reads it, "Hopkins's fascination with ancient African royalty, civilization, and patriarchal authority reflected a popular African American vision of Africa, and such diasporic yearnings were a central component of Black Nationalist and racial uplift ideology. Inevitably, however, the attempt to transcend the racialized circumstances of enslavement and Jim Crow through an identification with ancient Africa as the source of the race's origins imposed contemporary needs on its nostalgic vision of the past" (111).

9. General histories of the conflict are Barker, *Civilizing Mission;* Dugan and Lafore, *Days of Emperor and Clown;* and Brice Harris Jr., *United States and the Italo-Ethiopian Conflict.*

10. On the African American response to the Ethiopian crisis, see Hardie, *The Abyssinian Crisis;* Coffey, *Lion by the Tail;* and Baer, *Coming of the Italo-Ethiopian War.*

11. For work on Cooks, see Robert Harris, Nyota Harris, and Grandassa Harris, eds., *Carlos Cooks and Black Nationalism.*

12. For biographical and autobiographical analyses of the life of Adam Clayton Powell Jr., including his involvement in the Harlem boycotts, see Adam Clayton Powell Jr., *Adam by Adam* 55–69; Hamilton, *Adam Clayton Powell, Jr.* 91–93; Hickey and Edwin, eds., *Adam Clayton Powell and the Politics of Race* 52–53.

13. The "official" findings do not fault the Communists, either, but instead indict poor social conditions as the cause. See "Mayor LaGuardia's Commission on the Harlem Riot of March 19, 1935."

14. See the following *New York Times* articles: "Smith Is Named Tammany Delegate," August 25, 1932, 8; "Three Restored to Ballot," September 8, 1932, 4; "Negro's Name Barred from Ballot," September 9, 1932, 4; "Free in Anti-Semitic Case," October 12, 1932, 29.

15. On Divine, see Fauset, *Black Gods* 52–67; and Watts, *God, Harlem U.S.A.*

16. In *Wages of Whiteness,* Roediger contends that this is a reaction to the formation of white identity in terms of labor and the white American working class.

17. For the history of the U.S. occupation of Haiti, see Renda, *Taking Haiti;* and Hans Schmidt, *United States Occupation of Haiti.*

18. Johnson takes credit for a body of writing on Haiti that includes John W. Vandercook's *Black Majesty: The Life of Christophe, King of Haiti* and W. B. Seabrook's *The Magic Island,* but which perhaps begins properly with Victor Hugo's *Bug-Jargal.*

19. See Callow, "Voodoo Macbeth" 34–80.

20. For studies that recover the black Marxist tradition, see Naison, "Communism and Harlem Intellectuals" and *Communists in Harlem;* and Kelley, *Hammer and the Hoe.* Studies of the history of Communism in the United States and the interplay between Communists and African American intellectuals during the 1920s and 1930s I have found invaluable for this work are Foner and Allen, *American Communism and Black Americans, 1919–1929;* Foner

and Shapiro, *American Communism and Black Americans, 1930–1934*; Kate A. Baldwin, *Beyond the Color Line*; Solomon, *The Cry Was Unity*; and Record, *The Negro and the Communist Party*.

21. For histories of black conservatism, see Eisenstadt, ed., *Black Conservatism*; and Tate and Randolph, eds., *Dimensions of Black Conservatism*.

22. See Bauman, "Left as Counter-Culture." For histories of the Left in the United States, see Coombes, *Writing from the Left: Socialism, Liberalism, and the Popular Front*; Gorman, *Left Intellectuals*; Dietrich, *Old Left in History*; Buhle, *Marxism in the United States*; and Wald, *Writing from the Left: New Essays on Radical Culture and Politics*.

23. For the standard classical Marxist essays on fascism, see Bentham, ed., *Marxists in the Face of Fascism*, in particular Palmiro Togliatti's essay, "On the Question of Fascism (1928)" 136–48. See also Gramsci, *Prison Notebooks* 210–15.

24. See Nolte, *Three Faces of Fascism* 20–22.

25. For the liberal-humanist theory of fascism, see Lipset, *Political Man*.

26. On fascism's "Third Way," see Sutton, "Interpretation of 'Fascism.'" See also Mosse, "Towards a General Theory of Fascism" 1–41.

27. The best books on the presence of these places and themes in the African American literary imagination are Thomas, *From Folklore to Fiction*; Moses, *Wings of Ethiopia*; and Dash, *Haiti and the United States*.

28. On the "sense-making crisis" and how it engenders revolution, see Platt, "Thoughts on a Theory of Collective Action."

29. For an account of fascism in America, see Brinkley, *Voices of Protest* 273–83.

30. See Jameson, *Fables of Aggression*.

31. See North, *Dialect of Modernism* 77–125.

32. See Bhabha, "Of Mimicry and Man" 85–92.

33. See McElvaine, *Great Depression*; and Terkel, *Hard Times*.

34. See Hall, "Race, Articulation, and Societies Structured in Dominance."

35. A typical reaction of the fascist-leaning European modernist would be Bataille's. Bataille saw absolutely no alternative to either fascism or Communism. In fact, Bataille believed that the almost absolute repressiveness of fascism led to Communist revolution. See Bataille, "Psychological Structure of Fascism."

36. For general historical accounts and interpretations of the rise of fascism in Europe, see Carsten, *Rise of Fascism*; and Kedward, *Fascism in Western Europe*.

37. See Payne, *Fascism in Spain, 1923–1977*, 54, 89, 254.

38. Studies instrumental to my understanding of generic fascism are Payne, *Fascism: Comparison and Definition* (henceforth referred to as *FCD* in the text) and *A History of Fascism, 1914–1945*; Sternhell, *Birth of Fascist Ideology*; Laqueur, *Fascism: A Reader's Guide*; and Griffin, ed., *International Fascism* and *Fascism*.

39. For those against understanding Nazism as a form of fascism, see Sternhell, *Neither Right nor Left*; and de Felice, *Interpretations of Fascism*. See also Griffin, *Nature of Fascism*; and Nolte, *Three Faces of Fascism*.

40. Payne's sixth characteristic reads: "Exaltation of youth above other phases of life, emphasizing the conflict of generations, at least in effecting the initial political transformation" (7).

41. See Walter Benjamin, "Work of Art in the Age of Mechanical Reproduction," and "Theories of German Fascism."

42. See Jünger, "Total Mobilization;" Reich, *Mass Psychology of Fascism* 119–39; Freud, *Civilization and Its Discontents* and *Group Psychology*; and Adorno, "Freudian Theory and the Pattern of Fascist Propaganda."

43. On fascist aesthetics, see Sontag, "Fascinating Fascism;" Berman, "Aestheticization of Politics;" Ben-Ghiat, "Italian Fascism and the Aesthetics of the 'Third Way'"; Carlston, *Thinking Fascism*; and Koepnick, "Fascist Aesthetics Revisited."

44. For works specifically on the Leftist politics of the Renaissance, see Maxwell, *New Negro, Old Left*; Smethurst, *The New Red Negro*; and Vincent, *Keep Cool*.

45. For general evaluations of the Harlem Renaissance and its politics, see Hutchinson, *Harlem Renaissance in Black and White*; Allen, Jr., "The New Negro"; Huggins, *Harlem Renaissance*; Watson, *Harlem Renaissance: Hub of African American Culture*; Wintz, *Black Culture and the Harlem Renaissance*; Baker, Jr., *Modernism and the Harlem Renaissance*.

2. The Myth of Marcus Garvey

1. Garvey claimed this in his 1937 interview with Rogers (Rogers 420).

2. Garvey was in fact never truly forgotten. See Sewell for the ways in which the memory of Garvey shaped black political thought throughout the latter half of the twentieth century.

3. On Selassie, see Selassie I, *My Life and Ethiopia's Progress*; Lockot, *The Mission*; Mosley, *Haile Selassie*; and Gorham, *The Lion of Judah*. For his role in Rastafarianism, see V. Jacobs, *Roots of Rastafari*.

4. Quoted in Cronon, ed., *Marcus Garvey*.

5. Martin notes the core of Garvey's dissatisfaction with Selassie: "He argued that Haille Selassie should have modernized Ethiopia" (*Pan-African Connection* 24).

6. *The Black Man* July–August 1936, quoted in Fax, *Garvey* 268.

7. See Gillette, *Racial Theories in Fascist Italy*.

8. Garvey's anti-Semitism contradicts itself. Although Garvey clearly voiced anti-Semitic rhetoric, he also admired Zionism and what he believed to be Jewish self-reliance. For the best essay on Garvey's "Black Zionism" and anti-Semitism, see Hill, "Black Zionism."

9. Garvey seems to forget here that Jesus was a Jew.

10. One could object that Garvey cannot be grouped at all with Mussolini because Italian Fascism did not make race its centerpiece. Of course, I do not wish to identify Garvey with Mussolini, but with generic fascism. For a com-

parison of racial policies of fascist Italy and Nazi Germany, see Bessel, *Fascist Italy and Nazi Germany*.

11. Nazi "hygienic" practice relied on racial myths and "medical knowledge" of deformity and insanity. See Aly, Chroust, and Pross, eds., *Cleansing the Fatherland*; Friedlander, *The Origins of Nazi Genocide*; and Lifton, *The Nazi Doctors*.

12. Garvey echoes here the sentiments of the Negro history movement en vogue during the 1920s and 1930s. See Meier, *Negro Thought in America, 1880–1915*; and Schomburg, "The Negro Digs Up His Past."

13. "The brute who killed with bombs of liquid / flame; / We hate him, yes we hate him, good and plenty; / We hate the 'smell' of that most brutal / name." Elsewhere Garvey's verse again takes on "the Fascist Brute" and his lute-playing Blackshirts: "When changes come, the Fascist brute / Shall see his awful, foolish sin: / The blackshirts play upon the lute, / But vic'tr:es they shall never win" (*Poetical Works* 83–84).

14. Translation is altered slightly from that in Schnapp's *A Primer of Fascism*. The Italian reads: "Caposaldo della dottrina fascista e la concezione dello Stato, della sua essenza, de. suoi compiti, delle sue finalita. Per il fascismo lo Stato e un assoluto, davanti al quale individui e gruppi sono il relative. Individui e gruppi sono 'pensabili' in quanto siano nello Statu" (Mussolini 84).

15. See de Felice, *Mussolini*; and R. J. B. Bosworth, *Italian Dictatorship*.

16. See de Grand, *Italian Fascism*; Knox, *Common Destiny*; and Ben-Ghiat, *Fascist Modernities*.

17. This gives credence to traditional Marxist interpretations of fascism that see fascism as rising in response to a burgeoning proletarian revolution and as a way for the bourgeoisie to control the means of production. See Beetham, ed., *Marxists in Face of Fascism*.

18. In the sense that he believed in uplift through the "practical" training of the race, Garvey never relinquished his faith in Booker T. Washington, whom he originally came to the United States to see in hopes that the Tuskeegeeian would found a chapter of the Tuskeegee Institute in Jamaica. See Wintz, ed., *African American Political Thought, 1890–1930*.

19. Garvey believed, "All funds of the UNIA are supposed to be directed in these channels. The funds of the UNIA must be used for the race, and only the race" (*Message* 33).

20. Garvey paid close attention to what Mussolini had to say, and Mussolini's and Gentile's 1932 "Foundations and Doctrine of Fascism" was widely translated at the time. I find it hard to believe Garvey wasn't familiar with the text.

21. For the Derridean take on originary thought as it pertains to some of the more troubling political aspects of Heidegger's thought, see Derrida, *Of Spirit*. See also Lacoue-Labarthe's perhaps more politically relevant reading of the "Nazi myth" in Heideggerean thought, *Heidegger, Art and Politics*.

22. For Garvey's contextualized place in the history of Black Nationalist thought, see Moses, ed., *Classical Black Nationalism;* and Van Deburg, ed., *Modern Black Nationalism.*

23. For the variant of this idea in European fascist thought, see Schnapp, *The Manifesto of Race* (1938), *Critique of* The Manifesto of Race (1938), and *New Revised Draft of* The Manifesto of Race (1942). (All of these can be found in Schnapp, ed., *A Primer of Italian Fascism.*)

24. Mosse traces the history of the rise of the racialized State in Europe in *Toward the Final Solution.*

25. Bataille, "The Psychological Structure of Fascism."

26. This apotheosis amounts to little more than the mystification of man and signals a logical development in the project of enlightenment. See Horkheimer and Adorno, *Dialectic of Enlightenment* 3–43.

3. George S. Schuyler and the God of Love

1. "Views and Reviews," *Pittsburgh Courier,* November 30, 1935. Quoted in Joseph Harris, *African American Reactions to War in Ethiopia, 1936–1941.*

2. Scott relates, "Throughout 1935 and much of 1936, the Afro-American press overflowed with news relating to the Italo-Ethiopian crisis and war. News reports, special features, editorials, letters to the editor, and photographs concerning the conflict appeared abundantly in the pages of the nation's leading black publications. In their coverage of the conflict, black newspapers demonstrated a strong sense of racial patriotism, which transcended the borders of the United States and extended as far as the distant shores of Northeastern Africa. By publishing a multitude of pro-Ethiopian articles, columns and editorials, the national black press promoted the general cause of pan-Africanism in America and helped work thousands, if not millions, of Afro-Americans into a frenzy of support for the Ethiopians" (120).

The intense coverage in the black press of the Italo-Ethiopian conflict inspired Langston Hughes, in a poem entitled "Broadcast on Ethiopia," to write: "Addis Ababa / In headlines all year long. / Ethiopia—tragic-song." Hughes stresses that, despite the constant repetition of the coverage ("In headlines all year long"), the trauma of the event entails a reaction symptomatic of a psychic wound that never recovers from the initial blow but feels the shock of the impact as if it were the first time, each time it strikes. Thus, the invasion of Ethiopia remains both tragic and fodder for artistic production: trauma retains the initial potency of its event, defying any attempt to adequate the experience with its representation with any other means than that of "song," or poetry. "Broadcast on Ethiopia" was first published in *American Spectator*; rpt. in *Collected Poems of Langston Hughes.*

3. Quoted in R. Hill, *Ethiopian Stories* 17.

4. See Jünger, "Total Mobilization."

5. On the cult of the leader and generic fascism, see Mosse, "Towards a General Theory of Fascism;" and Payne, *Fascism: Comparison and Definition.*

6. On fascist theories of nation and nationalism, see Mussolini, "Foundations and Doctrine of Fascism"; and Hitler, *Mein Kampf* 284–329.

7. For example, Woodson concentrates his analysis of *Black Empire* on Schuyler's use of names in the text. Scanning his readership for what amounts to talented-tenth recruits, Woodson's Schuyler crafts his various pen names within an elaborate philosophical system that engages the cream of African America's crop for Gurdjieffian purposes—a reading Woodson does not support with anything outside of *Black Empire*. No doubt Schuyler gave to his characters' names, as well as his pen names, complex meanings designed to touch on a wide array of themes and philosophical insights. But this reading closes its eyes to a far more prevalent rhetoric of supermen in the latter half of the 1930s: fascism.

8. Belsidus's use of the occult falls neatly in line with the very basis for the recognition of the apotheosis of the fascist charismatic leader. See Goodrick-Clarke, *The Occult Roots of Nazism*.

9. The sculpture and architecture—the aesthetic sense of the temples—matches well with monumental Nazi art and construction typified in the designs and structures of Hitler's architect, Albert Speer. On Speer, see M. Schmidt, *Albert Speer* 37–56.

10. The quintessential study on the hypnotic, psychological ramifications of fascism for the masses is Reich's *Mass Psychology of Fascism*.

11. Schuyler takes pains to establish the theatrical element of the spectacle of power—an aspect of the stage put to good use by the Nazis, and fascists in general. For intersections between fascist power and the stage, see Berghaus, ed., *Fascism and Theatre*.

12. See Spackman, *Fascist Virilities*, and de Grazia, *How Fascism Ruled Women*, for readings on the formation of fascist ideology around the idea of virility as espoused by women. Whereas Spackman sees writing by fascist women as a form of Foucauldian reverse-discourse, no such claim can be made for Gaskin.

13. This sentiment echoes the common conception of the necessity for a battlefield consecration of the fascist State. See Marcuse, *Technology, War, and Fascism*, for an analysis of the positive interplay between technological advance and martial power as fascist ontological imperative.

14. For the gruesome history of Nazi medical practice, see Lifton, *The Nazi Doctors*.

15. See Herf, *Reactionary Modernism* 1–17, for a reading of the extreme and seemingly paradoxical importance fascism places on its technicians and technological advance.

4. "In Turban and Gorgeous Robe"

1. Schuyler's essay was published in his "Views and Reviews" column in the *Pittsburgh Courier* November 6, 1937: 10. The piece was Schuyler's reaction to McKay's "Labor Steps out in Harlem," *Nation* 145 (October 16, 1937): 399–402.

2. "McKay Says Schuyler Is Writing Nonsense," *The New York Amsterdam News* November 20, 1937: 12; reprinted as "Schuyler Lashes Here and There Like Mad Dog—Bites Everybody," *The Pittsburgh Courier* December 4, 1937: 14. Schuyler bit back again in "Views and Reviews," *The Pittsburgh Courier* December 11, 1937: 10.

3. Thus, this chapter disputes the claim that, as Keller puts it, "[Claude] McKay's agenda for social transformation does not involve fundamental change. He indicts America for its failure to live up to its own principles" ("'Chafing Savage'" 456).

4. See Winston C. McDowell, who writes: "The African American reporter Roi Ottley summed up the assessment of many black elites when he declared that Hamid was nothing more than a 'crude, racketeering giant . . . posing as an evangelist of Black labor'" ("'Same Boat Together'" 227).

5. Garvey met with Acting Imperial Wizard Edward Young Clarke in Atlanta on June 25, 1922. The meeting was taken so both parties could express their common goals, and to establish protection for UNIA members striving to achieve those goals. On the meeting, see Hill, in A. Garvey, ed., *Philosophy and Opinions* 401; and Cronon, *Black Moses* 189–90.

6. For an overview of the history of the African Blood Brotherhood, see Hill, "Cyril V. Briggs, *The Crusader* Magazine, and the African Blood Brotherhood, 1918–1922."

7. The best general study of the history of the interdependence of nationalism and masculinity, at least in the context of fascism, is Mosse, *Image of Man*.

8. For general accounts of the history of African American labor unions, including the attitudes of blacks to "open shops," see W. Harris, *The Harder We Run*.

9. The La Guardia report backs up this assumption ("Mayor La Guardia's Commission").

10. Ralph Ellison's fictional account in *Invisible Man* of the 1935 Harlem riot makes no bones about the riot's status as a racially motivated event. Although whites did not face attack during the riot and the rioters steered clear, for the most part, of white-owned businesses, this, as Ellison knew, does not mean that the event cannot be considered a race riot. Intraracial conflict (the narrator vs. Raz, for instance) and the fact of black Harlem as black Harlem rioting in reaction to overall poor social conditions—which are racially determined—decide the matter.

11. For narratives dealing with Black communities in the 1930s and their struggle for fair labor practices, see Sitkoff, *A New Deal for Blacks*; and A. Morris, *Origins of the Civil Rights Movement*.

12. The Harlem intelligentsia may not have taken the Sufi seriously, but his boycott campaigns occasioned public debates. George S. Schuyler participated in one such event-in-print over the value of the boycott campaigns in the *Crisis*. See Schuyler, "To Boycott or Not to Boycott."

13. For a general account of black-Jewish relations, see Salzman and West, eds., *Struggles in the Promised Land*.

14. For one of the most penetrating philosophical analyses of anti-Semitism, see Sartre's famous essay on the subject, *Anti-Semite and Jew*, in which he finds the anti-Semite to be one who is unwilling to take existential responsibility for his actions, and who is thus culpable for his perceptions of Jews and implicated in his hatred.

15. Nationalism, then, plays the quintessential role in the construction of the subject of black labor in class struggle. For a history of the part played by Black Nationalism in labor politics, see Bush, "*We are not what we seem.*"

16. W. E. B. Du Bois, "Of Our Spiritual Strivings," *The Souls of Black Folk* 9–16.

17. For a good summary of the state of Freudian theory and the analysis of fascism as a manifestation of mass psychosis, see Adorno, "Freudian Theory and the Pattern of Fascist Propaganda."

18. See Freud, *The Future of an Illusion*.

19. My understanding of Nazi ideology as a singular variant of fascist ideology comes from Mosse, *Crisis of German Ideology*. See also Pollock, "State Capitalism" 71–94.

20. McKay's new community, like any such construct, would be an "inoperative" one in that it rests on a foundational myth that it must, as a means maintaining its concrete structure, deny. See Nancy, *Inoperative Community* 1–70.

21. Fascism, when considered a bourgeois movement that answers to a crisis in capitalism—for example, a measure against a burgeoning proletarian revolution—eliminates class conflict as it subsumes class under the heading of the Volk. See Lyttelton, "Crisis of Bourgeois Society and the Origins of Fascism."

22. The most widely known advocate of the day for segregated unions was the great A. Philip Randolph. For biographical accounts of Randolph and his impact on black labor movements, see Cwiklik, *A. Philip Randolph and the Labor Movement*; W. Harris, *Keeping the Faith*; and Meier and Rudwick, "Attitudes of Negro Leaders toward the American Labor Movement."

23. On fascism and its putative anti-intellectualism, see Mosse, *Nazi Culture*. Fascism, although highly antagonistic to what it sees as thought without action, embraces forms of intellectualism that purport to either lead inevitably to, or be a form of, vital praxis.

24. Gramsci posits the existence of "organic" intellectuals, thinkers and representatives of a class whose ideas manifest the values and interests of their particular social milieu. See *Prison Notebooks* 3–23.

25. For the best study of African American cultural production during the late 1930s and early 1940s in relation to the Popular Front, see Mullen, *Popular Fronts*, particularly his discussion of Richard Wright, 19–43.

26. For a famously negative take on McKay's relationship with Mike Gold, see Cruse's *The Crisis of the Negro Intellectual*, in which he tacitly assigns Gold

the role of generic Jewish intellectual and then proceeds the show how Gold frustrated McKay's attempts at formulating a working theory of black self-reliance (51–54). See also Maxwell's counternarrative in *New Negro, Old Left*, which finds the at times troubled interplay between Gold and McKay as a predominantly positive dialogue in part generative of American proletarian literature (95–124).

27. For a taste of Gide's apologetic nature, see *The God That Failed*.

28. In this sense, McKay alters Lukács' teleological model of class-driven revolution, replacing class consciousness with racial consciousness that comes to realize itself through labor and so partially through class relations. See Lukács, *History and Class Consciousness* 46–82.

29. For a brilliant analysis of Nazism's obsession with the "beautiful" body, particularly in the work of Leni Riefenstahl, see Sontag, "Fascinating Fascism."

30. Thus Garvey turns into a black labor leader a posteriori.

31. Omar exalts male youth; he sees it, paradoxically, as the culmination of the (adult) masculine principle. On the role of youth as the promise and culmination of the new fascist man, see Stachura, *Nazi Youth in the Weimar Republic*.

5. His Rod of Power

1. Hurston describes the colonel as follows: "He is a tall, and slender black man around forty with the most beautiful hands and feet that I have ever beheld on a man. He is truly loved and honored by the three thousand men under him.... There is no doubt that the military love their chief.... Anyway, there is Colonel Calixe with his long tapering fingers and his beautiful slender feet, very honest and conscientious and doing a beautiful job keeping order in Haiti ... he is a man of arms and wishes no other job than the one he has. In fact we have a standing joke between us that when I become president of Haiti, he is going to be my chief of the army and I am going to allow him to establish state farms in all the departments ... a thing he has wanted to do in order to eliminate the beggars from the streets of Port Au Prince, and provide food for hospitals, jails and other state institutions ... He is pathetically eager to clear the streets of Haiti of beggars and petty thieves ... what a beautifully polished Sam Brown belt on his perfect figure and what lovely, gold looking buckles on his belt!" (*TMH* 89)

2. On Hurston's politics, see Headon, "'Beginning to See Things Really'"; Maxwell *New Negro, Old Left;* Trefzer, "'Let's Us All Be Kissing-Friends?'"; and Carby, "The Politics of Fiction, Anthropology, and the Folk."

3. Though Hurston's engagement with discourses on eugenics certainly informs any discussion of the genocidal bent of not only her Rameses, but her Moses, the task of this essay will be to establish the terms of Hurston's one-sided dialogue with National Socialism along the lines of the charismatic, authoritarian ruler. On Hurston's reaction to theories of eugenics, see Chuck Jackson, "Waste and Whiteness."

4. For a charting of Moses in the African American folk tradition, see H. Nigel Thomas, *From Folklore to Fiction*.

5. Johnson reads Hurston side by side with Freud's *Moses and Monotheism.* That Freud and Hurston both published works on Moses during the same year, as Johnson reminds us, does not, however, mean (as Johnson is aware) that we can ascertain the direct influence of Freud's Moses on Hurston's, or vice versa. This is not to say that such an influence on Hurston was not possible—the first two sections of Freud's text appeared, in *Imago* and in German, in 1937—but that there is no evidence that Hurston had read Freud's text before the publication of *Moses.*

6. Boas attempted to undermine the notion of racial purity by shifting the emphasis from a notion of divergent racial origins to racial mixture for the production of a superior civilization, thus supporting his claim for the possibility of contemporary racial equality in terms of innate ability.

7. Originally quoted in Lillie P. Howard (39), from ' an unpublished letter in the James Weldon Johnson Collection in the Beinecke Rare Books and Manuscripts Library of Yale University" (R. Morris 308, fn. 12).

8. The context in which I am speaking of the Mosaic myth is always that of Hurston's novel, and not that of the Bible.

9. I say the law here, as opposed to simply one law, because Pharaoh acts as the epistemological guarantor for all law; therefore, if the office of Pharaoh finds itself legally undermined in even one case, the entirety of the law falls into question in terms of its validity.

10. See Hitler, *Mein Kampf* 284–329.

11. Following Griffin's definition of generic fascism detailed previously.

12. Pharaoh's analysis of Egyptian history and national health echoes the protofascist cultural despair Stern has identified in the works of Paul de Lagarde, Julius Langbehn, and Moeller van den Bruck. See Stern, *The Politics of Cultural Despair.*

13. "Contagion" here refers to Rene Girard's reading of the term in *Violence and the Sacred,* in which he posits the primacy of "mimetic desire" (the desire not only to be the other, but to possess what the other possesses) as a form of contagion perpetuating the cycle of violence that characterizes any given society and which can be brought under control only by the sacrifice of a scapegoat. The scapegoat substitutes for the object of revenge, introducing a disinterested interest into the cycle of retribution and so ending the cycle (otherwise one would have to take revenge for the revenge taken upon him). See Girard 39–67.

14. This would be exactly the analysis of the relation between Nazism and myth Lacoue-Labarthe and Nancy, following Hannah Arendt's critique of Nazi ideology, bring to bear in their "The Nazi Myth."

15. See Sontag's discussion of the Leni Riefenstahl film in "Fascinating Fascism."

16. "Divine violence" means, in this context, that the foundational deed for a system of law, divine or secular, is premised on a violent act that leads to the creation, as an exculpatory measure, of the godhead. See Nietzsche, *On the Genealogy of Morals,* and *Ecce Homo* 57–96; and the Freud of *Totem and*

Taboo 125–200. See also Benjamin, "Critique of Violence". Reading Benjamin's essay, Derrida offers that divine violence "does not lend itself to any human determination, to any knowledge or decidable 'certainty' on our part. It is never known in itself, 'as such,' but only in its 'effects' and its effects are 'incomparable,' they do not lend themselves to any conceptual generalization. There is no certainty (*Gewissheit*) or determinant knowledge except in the realm of mythic violence, that is, of *droit,* that is, of the historical undecidable" ("Force of Law" 1033).

17. This would be commensurate with Benjamin's critique of the fascist state as aesthetic spectacle premised on violence for the sake of violence in his "Theories of German Fascism," discussed earlier.

18. For the state of exception as the site at which secular law reveals its authority as premised on a theological semantic structure, see Schmitt's *Political Theology,* to which Benjamin's "Critique of Violence" and notion of divine violence as absolute means, or means without ends, was a response and an alternative.

19. For foundational discussions of the nature and function of sacrifice, see Tylor, *Primitive Culture,* who understands sacrifice as a gift made to the godhead with the hope of the fulfillment of a wish. Building on Tylor's work, William Robertson Smith's *Lectures on the Religion of the Semites* theorizes that sacrifice establishes a momentary link between the godhead and the community of worshippers, such that the community itself—not the individual—is not only at stake but unified by the rite of sacrifice. Frazer believes that the sacrificial victim is a "dying god," or stand-in or double of the godhead itself *(Golden Bough).* See also Durkheim's *Elementary Forms of Religious Life,* in which he maintains that ritual sacrifice is a means by which communal being affirms itself, by proxy of the victim and the godhead, as divine. Hurston makes use at turns of all of these theories, as well as, as we shall see, Hubert and Mauss's tripartite structure of sacrificial victimization *(Sacrifice).*

20. Hubert and Mauss insist that the sacrificial victim has no definite character other than a conglomeration of the godhead, the sacrificer, and the *sacrifier. Sacrifier* is the term they use to denote the community engaged in the sacrifice. See Hubert and Mauss, *Sacrifice.*

21. Rameses gains his secular authority by surmounting a sacred order. This accomplishment must be recognized as an act of rising above gods. The necessary recognition of this feat cannot take place if the community to be sacrificed does not recognize the authority of the surmounted gods. Thus, conquered peoples whose systems of belief differ from those of the Egyptians are not adequate for Rameses' purposes.

22. For Hurston's attitude about the idea of race, biological and otherwise, see "My People, My People," and "Seeing the World as It Is" (*Dust Tracks* 235–46; 247–66).

23. As McDowell puts it: "in passing the mantle to Joshua [Moses] explains the 'chosen people must not take up too many habits from the nations they come

in contact with'" (xi). This is in direct contradiction to what Boas proposes as the method by which nations and races achieve a high level of civilization.

24. In this sense, one could see Moses in the light of Gates's trickster figure, but only before the Exodus out of Egypt. As Gates presents it, the trickster figure depends on, for his existence, his position as displaced and oppressed within a master discourse; otherwise, the trickster figure is no trickster but a law maker, a legally recognized judge. Once Moses defeats Pharaoh, Moses claims absolute power over Pharaoh, and so the power to decide the semantic and grammatical structure of the master tongue. See Gates, *The Signifying-Monkey*.

25. Hurston here calls on the figure of Hermes Trismagistus (thrice great), echoing both Hubert and Mauss's tripartite structure of sacrifice, and the Egyptian god Thoth, with whom Hermes is associated and who will make an appearance in Hurston's text in the form of a text. Thoth, it should be noted, is the Egyptian symbol of the moon and god of wisdom; he is the messenger of the gods (and so associated with sacrifice, as sacrifice is, ultimately, a form of communication between mortals and gods), born from language through an act of his own will, and the inventor of writing.

26. Moses is Hurston's Frazerian "dying god", both in *Moses* and in Hurston's prefatory meditation on the Mosaic myth and sovereignty, "The Fire and the Cloud" (1934).

27. For a reading of the falsity of the notions of the Negro as existing outside of history before his forcible entrance into the New World, see Hurston's other Barnard advisor, Herscovits *(Myth of the Negro Past)*, who argues against limited notions of Negro historicity in favor of following the timeline beyond or before the New World to Africa.

28. This echoes Ralph Ellison's analysis of the suppression of a three-dimensional image of the Negro in twentieth-century American fiction, which would, if present, challenge the basic tenets of American democracy and so the image of the "American." See Ellison, "Twentieth-Century Fiction and the Black Mask of Humanity," 81–99.

For readings of the Jim Crow Era South in terms of the creation of whiteness through exclusion and violence, as well as lynching as blood sacrifice, see Patterson, *Rituals of Blood;* and T. Harris, *Exorcising Blackness*.

29. Blydon Jackson writes: "If there was meant to be a lesson for the black leadership of Hurston's day in *Moses*, it is difficult to say of what that lesson was intended to consist. Hurston was no social visionary" ("A Study of Power" 153). Agreeing with Jackson, I would simply add that though Hurston was "no social visionary," her contribution to the "lesson of the day" was less systematic than it was derivative of a radical rethinking of race along lines of anti-essentialism and impurity. The word to black leadership would signify not a vacant racial signified but a cultural heteroglossia brought to the extreme of totalization such that the racial signifier stands for a concept of cultural racial identity and not biological determinism.

6. Richard Wright's Jealous Rebels

1. One way African Americans fought fascism was the "Double V" campaign. Begun by the *Pittsburgh Courier* and largely rhetorical, the Double V called for victory over fascism at home and abroad. For an account of the "Double V," see Mullen, *Popular Fronts* 47, 61. On the African American press during World War II, see Johnson and Johnson, *Propaganda and Aesthetics* 125–60.

2. Biographies of Wright include Fabre, *Unfinished Quest of Richard Wright*; Walker, *Richard Wright, Daemonic Genius*; and Rowley, *Richard Wright*.

3. For the best overview of Wright's aesthetic and political thought during the 1930s, see Yarborough's introduction to *Uncle Tom's Cabin*.

4. In the announcement in the *Daily Worker* for his new journal, Wright listed one of the explicit goals of the *New Challenge* as the presentation of "the literature and conditions of life of American Negroes in relationship to the struggle against war and Fascism" (Fabre, *Unfinished Quest* 142).

5. I'm referring here to Houston A. Baker Jr., *Blues, Ideology, and Afro-American Literature* 113–99.

6. Gilroy believes that *The Outsider* and Wright's travel literature and nonfiction of the 1950s has been and remains largely ignored or derided because of its transatlantic approach to race relations in the United States (*Black Atlantic* 146–86).

7. Although they did not charge that Wright went white, Baldwin and Ellison, in reflecting their respective relationships with Wright, both charged him with presenting two-dimensional accounts of African American life, largely owing to his dependency on naturalism—a mode of writing not overwhelmingly in evidence in *The Outsider*. See James Baldwin, "Everybody's Protest Novel" 13–23; Ralph Ellison, "The World and the Jug" 1549–71.

8. On Wright and existentialism, see Gordon, *Existentia Africana*; and Hayes III, "Concept of Double Vision."

9. I'm referring, of course, to Wright's "official" break with the Party, "I Tried to Be a Communist." The essay was excerpted from the second part of *Black Boy* (1944).

10. See Kierkegaard, *The Concept of Anxiety*.

11. For the seminal account of the concept of blackness as it pertains to Wright's thought vis-à-vis "western culture," see Kent, "Richard Wright" 76–97.

12. With this in mind, we can say that Wright believed himself to be practicing a type of existentialism that intervenes in the world and so operates outside the "ivory tower" Arendt accuses the philosophy of hiding in ("French Existentialism" 188–93).

13. For readings of the political uses of Kierkegaard's thought, both liberal and totalitarian, see Arendt, "Søren Kierkegaard"; Eagleton, "Absolute Ironies"; Bellinger, "Toward a Kierkegaardian Understanding"; and Connell and Evans, *Foundations of Kierkegaard's Vision of Community*.

14. Fromm traces the psychological impulse to fascism from the perspective of the dictator as a form of necrophilia, and more generally a cult of the dead. See his *Anatomy of Human Destructiveness*. See also *Escape from Freedom,* in which Fromm focuses on group psychology and posits that the fear of terrible freedom drives the herd into the clutches of the dictator.

15. Although Wright's book concentrates on a form of radical individuality as psychological event, his concern lies primarily with group consciousness as perceived and manipulated by the dictator. Wright marks the link between group and individual as a type of oceanic feeling akin to that which Freud stipulates to be the basis and illusion of group psychology. See Freud, *Civilization and Its Discontents.*

16. Before it became the dominant ideology in Italy and Germany, fascism positioned itself on the outside as a means of breaking in. In this sense, fascists play the part of political and philosophical outsider before taking control of that which demarcates such distinctions. For texts of fascist ideologues in Italy and Germany before each respective movement took power, see Griffin, ed., *Fascism* 23–44; 104–28. For a discussion of the various poses fascist ideology struck in order to take power, including that of outsider, see Taylor, *Prelude to Genocide.*

17. Damon marks, then, the essential moment of rebellion, in that his existence counters the essential basis of law; for if the individual ultimately accounts for her actions, she plays the role of lawgiver. Wright had read his Camus. See Albert Camus, *The Rebel,* in particular the section "Revolution and Murder" 279–93.

18. See Schmitt, *Political Theology.*

19. See Derrida's reading of the Kafka parable "Before the Law," in which Derrida, not surprisingly, de-centers, along with Kafka, the epistemological certainty of the rule of law ("Before the Law" 181–220). Damon, then, reinstates this certainty, after realizing it doesn't exist, through brute force.

20. Fascism and Marxism in *The Outsider* encompass Janus's two faces and interact together on a two-dimensional plane characteristic of cold war representations of both. See Nolte, *Marxism, Fascism.*

21. On questions of the nature and material existence of fascism after 1945, see Cheles, Ferguson, and Vaughan, eds., *Neo-Fascism in Europe.*

22. See Herndon, *You Cannot Kill the Working Class.* See also Langston Hughes's one-act play *Angelo Herndon Jones;* the Joint Committee to Aid the Herndon Defense's *The Case of Angelo Herndon;* and Charles H. Martin's *The Angelo Herndon Case and Southern Justice.* See also Solomon, *The Cry Was Unity* 219–21; 297–301.

23. Damon's inhumanity is, of course, essential; it underscores his essential otherness and makes of him a living, breathing *différend*. See Lyotard, *The Différend.*

24. What Wright appears to be positing can be summed up with reference to Baudrillard's understanding of Disneyland: in the same way that the theme

park hovers just outside of Los Angeles County to obscure the fact that L.A. exists in hyperreality, Herndon and Blount distract us from the fact that Damon himself fits the description of would-be totalitarian ruler (1–42).

25. For a reading of the seemingly inextricable link between violence, fascism, and the modern age, see Forgacs, "Fascism, Violence and Modernity."

26. Damon exists in a state of exception, which is, according to Agamben, "the very condition of possibility of juridical rule and, along with it, the very meaning of State authority" (*Homo Sacer* 17).

27. The idea that for an ideology to be considered fascist it must in some way harken back to a premodern, all-but-lost existence as primal, privileged, and pagan forebear forms a cornerstone of this study and has already been examined. For an interesting reading of the lesser-known but crucial link between Nazism and ancient Rome, see Losemann, "The Nazi Concept of Rome."

28. The sovereignty in question here, however, comes purely from Wright's philosophical encounter with the question and can be traced to Schopenhauer's belief in will as the final arbiter of social reality and creator of the fundamental frames of reference in which a concept such as sovereignty can function. See Schopenhauer, *The World as Will and Idea*.

29. Damon, as Nietzschean anti-Christ, moves beyond pagan belief—or before it—into a realm disencumbered of binary distinctions, like good and evil. See Friedrich Nietzsche, *Twilight of the Idols*; and *The Anti-Christ*.

30. See Marcuse, *One-Dimensional Man*.

31. Damon displays his Girardian mimetic desire in that he kills that which he wishes to be as the only way to become it without contradiction. Damon sacrifices much in this text to be the man he wants to be (Girard, *Violence and the Sacred* 39–67).

32. A fact seen clearly by critics of Nazi Germany. See Neumann, *Behemoth*.

33. The "smoke-screen" acts as the backdrop for the projection of power's necessary spectacle. Wright posits here, as do Guy Debord and the Situationists shortly after him, that power's vehicle in putative mass democracies must be wide-ranging in scope and easily consumable, and so take the form of the spectacle (*Society of the Spectacle*).

34. I'm thinking here, of course, of Michel Foucault's, *Discipline and Punish*, in which writing, recording, confinement, and information sciences in general arise as a means of determining the nature of one's "soul" and producing, in effect, an almost invisible, coercive means of social control.

35. Fear stands as one of the most important emotions in Sartrean existentialism; it announces the moment of human choice and decision as direct acknowledgement of, and confrontation with, the ultimate horizon of existence, death. See Sartre, *Existentialism and Humanism*.

36. This is a Hobbesian principle in that Leviathan does not name a singular being but an organic collective by consent, which exists because without it, we would operate in a constant state of warfare—we would each of us be Cross Damon. See Hobbes, *Leviathan*.

37. Wright articulates a vague formulation of Fanon's analysis of the psychological disposition toward violence of the dispossessed, as well as Sartre's prefatory comments to Fanon's psychoanalytical exploration. Fanon writes, "For the native, life can only spring up again out of the rotting corpse of the settler." This violent rebirth "invests [the colonized people] with positive and creative qualities"—a statement with which Cross Damon would readily agree (*Wretched of the Earth* 93). See also Sartre's preface to *The Wretched of the Earth* 7–34.

38. The very idea that Damon could be beyond Althusserian ideology and ideological state apparatuses strikes one as Wright dealing in bad faith. See Althusser, "Ideology and Ideological State Apparatuses" 127–86.

39. Which describes precisely the dilemma facing parliamentary democracy diagnosed by Carl Schmitt and exploited by fascist ideology (*Crisis of Parliamentary Democracy* 65–76).

40. The anti-evolutionary, antimechanistic creative vitalism Wright writes into his text is Bergsonian in character and articulates, however abstractly, a basic tent of fascist ideology, namely, the need for vital, creative masculine health to combat the effects of western degeneration so graphically described in books like Max Nordau's *Degeneration*. See also Bergson, *Creative Evolution*.

Bibliography

Adamson, Walter L. *Avant-Garde Florence: From Modernism to Fascism.* Cambridge, MA: Harvard University Press, 1993.
Adell, Sandra. "Richard Wright's *The Outsider* and the Kierkegaardian Concept of Dread." *Comparative Literature Studies* 28 (Fall 1991): 379–95.
Adorno, Theodor W. "Freudian Theory and the Pattern of Fascist Propaganda." *The Essential Frankfurt School Reader.* Ed. Andrew Arato and Eike Gebhardt. New York: Continuum, 1982. 118–37.
———. *The Jargon of Authenticity.* Trans. Knut Tarnowski and Frederic Will. Evanston, IL: Northwestern University Press, 1973.
———. "Perennial Fashion—Jazz." 1953. *Prisms.* Trans. Samuel M. Weber. Cambridge, MA: MIT Press, 1994. 119–32.
Adorno, Theodor W., et al. "Introduction to *The Authoritarian Personality*." *Critical Theory and Society: A Reader.* Eds. Stephen Eric Bronner and Douglas MacKay. New York: Routledge, 1989.
Agamben, Giorgio. *Homo Sacer: Sovereign Power and Bare Life.* Trans. Daniel Heller-Roazen. Stanford, CA: Stanford University Press, 1998.
Allen, Ernest, Jr. "The New Negro: Explorations in Identity and Social Consciousness, 1910–1922." *1915, the Cultural Moment: The New Politics, the New Woman, the New Psychology, the New Art, and the New Theater in America.* Eds. Adele Heller and Lois Rudnick. New Brunswick, NJ: Rutgers University Press, 1991. 48–68.
Althusser, Louis. "Ideology and Ideological State Apparatuses." *Lenin and Philosophy, and Other Essays.* Trans. Ben Brewster. New York: Monthly Review Press, 1972. 127–86.
———. *Machiavelli and Us.* Trans. Gregory Elliott. Ed. François Matheron. New York: Verso, 2001.
Althusser, Louis, and Étienne Balibar. *Reading Capital.* Trans. Ben Brewster. New York: Verso, 1998.
Aly, Götz, Peter Chroust, and Christian Pross, eds. *Cleansing the Fatherland: Nazi Medicine and Racial Hygiene.* Trans. Belinda Cooper. Baltimore, MD: Johns Hopkins University Press, 1994.

Anderson, Jervis. *This Was Harlem: A Cultural Portrait, 1900–1950.* New York: Farrar, Straus, Giroux, 1982.
Antliff, Mark. "Fascism, Modernism and Modernity." *Art Bulletin* (March 2002): 148–69.
Arendt, Hannah. "French Existentialism." *Essays in Understanding, 1930–1954.* Ed. Jerome Kohn. New York: Harcourt, Brace, 1994. 188–93.
———. "Søren Kierkegaard." *Essays in Understanding, 1930–1954.* 44–49.
———. *The Origins of Totalitarianism.* New York: Harcourt Brace Jovanovich, 1973.
Baer, George. *The Coming of the Italo-Ethiopian War.* Cambridge, MA: Harvard University Press, 1967.
Baker, Houston A., Jr. *Blues, Ideology, and Afro-American Literature: A Vernacular Theory.* Chicago, IL: University of Chicago Press, 1987.
———. *Modernism and the Harlem Renaissance.* Chicago, IL: University of Chicago Press, 1987.
Balch, Emily Greene, ed. *Occupied Haiti; Being the Report of a Committee of Six Disinterested Americans Representing Organizations Exclusively American, Who, Having Personally Studied Conditions in Haiti in 1926, Favor the Restoration of the Independence of the Negro Republic.* New York: Writers Publishing Company, 1927.
Baldwin, James. "Everybody's Protest Novel." 1955. *Notes of a Native Son.* Boston, MA: Beacon Press, 1984. 13–23.
———. *The Fire Next Time.* 1962. New York: Random House, 1993.
Baldwin, Kate A. *Beyond the Color Line and the Iron Curtain: Reading Encounters between Black and Red, 1922–1963.* Durham, NC: Duke University Press, 2002.
Bambery, Chris. "The Revival of the Fascist Menace." R. Griffin, *International Fascism* 295–304.
Baraka, Amiri. "The Revolutionary Theater." Gates and McKay 1899–1902.
"Baraka Abandons 'Racism' as Ineffective and Joseph F. Sullivan Shifts to 'Scientific Socialism.'" *New York Times* December 27, 1974, 35.
Barker, A. J. *The Civilizing Mission; a History of the Italo-Ethiopian War of 1935–1936.* New York: Dial Press, 1968.
Barrett, William. *Irrational Man: A Study in Existential Philosophy.* Garden City, NY: Doubleday, 1962.
Bataille, George. "The Psychological Structure of Fascism." *Visions of Excess: Selected Writings, 1927–1939.* Ed. Allan Stoekl, trans. Allan Stoekl, with Carl R. Lovitt and Donald M. Leslie Jr. Minneapolis: University of Minnesota Press, 1985. 137–60.
Baudrillard, Jean. "The Precession of Simulacra." *Simulacra and Simulation.* Trans. Sheila Faria Glaser. Ann Arbor: University of Michigan Press, 1994. 1–42.
Bauman, Zygmunt. "The Left as the Counter-Culture of Modernity." *Telos* 70 (Winter 1986–87): 81–93.

Beard, Rev. John R. *The Life of Toussaint L'Ouverture: The Negro Patriot of Hayti: Comprising an Account of the Struggle for Liberty in the Island, and a Sketch of Its History to the Present Period*. Westport, CT: Negro Universities Press, 1970.

Beetham, David, ed. *Marxists in Face of Fascism: Writings by Marxists on Fascism from the Inter-War Period*. Manchester, UK: Manchester University Press, 1983.

Bell, Bernard W. *The Afro-American Novel and Its Tradition*. Amherst: University of Massachusetts Press, 1987.

Bellinger, Charles. "Toward a Kierkegaardian Understanding of Hitler, Stalin, and the Cold War." Connell and Evans 218–30.

Benedict Anderson. *Imagined Communities: Reflections on the Origin and Spread of Nationalism*. New York: Verso, 1991.

Ben-Ghiat, Ruth. *Fascist Modernities: Italy, 1922–45*. Berkeley: University of California Press, 2001.

———. "Italian Fascism and the Aesthetics of the 'Third Way.'" *Journal of Contemporary History: The Aesthetics of Fascism* 31 (1996): 293–316.

Benjamin, Walter. "Critique of Violence." 1920–21. Trans. Edmund Jephcott. *Reflections: Essays, Aphorisms, Autobiographical Writings*. Ed. Peter Demetz. New York: Harcourt, Brace, Jovanovich, 1978. 277–300.

———. "Theories of German Fascism: On the Collection of Essays *War and Warrior*, edited by Ernst Jünger." *New German Critique* 17 (Spring 1979): 120–28.

———. "The Work of Art in the Age of Mechanical Reproduction." *Illuminations*. Ed. Hannah Arendt. Trans. Harry Zohn. New York: Harcourt, Brace and World, 1968. 217–52.

Bentham, David, ed. *Marxists in the Face of Fascism: Writing by Marxists on Fascism from the Inter-War Period*. Totowa, NJ: Manchester University Press, 1984.

Berghahn, Marion. *Images of Africa in Black American Literature*. Totowa, NJ: Rowman and Littlefield, 1977.

Berghaus, Günter, ed. *Fascism and Theatre: Comparative Studies on the Aesthetics and Politics of Performance in Europe, 1925–1945*. Providence, RI: Berghahn Books, 1996.

Bergmeier, Horst J. P., and Rainer E. Lotz. *Hitler's Airwaves: The Inside Story of Nazi Broadcasting and Propaganda Swing*. New Haven, CT: Yale University Press, 1997.

Bergson, Henri. *Creative Evolution*. Trans. Arthur Mitchell. Westport, CT: Greenwood Press, 1975.

Berman, Russell A. "The Aestheticization of Politics: Walter Benjamin on Fascism and the Avant-Garde." *Stanford Italian Review* 8.1–2 (1990): 35–52.

———. "Written Right across Their Faces: Ernst Jünger's Fascist Modernism." *Modernity and the Text: Revisions of German Modernism*. Ed. Andreas Huyssen and David Bathrick. New York: Columbia University Press, 1989. 60–80.

Bessel, Richard, ed. *Fascist Italy and Nazi Germany: Comparisons and Contrasts*. New York: Cambridge University Press, 1996.
Bhabha, Homi K. "Of Mimicry and Man: The Ambivalence of Colonial Discourse." *The Location of Culture*. New York: Routledge, 1994. 85–92.
Boas, Franz. "Human Faculty as Determined by Race." *A Franz Boas Reader: The Shaping of American Anthropology, 1883–1911*. Ed. George Stocking Jr. Chicago: University of Chicago Press, 1982. 219–42.
Bogues, Anthony. *Black Heretics, Black Prophets: Radical Political Intellectuals*. New York: Routledge, 2003.
Bone, Robert. *The Negro Novel in America*. New Haven, CT: Yale University Press, 1965.
Bontemps, Arna. *Black Thunder*. 1936. Boston, MA: Beacon Press, 1968.
———. *Drums at Dusk: A Novel*. New York: Macmillan, 1939.
———. Rev. of *The Outsider*, by Richard Wright. *Saturday Review* 36 (March 28, 1953): 15–16. Rpt. in *Richard Wright: The Critical Reception*, ed. John M. Reilly. New York: Burt Franklin, 1978. 207–9.
Bontemps, Arna, and Langston Hughes. *Popo and Fifina: Children of Haiti*. 1932. New York: Oxford University Press, 1993.
Bosworth, R. J. B. *The Italian Dictatorship: Problems and Perspectives in the Interpretation of Mussolini and Fascism*. London: Arnold, 1998.
Brearley, H. C. "The Negro's New Belligerency." *Phylon* 5 (1944): 343.
Brinkley, Alan. *Voices of Protest: Huey Long, Father Coughlin, and the Great Depression*. New York: Knopf, 1982. 273–83.
Brooks, Joanna, and John Saillant, eds. *"Face Zion Forward": First Writers of the Black Atlantic, 1785–1798*. Boston, MA: Northeastern University Press, 2002.
Brown, Michael E. "The History of the History of U.S. Communism." *New Studies in the Politics and Culture of U.S. Communism*. Ed. Michael E. Brown et al. New York: Monthly Review Press, 1993. 15–44.
Buhle, Paul. *Marxism in the United States: Remapping the History of the American Left*. London: Verso, 1987.
Bush, Rod. *"We are not what we seem": Black Nationalism and Class Struggle in the American Century*. New York: New York University Press, 1999.
Callow, Simon. "Voodoo Macbeth." *Rhapsodies in Black: Art of the Harlem Renaissance*. Berkeley: University of California Press, 1997. 34–80.
Campbell, Jane. *Mythic Black Fiction: The Transformation of History*. Knoxville: University of Tennessee Press, 1986.
Camus, Albert. *The Rebel; An Essay on Man in Revolt*. 1951. Trans. Anthony Bower. New York: Vintage Books, 1956.
Canetti, Elias. *Crowds and Power*. 1960. Trans. Carol Stewart. New York: Seabury Press, 1978.
Carby, Hazel V. "Ideologies of Black Folk." *Slavery and the Literary Imagination*. Ed. Deborah E. McDowell and Arnold Rampersad. Baltimore, MD: Johns Hopkins University Press, 1989. 125–43.

———. "Policing the Black Woman's Body in an Urban Context." *Critical Inquiry* 18.4 (1992): 738–55.

———. "The Politics of Fiction, Anthropology, and the Folk: Zora Neale Hurston." *History and Memory in African American Culture*. Ed. Genevieve Fabre and Robert O'Meally. New York: Oxford University Press, 1994. 28–44.

Carlston, Erin G. *Thinking Fascism: Sapphic Modernism and Fascist Modernity*. Palo Alto: Stanford University Press, 1998.

Carsten, F. L. *The Rise of Fascism*. Berkeley: University of California Press, 1967, 1980.

Cheles, Luciano, Ronnie Ferguson, and Michalina Vaughan, eds. *Neo-Fascism in Europe*. London: Longman, 1991.

Chireau, Yvonne, and Nathaniel Deutsch, eds. *Black Zion: African American Religious Encounters with Judaism*. New York: Oxford University Press, 2000.

Chirenje, J. Mutero. *Ethiopianism and Afro-Americans in Southern Africa, 1883–1916*. Baton Rouge: Louisiana State University Press, 1987.

Chytry, Josef. *The Aesthetic State: A Quest in Modern German Thought*. Berkeley: University of California Press, 1989.

Clayton, Horace R. *Black Workers and the New Unions* Chapel Hill: University of North Carolina Press, 1939.

Clifford, James. *The Predicament of Culture: Twentieth-Century Ethnography, Literature, and Art*. Cambridge, MA: Harvard University Press, 1988.

Coffey, Thomas M. *Lion by the Tail: The Story of the Italian-Ethiopian War*. New York: Viking Press, 1974.

Coles, Robert A. "Richard Wright's *The Outsider:* A Novel in Transition." *Modern Language Studies* 13 (Summer 1983): 53–61.

Connell, George B., and C. Stephen Evans, eds. *Foundations of Kierkegaard's Vision of Community: Religion, Ethics, and Politics in Kierkegaard*. Atlantic Highlands, NJ: Humanities Press International, 1992.

Coombes, John E. *Writing from the Left: Socialism, Liberalism and the Popular Front*. New York: Harvester Wheatsheaf, 1989.

Cooper, Wayne. "Claude McKay and the New Negro." *Phylon* 25 (1964): 297–306.

Cronon, Edmund David. *Black Moses: The Story of Marcus Garvey and the Universal Negro Improvement Association*. Madison: University of Wisconsin Press, 1955.

———, ed. *Marcus Garvey*. Englewood Cliffs, NJ: Prentice-Hall, 1973.

Cruse, Harold. *The Crisis of the Negro Intellectual*. New York: Quill, 1984.

Cwiklik, Robert. *A. Philip Randolph and the Labor Movement*. Brookfield, CT: Millbrook Press, 1993.

Dash, J. Michael. *Haiti and the United States: National Stereotypes and the Literary Imagination*. New York: St. Martin's Press, 1997.

Davis, Arthur P. *From the Dark Tower: Afro-American Writers (1900 to 1960)*. Washington, DC: Howard University Press, 1974.

Dawson, Michael C. *Black Visions: The Roots of Contemporary African American Political Ideologies.* Chicago, IL: University of Chicago Press, 2001.

Dayan, Joan. *Haiti, History, and the Gods.* Berkeley: University of California Press, 1995.

Debord, Guy. *Society of the Spectacle.* Trans. Donald Nicholson-Smith. New York: Zone Books, 1995.

de Felice, Renzo. *Interpretations of Fascism.* Trans. Brenda Huff Everett. Cambridge, MA: Harvard University Press, 1977.

———. *Mussolini.* 4 vols. Turin: Einaudi, 1965–97.

de Grand, Alexander. *Italian Fascism: Its Origins and Development.* Lincoln: University of Nebraska Press, 1978.

de Grazia, Victoria. *How Fascism Ruled Women: Italy, 1922–1945.* Berkeley: University of California Press, 1992.

Deleuze, Gilles, and Guattari, Félix. *Anti-Oedipus: Capitalism and Schizophrenia.* Trans. Robert Hurley, Mark Seem, and Helen R. Lane. New York: Viking Press, 1977.

Denning, Michael. *The Cultural Front: The Laboring of American Culture in the Twentieth Century.* New York: Verso, 1996.

Derrida, Jacques. "Before the Law." *Acts of Literature.* Ed. Derek Attridge. New York: Routledge, 1992. 181–220.

———. "Force of Law: The Mystical Foundation of Authority." *Cardozo Law Review* 11 (July/August 1990): 1033.

———. *Of Spirit: Heidegger and the Question.* Trans. Geoffrey Bennington and Rachel Bowlby. Chicago, IL: University of Chicago Press, 1989.

Diedrich, Maria. "'Power to Command God': Zora Neale Hurston's *Moses, Man of the Mountain* and Black Folk Religion." *Studien zur englischen und amerikanischen Prosa nach dem Ersten Weltkrieg.* Darmstadt: Wissenschaftliche Buchgesellschaft, 1986. 176–85.

Dietrich, Julia. *The Old Left in History and Literature.* New York: Prentice Hall International, 1996.

Dixon, Chris. *African America and Haiti: Emigration and Black Nationalism in the Nineteenth Century.* Westport, CT: Greenwood Press, 2000.

Draper, Theodore. *American Communism and Soviet Russia.* New York: Viking Press, 1960.

Du Bois, W. E. B. *Dark Princess: A Romance.* 1928. Boston, MA: Northeastern University Press, 1995.

———. *The Souls of Black Folk: Authoritative Text, Contexts, Criticism.* Ed. Henry Louis Gates Jr. and Terri Hume Oliver. New York: W. W. Norton, 1999.

———. "Toussaint L'Ouverture." *The Oxford W. E. B. Du Bois Reader.* Ed. Eric J. Sundquist. New York: Oxford University Press, 1996. 296–302.

Dugan, James, and Laurence Lafore. *Days of Emperor and Clown: The Italo-Ethiopian War, 1935–1936.* Garden City, NY: Doubleday, 1973.

Durkheim, Emile. *The Elementary Forms of Religious Life.* Trans. Joseph Ward Swain. New York: Free Press, 1965.

Eagleton, Terry. "Absolute Ironies: Søren Kierkegaard." *The Ideology of the Aesthetic*. Cambridge, MA: Basil Blackwell, 1990. 173–95.
Eatwell, Roger. "The Drive toward Synthesis." R. Griffin, *International Fascism* 189–203.
Eisenstadt, Peter, ed. *Black Conservatism: Essays in Intellectual and Political History*. Garland Reference Library of the Humanities 2016. Crosscurrents in African American History 3. New York: Garland, 1999.
Ellison, Ralph Waldo. *Invisible Man*. New York: Random House, 1989.
———. "Recent Negro Fiction." *New Masses* 5 (1941): 24.
———. "Twentieth-Century Fiction and the Black Mask of Humanity." *The Collected Essays of Ralph Ellison*. Ed. John F. Callahan. New York, NY: Random House, 1995. 81–99.
———. "The World and the Jug." Gates and McKay 1549–71.
Esedebe, P. Olisanwuche. *Pan-Africanism: The Idea and Movement, 1776–1963*. Washington, DC: Howard University Press, 1982.
Fabre, Michel. *The Unfinished Quest of Richard Wright*. Trans. Isabel Barzun. New York: Morrow, 1973.
Falasca-Zamponi, Simonetta. *Fascist Spectacle: The Aesthetics of Power in Mussolini's Italy*. Berkeley: University of California Press, 1997.
Fanon, Frantz. *The Wretched of the Earth*. Preface by Jean-Paul Sartre. Trans. Constance Farrington. New York: Grove Press, 1968.
Fauset, Arthur Huff. *Black Gods of the Metropolis; Negro Religious Cults of the Urban North*. 1944. New York: Octagon Books, 1970.
Fax, Elton C. *Garvey: The Story of a Pioneer Black Nationalist*. New York: Dodd, Mead, 1972.
Foley, Barbara. *Radical Representations: Politics and Form in U.S. Proletarian Fiction, 1929–1941*. Durham, NC: Duke University Press, 1993.
Foner, Philip S., and James S. Allen, eds. *American Communism and Black Americans: A Documentary History, 1919–1929*. Philadelphia, PA: Temple University Press, 1987.
Foner, Philip S., and Herbert Shapiro, eds. *American Communism and Black Americans: A Documentary History, 1930–1934*. Philadelphia, PA: Temple University Press, 1991.
Forgacs, David. "Fascism, Violence and Modernity." *The Violent Muse: Violence and the Artistic Imagination in Europe, 1910–1939*. Ed. Jana Howlett and Rod Mengham. New York: Manchester University Press, 1994.
Foucault, Michel. *Discipline and Punish: The Birth of the Prison*. Trans. Alan Sheridan. New York: Vintage Books, 1979.
———. Preface. *Anti-Oedipus: Capitalism and Schizophrenia*. Gilles Deleuze and Félix Guattari. Trans. Robert Hurley, Mark Seem, and Helen R Lane. New York: Viking Press, 1977. xi–xiv.
Frazer, Sir James George. *The Golden Bough*. New York: Simon and Schuster, 1996.
"Free in Anti-Semitic Case." *New York Times* October 12, 1932, 29.

Freud, Sigmund. *Civilization and Its Discontents*. Ed. and trans. James Strachey. New York: W. W. Norton, 1962.
——. *The Future of an Illusion*. Ed. and trans. James Strachey. New York: W. W. Norton, 1989.
——. *Group Psychology and the Analysis of the Ego*. Ed. and trans. James Strachey. New York: W. W. Norton, 1989.
——. *Totem and Taboo: Resemblances between the Psychic Lives of Savages and Neurotics*. Ed. and trans. James Strachey. New York: W. W. Norton, 1962.
Friedlander, Henry. *The Origins of Nazi Genocide: From Euthanasia to the Final Solution*. Chapel Hill: University of North Carolina Press, 1995.
Fromm, Erich. *The Anatomy of Human Destructiveness*. New York: Holt, Rinehart, and Winston, 1973.
——. *Escape from Freedom*. 1941. New York: Holt, Rinehart and Winston, 1964.
Fuller, Hoyt. "Towards a Black Aesthetic." Gates and McKay. 1810–16.
Gabbin, Joanne V., ed. *The Furious Flowering of African American Poetry*. Charlottesville: University Press of Virginia, 1999.
Gaines, Kevin K. *Uplifting the Race: Black Leadership, Politics, and Culture in the Twentieth Century*. Chapel Hill: University of North Carolina Press, 1996.
Garvey, Amy Jacques, ed. *Garvey and Garveyism*. Kingston, Jamaica: A. Jacques Garvey, 1963.
——, ed. *The Philosophy and Opinions of Marcus Garvey, Or, Africa for the Africans*. 1925. Introduction by Robert A. Hill. Dover, MA: Majority Press, 1986.
Garvey, Marcus. *Marcus Garvey*. Ed. E. David Cronon. Englewood Cliffs, NJ: Prentice-Hall, 1973.
——. *Marcus Garvey: Life and Lessons: A Centennial Companion to the Marcus Garvey and Universal Negro Improvement Association Papers*. Ed. Robert A. Hill, assoc. ed. Barbara Bair. Los Angeles: University of California Press, 1987.
——. *Message to the People: The Course in African Philosophy*. 1937. Ed. Tony Martin. Dover, MA: Majority Press, 1986.
——. *The Poetical Works of Marcus Garvey*. Ed. Tony Martin. Dover, MA: Majority Press, 1983.
Gates, Henry Louis, Jr. "A Fragmented Man: George Schuyler and the Claims of Race." *New York Times Book Review* September 20, 1992: 42–43.
——. *The Signifying Monkey: A Theory of African American Literary Criticism*. New York: Oxford University Press, 1988.
Gates, Henry Louis, Jr., and Nellie Y. McKay, eds. *The Norton Anthology of African American Literature*. New York: W. W. Norton, 1997.
Gättens, Marie-Luise. *Women Writers and Fascism: Reconstructing History*. Gainesville: University Press of Florida, 1995.
Gayle, Addison, Jr. "The Black Aesthetic." Gates and McKay. 1870–77.

———. *The Way of the New World: The Black Novel in America.* Garden City, NY: Anchor Press, 1975.
Gentile, Emilio. *The Sacralization of Politics in Fascist Italy.* Trans. Keith Botsford. Cambridge, MA: Harvard University Press, 1996.
Gide, Andre. *The God that Failed.* 1949. Ed. R. H. S. Crossman. New York: Bantam Books, 1965.
Giles, James R. *Claude McKay.* Boston, MA: Twayne, 1976.
Gillette, Aaron. *Racial Theories in Fascist Italy.* New York: Routledge, 2002.
Gilroy, Paul. *Against Race: Imagining Political Culture beyond the Color Line.* Cambridge, MA: Belknap-Harvard, 2000.
———. *The Black Atlantic: Modernity and Double Consciousness.* Cambridge, MA: Harvard University Press, 1993.
———. "Black Fascism." *Transition* 80/81 (Spring 2000): 70–91.
Girard, Rene. *Violence and the Sacred.* Trans. Patrick Gregory. Baltimore, MD: Johns Hopkins University Press, 1977.
Golsan, Richard J., ed. *Fascism, Aesthetics, and Culture.* Hanover, NH: University Press of New England, 1992.
———, ed. *Fascism's Return: Scandal, Revision, and Ideology since 1980.* Lincoln: University of Nebraska Press, 1998.
Goodrick-Clarke, Nicholas. *The Occult Roots of Nazism: Secret Aryan Cults and Their Influence on Nazi Ideology: The Ariosophists of Austria and Germany, 1890–1935.* New York: New York University Press, 1992.
Gorham, Charles. *The Lion of Judah; A Life of Haile Selassie I, Emperor of Ethiopia.* New York: Ariel Books, 1966.
Gordon, Lewis R. *Existentia Africana: Understanding Africana Existential Thought.* New York: Routledge, 2000.
Gorman, Paul R. *Left Intellectuals and Popular Culture in Twentieth-Century America.* Chapel Hill: University of North Carolina Press, 1996.
Gornick, Vivian. *The Romance of American Communism.* New York Basic Books, 1977.
Gramsci, Antonio. *Selections from the Prison Notebooks.* Ed. and trans. Quintin Hoare and Geoffrey Nowell Smith. New York: International Publishers, 1987.
Greenberg, Cheryl Lynn. *"Or Does It Explode": Black Harlem in the Great Depression.* New York: Oxford University Press, 1997.
Greenberg, Robert M. "Idealism and Realism in the Fiction of Claude McKay." *College Language Association Journal* 24.3 (1981): 237–61.
Gregor, A. James. *Faces of Janus: Marxism and Fascism in the Twentieth Century.* New Haven, CT: Yale University Press, 2004.
Griffin, Barbara Jackson. "The Last Word: Claude McKay's Unpublished 'Cycle Manuscript.'" *MELUS* 21.1 (1996): 41–57.
Griffin, Roger K., ed. *Fascism.* New York: Oxford University Press, 1995.
———, ed. *International Fascism: Theories, Causes and the New Consensus.* New York: Oxford University Press, 1998.

———. *The Nature of Fascism*. New York, NY: St. Martin's Press, 1991.
Gruesser, John Cullen. *Black on Black: Twentieth-Century African American Writing about Africa*. Lexington, KY: University Press of Kentucky, 2000.
Gysin, Fritz. "Black Pulp Fiction: George Schuyler's Caustic Vision of a Panafrican Empire." *Empire: American Studies*. Eds. John G. Blair and Reinhold Wagnleitner. Tübingen: Narr, 1997.
Hakutani, Yoshinobu. "Richard Wright's *The Outsider* and Albert Camus's *The Stranger*." *Mississippi Quarterly* 42 (Fall 1989): 365–78.
Hall, Stuart. "Race, Articulation, and Societies Structured in Dominance." *Black British Cultural Studies: A Reader*. Ed. Houston A. Baker Jr., Manthia Diawara, and Ruth H. Lindeborg. Chicago, IL: University of Chicago Press, 1996. 16–60.
Hamilton, Charles V. *Adam Clayton Powell, Jr.: The Political Biography of an American Dilemma*. New York: Maxwell Macmillan International, 1991.
Hansberry, Lorraine. Rev. of *The Outsider*, by Richard Wright. *Freedom* 14 (April 1953), 7. Rpt. in *Richard Wright: The Critical Reception*, ed. John M. Reilly. New York: Burt Franklin, 1978. 219–20.
Hardie, Frank. *The Abyssinian Crisis*. London: B. T. Batsford, 1974.
"Harlem's Hitler Brought to Court." *New York Times* October 9, 1934, 2.
Harris, Brice, Jr. *The United States and the Italo-Ethiopian Crisis*. Stanford, CA: Stanford University Press, 1964.
Harris, Joseph E. *African American Reactions to War in Ethiopia, 1936–1941*. Baton Rouge: Louisiana State University Press, 1994.
Harris, Robert, Nyota Harris, and Grandassa Harris, eds. *Carlos Cooks and Black Nationalism from Garvey to Malcolm*. Dover, MA: Majority Press, 1992.
Harris, Trudier. *Exorcising Blackness: Historical and Literary Lynching and Burning Rituals*. Bloomington: Indiana University Press, 1984.
Harris, William H. *The Harder We Run: Black Workers since the Civil War*. New York: Oxford University Press, 1982.
———. *Keeping the Faith: A. Philip Randolph, Milton P. Webster, and the Brotherhood of Sleeping Car Porters, 1925–37*. Urbana: University of Illinois Press, 1991.
Hatlen, Burton. "Ezra Pound and Fascism." *Ezra Pound and History*. Ed. Marianne Korn. Orono: National Poetry Foundation, University of Maine Press, 1985. 145–72.
Hayes, Floyd W., III. "The Concept of Double Vision in Richard Wright's *The Outsider*: Fragmented Blackness in the Age of Nihilism." *Existence in Black: An Anthology of Black Existential Philosophy*. Ed. Lewis R. Gordon. New York: Routledge, 1997. 173–84.
Headon, David. "'Beginning to See Things Really': The Politics of Zora Neale Hurston." *Zora in Florida*. Ed. Elizabeth T. Hayes. Gainesville: University Press of Florida, 1994. 170–94.

Heinl, Robert Debs, and Nancy Gordon Heinl. *Written in Blood: The Story of the Haitian People, 1492–1971.* Boston, MA: Houghton Mifflin, 1978.

Helbing, Mark I. "Claude McKay: Art and Politics." *Negro American Literature Forum* 7 (1973): 49–52.

Herf, Jeffrey. *Reactionary Modernism: Technology, Culture, and Politics in Weimar and the Third Reich.* New York: Cambridge University Press, 1984.

Herndon, Angelo. *You Cannot Kill the Working Class.* New York: International Labor Defense and the League of Struggle for Negro Rights. Ca. 1937.

Herscovits, Melville J. *Life in a Haitian Valley.* 1937. Garden City, NY: Anchor Books, 1971.

———. *The Myth of the Negro Past.* New York: Harper and Brothers, 1941.

Hewitt, Andrew. *Fascist Modernism: Aesthetics, Politics, and the Avant-Garde.* Stanford, CA: Stanford University Press, 1993.

Hickey, Neil, and Ed Edwin, eds. *Adam Clayton Powell and the Politics of Race.* New York: Fleet, 1965.

Hicks, Granville. "The Portrait of a Man Searching." *New York Times Review of Books* March 22, 1953, 1, 35. Rpt. in *Richard Wright: The Critical Reception,* ed. John M. Reilly. New York: Burt Franklin, 1978. 198–201.

Hill, Robert A. "Black Zionism: Marcus Garvey and the Jewish Question." *African Americans and Jews in the Twentieth Century: Studies in Convergence and Conflict.* Ed. V. P. Franklin. Columbia: University of Missouri Press, 1998. 105–22.

———. "Cyril V. Briggs, *The Crusader* Magazine, and the African Blood Brotherhood, 1918–1922." *The Crusader.* Ed. Robert A. Hill. New York: Garland Press, 1987. v–lxvi.

———. Introduction. *Ethiopian Stories.* Ed. Robert A. Hill. Boston, MA: Northeastern University Press, 1994. 1–50.

Hill, Robert A., ed., and Barbara Bair, assoc. ed. *Marcus Garvey: Life and Lessons: A Centennial Companion to The Marcus Garvey and the Universal Negro Improvement Papers.* Berkeley: University of California Press, 1987.

Hill, Robert A., and R. Kent Rasmussen. Afterword. *Black Empire.* Ed. Robert A. Hill and R. Kent Rasmussen. Boston, MA: Northeastern University Press, 1991. 259–310

Hitler, Adolf. *Mein Kampf.* 1922. Trans. Ralph Manheim. New York: Houghton Mifflin, 1943, 1971.

Hobbes, Thomas. *Leviathan: Authoritative Text, Backgrounds, Interpretations.* Eds. Richard E. Flathman and David Johnston. New York: W. W. Norton, 1997.

Hopkins, Pauline E. *Of One Blood.* Serialized in the *Colored American Magazine,* 6.1–11 (1902–3).

Horkheimer, Max, and Theodor W. Adorno. *Dialectic of Enlightenment.* 1944. Trans. John Cumming. New York: Continuum, 1995.

Howard, Lillie P. *Zora Neale Hurston.* Boston: Twayne, 1980.

Hubert, Henri, and Marcel Mauss. *Sacrifice: Its Nature and Function.* Trans. W. D. Halls. Chicago: University of Chicago Press, 1981.
Huggins, Nathan Irvin. *Harlem Renaissance.* New York: Oxford University Press, 1973.
Hughes, Langston. *Angelo Herndon Jones: A One-Act Play of Negro Life.* The Political Plays of Langston Hughes. Carbondale: Southern Illinois University Press, 2000. 147–62.
———. "Broadcast on Ethiopia." *American Spectator* (July/August 1936): 16–17.
———. "Call of Ethiopia." *Opportunity: Journal of Negro Life.* 13.9 (September 28, 1935): 276. Rpt. in *Collected Poems of Langston Hughes* 192–93.
———. *The Collected Poems of Langston Hughes,* ed. Arnold Rampersad, associate ed. David Roessel. New York: Knopf, 1994.
———. *I Wonder as I Wander: An Autobiographical Journey.* New York: Hill and Wang, 1964.
Hurston, Zora Neale. *Dust Tracks on the Road.* 1942. New York: HarperPerennial, 1991.
———. "The Fire and the Cloud. " 1934. *The Complete Stories.* New York: HarperPerennial, 1995. 117–21.
———. *Moses, Man of the Mountain.* 1939. Ed. Deborah McDowell. New York: Harper Perennial, 1991.
———. *Tell My Horse: Voodoo and Life in Haiti and Jamaica.* 1937. New York: Perennial Library, 1990.
Hutchinson, George. *The Harlem Renaissance in Black and White.* Cambridge, MA: Belknap-Harvard, 1995.
Jackson, Blyden. *"Moses, Man of the Mountain:* A Study of Power." *Modern Critical Views: Zora Neale Hurston.* Ed. Harold Bloom. Broomall, PA: Chelsea House, 1986.
Jackson, Chuck. "Waste and Whiteness: Zora Neale Hurston and the Politics of Eugenics." *African American Review* 34.4 (1997): 329–60.
Jacobs, Sylvia M. *The African Nexus: Black American Perspectives on the European Partitioning of Africa, 1880–1920.* Westport, CT: Greenwood Press, 1981.
Jacobs, Virginia Lee. *Roots of Rastafari.* San Diego, CA: Avant Books, 1985.
James, C. L. R. *At the Rendezvous of Victory: Selected Writings.* London: Allison and Busby, 1984.
———. *The Black Jacobins: Toussaint L'Ouverture and the San Domingo Revolution.* 1938. London: Allison and Busby, 1980.
Jameson, Fredric, ed. *Aesthetics and Politics.* Trans. Ronald Taylor. New York: Verso, 1980.
———. *Fables of Aggression: Wyndham Lewis, the Modernist as Fascist.* Berkeley: University of California Press, 1979.
———. *Marxism and Form; Twentieth-Century Dialectical Theories of Literature.* Princeton, NJ: Princeton University Press, 1972.
———. *The Political Unconscious: Narrative as a Socially Symbolic Act.* Ithaca, NY: Cornell University Press, 1981.

Jelavich, Peter. *Berlin Cabaret*. Cambridge, MA: Harvard University Press, 1993.
Jenkins, David. *Black Zion: The Return of Afro-Americans and West Indians to Africa*. London: Wildwood House, 1975.
Johnson, Abby Arthur, and Ronald Maberry Johnson. *Propaganda and Aesthetics: The Literary Politics of Afro-American Magazines in the Twentieth Century*. Amherst, MA: University of Massachusetts Press, 1979.
Johnson, Barbara. "Moses and Intertextuality: Sigmund Freud, Zora Neale Hurston, and the Bible." *Poetics of the Americas: Race, Founding, and Textuality*. Ed. Bainard Cowan and Jefferson Humphries. Baton Rouge: Louisiana State University Press, 1997.
Johnson, James Weldon. *Along This Way; The Autobiography of James Weldon Johnson*. New York: Viking Press, 1933.
Joint Committee to Aid the Herndon Defense. *The Case of Angelo Herndon*. New York, NY: Joint Committee to Aid the Herndon Defense, 1935.
Joyce, Joyce A. "Bantu, Nkodi, Ndungu, and Nganga Language, Politics, Music, and Religion in African American Poetry." Gabbin 99–117.
Jünger, Ernst. "Total Mobilization." *The Heidegger Controversy*. Ed. Richard Wolin. Trans. Joel Golb and Richard Wolin. Cambridge, MA: MIT Press, 1993. 119–39.
Kalaidjian, Walter. *American Culture between the Wars: Revisionary Modernism and Postmodern Critique*. New York: Columbia University Press, 1993.
Kantorowicz, Ernst H. *The King's Two Bodies: A Study of Mediaeval Political Theology*. Princeton, NJ: Princeton University Press, 1997.
Kater, Michael H. *Different Drummers: Jazz in the Culture of Nazi Germany*. New York: Oxford University Press, 1992.
Karenga, Maulana. "Black Art: Mute Matter Given Force and Function." Gates and McKay 1973–77.
Kedward, H. R. *Fascism in Western Europe, 1900–45*. London: Blackie, 1969.
Keller, James R. "'A Chafing Savage, Down the Decent Street': The Politics of Compromise in Claude McKay's Protest Sonnets." *African American Review* 218.3 (1994): 447–56.
Kelley, Robin D. G. *Freedom Dreams: The Black Radical Imagination*. Boston, MA: Beacon Press, 2002.
———. *Hammer and the Hoe: Alabama Communists during the Great Depression*. Chapel Hill: University of North Carolina Press, 1990.
———. *Race Rebels: Culture, Politics, and the Black Working Class*. New York: Free Press, 1994. 123–58.
Kent, George E. "Richard Wright: Blackness and the Adventure of Western Culture." *Blackness and the Adventure of Western Culture*. Chicago, IL: Third World Press, 1972.
Kierkegaard, Søren. *The Concept of Anxiety: A Simple Psychologically Orienting Deliberation on the Dogmatic Issue of Hereditary Sin*. Ed. and trans. Reidar Thomte, with Albert B. Anderson. Princeton, NJ: Princeton University Press, 1980.

Kinnamon, Keneth, and Michel Fabre. *Conversations with Richard Wright.* Jackson: University Press of Mississippi, 1993.
Klehr, Harvey, and John Earl Haynes. *The American Communist Movement: Storming Heaven Itself.* New York: Maxwell Macmillan International, 1992.
Knox, MacGregor. *Common Destiny: Dictatorship, Foreign Policy, and War in Fascist Italy and Nazi Germany.* New York: Cambridge University Press, 2000.
Koepnick, Lutz P. "Fascist Aesthetics Revisited." *Modernism/Modernity* 6.1 (January 1999): 51–73.
Korn, Marianne, ed. *Ezra Pound and History.* Orono: National Poetry Foundation, University of Maine, 1985.
Korngold, Ralph. *Citizen Toussaint.* 1944. New York: Hill and Wang, 1965.
Kracauer, Siegfried. "Das Ornament der Masse." *Das Ornament der Masse.* 1927. Frankfurt a.M.: Suhrkamp Verlag, 1977. 50–63.
Laclau, Ernesto. *Politics and Ideology in Marxist Theory: Capitalism, Fascism, Populism.* 1977. New York: Verso, 1979.
Lacoue-Labarthe, Philippe. *Heidegger, Art and Politics.* Trans. Chris Turner. Cambridge, MA: Basil Blackwell, 1990.
Lacoue-Labarthe, Philippe, and Nancy, Jean-Luc. "The Nazi Myth." Trans. Brian Holmes. *Critical Inquiry* 16 (Winter 1990): 291–312.
Laqueur, Walter. *Fascism: Past, Present, Future.* New York: Oxford University Press, 1996.
———, ed. *Fascism: A Reader's Guide: Analyses, Interpretations, Bibliography.* Berkeley: University of California Press, 1976.
Lemke, Sieglinde. *Primitivist Modernism: Black Culture and the Origins of Transatlantic Modernism.* New York: Oxford University Press, 1998.
LeSeur, Geta. "Claude McKay's Marxism." *The Harlem Renaissance: Revaluations.* Ed. Amritjit Singh, William S. Shiver, and Stanley Brodwin. New York, NY: Garland, 1989. 219–31.
Levecq, Christine. "'Mighty Strange Threads in Her Loom': Laughter and Subversive Heteroglossia in Zora Neale Hurston's *Moses, Man of the Mountain.*" *Texas Studies in Literature and Language* 36.4 (Winter 1994): 436–61.
Levine, Lawrence W. "Marcus Garvey and the Politics of Revitalization." *Black Leaders of the Twentieth Century.* Ed. John Hope Franklin and August Meier. Urbana: University of Illinois Press, 1982. 104–38.
Lewis, David Levering. *When Harlem Was in Vogue.* New York: Random House, 1981.
Lewis, Rupert. *Marcus Garvey: Anti-Colonial Champion.* Trenton, NJ: Africa World Press, 1988.
Lewy, Guenter. *The Cause that Failed: Communism in American Political Life.* New York: Oxford University Press, 1990.
Lifton, Robert Jay. *The Nazi Doctors: Medical Killing and the Psychology of Genocide.* New York: Basic Books, 1986.

Linz, Juan. "Some Notes towards a Comparative Study of Fascism in Sociological Perspective." Laqueur, *Fascism: A Reader's Guide* 3–121.
Lipset, Seymour Martin. *Political Man: The Social Bases of Politics.* Garden City, NY: Doubleday, 1960.
Locke, Alain. "Dry Fields and Green Pastures." *Opportunity* 18 (1940): 7.
Lockot, Hans Wilhelm. *The Mission: The Life, Reign, and Character of Haile Sellassie I.* New York: St. Martin's Press, 1989.
Losemann, Volker. "The Nazi Concept of Rome." *Roman Presences: Receptions of Rome in European Culture, 1789–1945.* Ed. Catharine Edwards. New York: Cambridge University Press, 1999. 221–35.
Lukács, Georg. *The Historical Novel.* Trans. Hannah and Stanley Mitchell. Lincoln: University of Nebraska Press, 1983.
———. *History and Class Consciousness: Studies in Marxist Dialectics.* Trans. Rodney Livingstone. Cambridge, MA: MIT Press, 1971.
Lyotard, Jean-François. *The Differend: Phrases in Dispute.* Trans. Georges Van Den Abbeele. Minneapolis: University of Minnesota Press, 1988.
Lyttelton, A. "The Crisis of Bourgeois Society and the Origins of Fascism." *Fascist Italy and Nazi Germany: Comparisons and Contrasts.* Ed. R. Bessel. Cambridge: Cambridge University Press. 12–22.
Maduka, Chidi. "The Revolutionary Hero and Strategies for Survival in Richard Wright's *The Outsider.*" *Presence Africaine: Revue Culturelle du Monde Noir/Cultural Review of the Negro World* 135 (1985): 56–70.
Marcuse, Herbert. *One-Dimensional Man: Studies in the Ideology of Advanced Industrial Society.* Boston, MA: Beacon Press, 1966.
———. *Technology, War, and Fascism: The Collected Papers of Herbert Marcuse, Volume One.* Ed. Douglas Kellner. New York: Routledge, 1998.
Martin, Charles H. *The Angelo Herndon Case and Southern Justice.* Baton Rouge: Louisiana State University Press, 1976.
Martin, Elaine. *Gender, Patriarchy, and Fascism in the Third Reich: The Response of Women Writers.* Detroit, MI: Wayne State University Press, 1993.
Martin, Tony. *Literary Garveyism: Garvey, Black Arts and the Harlem Renaissance.* Dover, MA: Majority Press, 1983.
———. *Marcus Garvey, Hero: A First Biography.* Dover, MA: Majority Press, 1983.
———. *The Pan-African Connection: From Slavery to Garvey and Beyond.* Dover, MA: Majority Press, 1998.
———. *Race First.* Dover, MA: Majority Press, 1986.
Marx, Karl. *The Eighteenth Brumaire of Louis Bonaparte.* Trans. Daniel De Leon. New York: Labor News, 1951.
Maxwell, William J. *New Negro, Old Left: African American Writing and Communism between the Wars.* New York: Columbia University Press, 1999.
"Mayor LaGuardia's Commission on the Harlem Riot of March 19, 1935." *The Complete Report of Mayor LaGuardia's Commission on the Harlem Riot of March 19, 1935.* New York: Arno Press, 1969.

McDowell, Deborah. "Foreword: Lines of Descent/Dissenting Lines." Hurston, *Moses, Man of the Mountain* vii–xxii.
McDowell, Winston C. "Keeping Them 'In the Same Boat Together'? Sufi Abdul Hamid, African Americans, Jews, and the Harlem Jobs Boycotts." *African Americans and Jews in the Twentieth Century.* Columbia: University of Missouri Press, 1998. 208–36.
McElvaine, Robert S. *The Great Depression: America, 1929–1941.* New York: Times Books, 1984.
McKay, Claude. *Banana Bottom.* 1933. Chatham, NJ: Chatham Bookseller, 1970.
———. *Harlem: Negro Metropolis.* 1940. New York: Harcourt Brace Jovanovich, 1968.
———. "Harlem Runs Wild." 1935. Gates and McKay 993–96.
———. *Home to Harlem.* 1928. Boston, MA: Northeastern University Press, 1987.
———. *A Long Way from Home.* 1937. New York: Harcourt Brace Jovanovich, 1970.
———. "Negroes Are Anti-Nazi, but Fight Anglo-US Discrimination. Soap-Boxers in Harlem Typify Negro Resentments." *New Leader* (October 25, 1941): 4. Rpt. in McKay, *Passion of Claude McKay* 277–80.
———. *The Passion of Claude McKay: Selected Prose and Poetry, 1912–1948.* Ed. Wayne Cooper. New York: Schocken Books, 1973.
———. "Sufi Abdul Hamid." ca. 1940. *The Complete Poems of Claude McKay.* Ed. William J. Maxwell. Urbana: University of Illinois Press, 2004.
McLeod, Marian B. "Claude McKay's Russian Interpretation: The Negroes in America." *College Language Association Journal* 23.3 (1980): 336–51.
Meier, August. *Negro Thought in America, 1880–1915: Racial Ideologies in the Age of Booker T. Washington.* Ann Arbor: University of Michigan Press, 1963.
Meier, August, and Elliot Rudwick. "Attitudes of Negro Leaders toward the American Labor Movement from the Civil War to World War I." *The Negro and the American Labor Movement.* Ed. Julius Jacobson. Garden City, NY: Anchor Books, 1968. 27–48.
Métraux, Alfred. *Voodoo in Haiti.* Trans. Hugo Charteris. New York: Oxford University Press, 1959.
Michaelis, Meir. *Mussolini and the Jews: German-Italian Relations and the Jewish Question in Italy, 1922–1945.* New York: Oxford University Press, 1978.
Miller, James A. "African American Writing of the 1930s: A Prologue." *Radical Revisions: Rereading 1930s Culture.* Ed. Bill Mullen and Sherry Lee Linkon. Urbana: University of Illinois Press, 1996. 78–90.
Mitchell, Angelyn, ed. *Within the Circle: An Anthology of African American Literary Criticism from the Harlem Renaissance to the Present.* Durham, NC: Duke University Press, 1994.
Moore, Richard B. "The Critics and Opponents of Marcus Garvey." *Marcus Garvey and the Vision of Africa.* Ed. John Henrik Clarke, with the assistance of Amy Jacques Garvey. New York: Random House, 1974. 210–35.

Morris, Aldon D. *The Origins of the Civil Rights Movement: Black Communities Organizing for Change*. New York: Free Press; London: Collier Macmillan, 1984.

Morris, Robert J. "Zora Neale Hurston's Ambitious Enigma: *Moses, Man of the Mountain*." *CLA Journal* 40.3 (1977): 308.

Morrison, Paul. *The Poetics of Fascism: Ezra Pound, T. S. Eliot, Paul de Man*. New York: Oxford University Press, 1996.

Moses, Wilson Jeremiah, ed. *Classical Black Nationalism: From the American Revolution to Marcus Garvey*. New York: New York University Press, 1996.

———. *The Wings of Ethiopia: Studies in African-American Life and Letters*. Ames: Iowa State University Press, 1990.

Mosley, Leonard. *Haile Selassie: The Conquering Lion*. Englewood Cliffs, NJ: 1965.

Mosse, George L. *The Crisis of German Ideology: Intellectual Origins of the Third Reich*. 1964. New York: Schocken Books, 1981.

———. *The Image of Man: The Creation of Modern Masculinity*. New York: Oxford University Press, 1996.

———, ed. *Nazi Culture: Intellectual, Cultural, and Social Life in the Third Reich*. New York: Schocken Books, 1981.

———. "Towards a General Theory of Fascism." *International Fascism. New Thoughts and New Approaches*. Ed. George L. Mosse. New York: Howard Fertig, 1979. 1–41.

———. *Toward the Final Solution: A History of European Racism*. New York: H. Fertig, 1978.

Mullen, Bill V. *Popular Fronts: Chicago and African-American Cultural Politics, 1935–46*. Urbana: University of Illinois Press, 1999.

Mussolini, Benito, and Giovanni Gentile. "La Dottrina del fascismo." *Scritti e Discorsi, 1932–1933*. Vol. 8. Milan: Ulrico Hoepli, 1934. 67–96. Translated as "Foundations and Doctrine of Fascism" in Schnapp 46–71.

Naison, Mark. "Communism and Harlem Intellectuals in the Popular Front: Anti-Fascism and the Politics of Black Culture." *Journal of Ethnic Studies* 9.1 (Spring 1981): 1–26.

———. *Communists in Harlem during the Depression*. Urbana: University of Illinois Press, 1983.

Nancy, Jean-Luc. *The Inoperative Community*. Ed. Peter Connor. Trans. Peter Connor, Lisa Garbus, Michael Holland, and Simona Sawhney. Minneapolis: University of Minnesota Press, 1991.

"Negro's Name Barred from Ballot." *New York Times* September 9, 1932, 4.

Nelson, Cary. *Repression and Recovery: Modern American Poetry and the Politics of Cultural Memory, 1910–1945*. Madison: University of Wisconsin Press, 1989.

Nembhard, Lens S. *Trials and Tribulations of Marcus Garvey*. Millwood: Kraus Reprint Co., 1978.

Neocleous, Marc. *Fascism*. Minneapolis: University of Minnesota Press, 1997.

Neumann, Franz. *Behemoth: The Structure and Practice of National Socialism, 1933–1944*. 1944. New York: Octagon Books, 1972.

Nicholls, David. *From Dessalines to Duvalier: Race, Colour, and National Independence in Haiti*. New York: Cambridge University Press, 1979.

Nietzsche, Friedrich. *The Gay Science: With a Prelude in Rhymes and an Appendix of Songs*. Trans. Walter Kaufmann. New York: Random House, 1974.

———. On the Genealogy of Morals *and* Ecce Homo. Trans. Walter Kaufmann and R. J. Hollingdale. New York: Random House, 1989.

———. *Twilight of the Idols; and* The Anti-Christ. Trans. R. J. Hollingdale. Baltimore, MD: Penguin Books, 1968.

Noerr, Gunzelin Schmid. *Philosophical Fragments*. Ed. and trans. Edmund Jephcott. Stanford, CA: Stanford University Press, 2002.

Nolte, Ernst. *Marxism, Fascism, Cold War*. Assen: Van Gorcum, 1982.

———. *Three Faces of Fascism: Action Française, Italian Fascism, and National Socialism*. New York: Holt, Rinehart and Winston, 1966.

Nordau, Max. *Degeneration*. Lincoln: University of Nebraska Press, 1993. Originally appeared as *Entartung*. Berlin: C. Duncker, 1892–1893.

North, Michael. *The Dialect of Modernism: Race, Language, and Twentieth-Century Literature*. New York: Oxford University Press, 1994.

Ottanelli, Fraser M. *The Communist Party of the United States: From the Depression to World War II*. New Brunswick, NJ: Rutgers University Press, 1991.

Ottley, Roi. *New World A-Comin': Inside Black America*. 1943. New York: Arno Press, 1968.

———. "Wright Adds a New Monster to the Gallery of the Dispossessed." *Chicago Sunday Tribune Magazine of Books* March 22, 1953, 3. Rpt. in *Richard Wright: The Critical Reception*, ed. John M. Reilly. New York: Burt Franklin, 1978. 205.

Passmore, Kevin. *Fascism: A Very Short Introduction*. New York: Oxford University Press, 2002.

Patterson, Orlando. *Rituals of Blood: Consequences of Slavery in Two American Centuries*. New York: Basic Books, 1998.

Payne, Stanley G. *Fascism: Comparison and Definition*. Madison: University of Wisconsin Press, 1980.

———. *Fascism in Spain, 1923–1977*. Madison: University of Wisconsin Press, 1999.

———. *A History of Fascism, 1914–1945*. Madison: University of Wisconsin Press, 1995.

Pickering-Iazzi, Robin. *Politics of the Visible: Writing Women, Culture, and Fascism*. Minneapolis: University of Minnesota Press, 1997.

Platt, Gerald M. "Thoughts on a Theory of Collective Action: Language, Affect, and Ideology in Revolution." *New Directions in Psychohistory*. Ed. M. Albin. Lexington, MA: Lexington Books, 1980. 69–94.

Plummer, Brenda Gayle. *Haiti and the United States: The Psychological Moment.* Athens: University of Georgia Press, 1992.
Pollock, Friedrich. "State Capitalism: Its Possibilities and Limitations." *The Essential Frankfurt School Reader.* Ed. Andrew Arato and Eike Gebhardt. New York: Continuum, 1982. 71–94.
Powell, Adam Clayton, Jr. *Adam by Adam; The Autobiography of Adam Clayton Powell, Jr.* New York: Dial Press, 1971.
Prescott, Orville. Rev. of *The Outsider,* by Richard Wright. *New York Times* March 18, 1953, 29. Rpt. in *Richard Wright: The Critical Reception,* ed. John M. Reilly. New York: Burt Franklin, 1978. 193–94.
Prowe, Diethelm. "Fascism, Neo-fascism, New Radical Right?" R. Griffin. *International Fascism* 305–24.
Rainey, Lawrence S. *Ezra Pound and the Monument of Culture: Text, History, and the Malatesta Cantos.* Chicago, IL: University of Chicago Press, 1991.
Ravetto, Kriss. *The Unmaking of Fascist Aesthetics.* Minneapolis: University of Minnesota Press, 2001.
Record, Wilson. *The Negro and the Communist Party.* 1951. New York: Atheneum, 1971.
Redkey, Edwin S. *Black Exodus; Black Nationalist and Back-to-Africa Movements, 1890–1910.* New Haven, CT: Yale University Press, 1969.
Redman, Tim. *Ezra Pound and Italian Fascism.* New York: Cambridge University Press, 1991.
Reich, Wilhelm. *The Mass Psychology of Fascism.* Trans. Vincent R. Carfagno. New York: Farrar, Straus and Giroux, 1970.
Renda, Mary A. *Taking Haiti: Military Occupation and the Culture of U.S. Imperialism, 1915–1940.* Chapel Hill: University of North Carolina Press, 2001.
Rideout, Walter B. *The Radical Novel in the United States, 1900–1954: Some Interrelations of Literature and Society.* Cambridge, MA: Harvard University Press, 1956.
Robinson, Cedric J. *Black Marxism: The Making of the Black Radical Tradition.* London: Zed; Totowa, NJ: Biblio Distribution Center, 1983.
Robinson, J. Bradford. "Jazz Reception in Weimar Germany: In Search of a Shimmy Figure." *Music and Performance during the Weimar Republic.* Ed. Bryan Gilliam. Cambridge, MA: Cambridge University Press, 1994. 107–35.
Roediger, David R. *The Wages of Whiteness: Race and the Making of the American Working Class History.* New York: Verso, 1991.
Rogers, Joel Augustus. *World's Great Men of Color.* 1946–47. Ed. John Henrik Clarke. New York: Macmillan, 1972.
Rowley, Hazel. *Richard Wright: The Life and Times.* New York: Henry Holt, 2001.
Rubin, Steven J. "Richard Wright and Albert Camus: The Literature of Revolt." *International Fiction Review* 8 (Winter 1981): 12–16.
Rugoff, Milton. "The Existential Darkness: Richard Wright's *The Outsider.*" *New York Herald Tribune Book Review* March 22, 1953, 4. Rpt. in *Richard*

Wright: The Critical Reception, ed. John M. Reilly. New York: Burt Franklin, 1978. 196–97.

Salzman, Jack, and Cornel West, eds. *Struggles in the Promised Land: Toward a History of Black-Jewish Relations in the United States.* New York: Oxford University Press, 1997.

Sartre, Jean Paul. *Anti-Semite and Jew.* Trans. George J. Becker. New York: Schocken Books, 1970.

———. *Existentialism and Humanism.* Trans. Philip Mairet. Brooklyn, NY: Haskell House, 1977.

Schmidt, Hans. *The United States Occupation of Haiti, 1915–1934.* New Brunswick, NJ: Rutgers University Press, 1971.

Schmidt, Matthias. *Albert Speer: The End of a Myth.* Trans. Joachim Neugroschel. New York: St. Martin's Press, 1984.

Schmitt, Carl. *The Crisis of Parliamentary Democracy.* Trans. Ellen Kennedy. Cambridge, MA: MIT Press, 1985.

———. *Political Theology: Four Chapters on the Concept of Sovereignty.* Trans. George Schwab. Cambridge, MA: MIT Press, 1985.

Schnapp, Jeffrey T., ed. *A Primer of Italian Fascism.* Ed. and trans. Jeffrey T. Schnapp, Olivia E. Sears, and Maria G. Stampino. Lincoln: University of Nebraska Press, 2000.

Schomburg, Arthur A. "The Negro Digs Up His Past." 1925. Gates and McKay 937–942.

Schopenhauer, Arthur. *The World as Will and Idea.* Trans. R. B. Haldane and J. Kemp. Garden City, NY: Doubleday, 1961.

Schuyler, George S. *Black and Conservative: The Autobiography of George S. Schuyler.* New Rochelle, NY: Arlington House, 1966.

———. *Black Empire.* 1936–38. Ed. Robert A. Hill and R. Kent Rasmussen. Boston, MA: Northeastern University Press, 1991.

———. *Black No More: Being an Account of the Strange and Wonderful Workings of Science in the Land of the Free, A.D. 1933–1940.* 1931. Boston, MA: Northeastern University Press, 1989.

———. "The Negro and Nordic Civilization." 1925. Schuyler, *Rac(e)ing to the Right* 3–12.

———. "The Negro-Art Hokum." 1926. *Within the Circle: An Anthology of African American Literary Criticism from the Harlem Renaissance to the Present.* Ed. Angelyn Mitchell. Durham, NC: Duke University Press, 1994.

———. *Rac(e)ing to the Right: Selected Essays of George S. Schuyler.* Ed. Jeffrey B. Leak. Knoxville: University of Tennessee Press, 2001.

———. "The Rise of the Black Internationale." 1938. Schuyler, *Rac(e)ing to the Right* 29–36.

———. *Slaves Today: A Story of Liberia.* 1931. College Park, MD: McGrath, 1969.

———. "To Boycott or Not to Boycott." *Crisis* 41 (September 1934): 258–60, 274.

———. "Uncle Sam's Black Step-Child." 1933. Schuyler, *Rac(e)ing to the Right* 17–28.
Scott, William R. "Black Nationalism and the Italo-Ethiopian Conflict 1934–1936." *Journal of Negro History* 63.2 (April 1978): 118–34.
Selassie, Haile, I. *My Life and Ethiopia's Progress.* 1966. Ed. Harold Marcus, with Ezekiel Gebissa and Tibebe Eshete. Trans. Ezekiel Gebissa with Guluma Gemeda. East Lansing: Michigan State University Press, 1994.
Sewell, Tony. *Garvey's Children: The Legacy of Marcus Garvey.* Trenton, NJ: Africa World Press, 1990.
Sherry, Vincent. *Ezra Pound, Wyndham Lewis, and Radical Modernism.* New York: Oxford University Press, 1993.
Singh, Ameritjit. "Richard Wright's *The Outsider:* Existentialist Exemplar or Critique?" *CLA Journal* 27 (June 1984): 357–70.
Sitkoff, Harvard. *A New Deal for Blacks: The Emergence of Civil Rights as a National Issue.* New York: Oxford University Press, 1978.
Smethurst, James Edward. *The New Red Negro: The Literary Left and African American Poetry, 1930–1946.* New York: Oxford University Press, 1999.
———. "'Pat Your Foot and Turn the Corner': Amiri Baraka, the Black Arts Movement, and the Poetics of a Popular Avant-Garde." *African American Review* 37.2 (Summer 2003): 261–70.
Smith, David Lionel. "The Black Arts Movement and Its Critics." *American Literary History* 3 (1991): 93–110.
Smith, William Robertson. *Lectures on the Religion of the Semites.* 1889. New York: Schocken Books, 1972.
"Smith Is Named Tammany Delegate." *New York Times* August 25, 1932, 8.
Snowball, David. "Controlling Degenerate Music: Jazz in the Third Reich." *Jazz and the Germans.* Ed. Michael J. Budds. Hillsdale, NY: Pendragon Press, 2002. 149–66.
Solomon, Mark. *The Cry Was Unity: Communists and African Americans, 1917–36.* Jackson: University Press of Mississippi, 1998.
Sontag, Susan. "Fascinating Fascism." *Under the Sign of Saturn.* New York, NY: Farrar, Straus and Giroux, 1980. 73–105.
Spackman, Barbara. *Fascist Virilities: Rhetoric, Ideology, and Social Fantasy in Italy.* Minneapolis: University of Minnesota Press, 1996.
Stachura, Peter D. *Nazi Youth in the Weimar Republic.* Santa Barbara, CA: Clio Books, 1975.
Stein, Judith. *The World of Marcus Garvey: Race and Class in Modern Society.* Baton Rouge: Louisiana State University Press, 1986.
Stephens, Michelle A. "Black Transnationalism and the Politics of National Identity: West Indian Intellectuals in Harlem in the Age of War and Revolution." *American Quarterly* 50.3 (1998): 592–608.
Stern, Fritz. *The Politics of Cultural Despair: A Study in the Rise of the Germanic Ideology.* Berkeley: University of California Press, 1961.

Sternhell, Zeev. *The Birth of Fascist Ideology: From Cultural Rebellion to Political Revolution.* Trans. David Maisel. Princeton, NJ: Princeton University Press, 1994.

———. *Neither Right nor Left: Fascist Ideology in France.* Trans. David Maisel. Berkeley: University of California Press, 1986.

Sundquist, Eric J. *The Hammers of Creation: Folk Culture in Modern African American Fiction.* Athens: University of Georgia Press, 1992.

———. *To Wake the Nations: Race in the Making of American Literature.* Cambridge, MA: Belknap-Harvard, 1993.

Sutton, Claude. "An Interpretation of 'Fascism.'" *British Union Quarterly* 2 (April–July 1937): 67–77.

Tarchi, Marco. "Between Festival and Revolution." R. Griffin, *International Fascism* 264–74.

Tate, Claudia. "Christian Existentialism in Richard Wright's *The Outsider.*" *CLA Journal* 25 (1982): 371–95.

Tate, Gayle T., and Lewis A. Randolph, eds. *Dimensions of Black Conservatism in the United States: Made in America.* New York: Palgrave, 2002.

Taylor, Simon. *Prelude to Genocide: Nazi Ideology and the Struggle for Power.* London: Duckworth, 1985.

Terkel, Studs. *Hard Times: An Oral History of the Great Depression.* New York: Pantheon Books, 1970.

Theweleit, Klaus. *Male Fantasies.* 2 vols. Trans. Stephen Conway in collaboration with Erica Carter and Chris Turner. Minneapolis: University of Minnesota Press, 1987–89.

Thomas, H. Nigel. *From Folklore to Fiction: A Study of Folk Heroes and Rituals in the Black American Novel.* Westport CT: Greenwood Press, 1988.

Thomas, Lorenzo. "The Shadow World: New York's Umbra Workshop and Origins of the Black Arts Movement." *Callaloo* 4 (October 1978): 53–72.

"Three Restored to Ballot." *New York Times* September 8, 1932, 4.

Tillery, Tyrone. *Claude McKay: A Black Poet's Struggle for Identity.* Amherst: University of Massachusetts Press, 1992.

Togliatti, Palmiro. "On the Question of Fascism." 1928. Bentham 136–48.

Trefzer, Annette. "'Let's Us All Be Kissing-Friends?': Zora Neale Hurston and Race Politics in Dixie." *Journal of American Studies* 31.1 (1997): 69–78.

Tucker, Jeffrey A. "'Can Science Succeed Where the Civil War Failed?' George S. Schuyler and Race." *Race Consciousness: African American Studies for the New Century.* Ed. Judith Jackson Fossett and Jeffrey A. Tucker. New York: New York University Press, 1997. 136–53.

Turner, Darwin T. "*The Outsider:* Revision of an Idea." *CLA Journal* 12 (1969): 310–21.

Tylor, Edward B. *Primitive Culture.* 7th ed. New York: Brentano's, 1924.

Van Deburg, William L., ed. *Modern Black Nationalism: From Marcus Garvey to Louis Farrakhan.* New York: New York University Press, 1997.

Vincent, Ted. *Keep Cool: The Black Activists Who Built the Jazz Age*. East Haven, CT: Pluto Press, 1995.
Wald, Alan M. *Writing from the Left: New Essays on Radical Culture and Politics*. New York: Verso, 1994.
Walker, Margaret. *Richard Wright, Daemonic Genius: A Portrait of the Man, a Critical Look at His Work*. New York: Warner Books, 1988.
Watson, Steven. *The Harlem Renaissance: Hub of African American Culture, 1920–1930*. New York: Pantheon Books, 1995.
Watts, Jill. *God, Harlem U.S.A.: The Father Divine Story*. Berkeley: University of California Press, 1992.
Waxman, Percy. *The Black Napoleon: The Story of Toussaint L'Ouverture*. New York: Harcourt, Brace, 1931.
Webb, Constance. *Richard Wright: A Biography*. New York: Putnam, 1968.
Weil, Dorothy. "Folklore Motifs in Arna Bontemps' *Black Thunder*." *SFQ* 35 (March 1971): 1–14.
Weisbord, Robert. *Father Divine*. Boston, MA: Beacon Press, 1984.
Weisbord, Robert G. *Ebony Kinship: Africa, Africans, and the Afro-American*. Westport, CT: Greenwood Press, 1973.
West, Cornel. "Marxist Theory and the Specificity of Afro-American Oppression." *Marxism and the Interpretation of Culture*. Ed. Cary Nelson and Lawrence Grossberg. Urbana: University of Illinois Press, 1988. 17–26.
Williams, John A. Foreword. Schuyler, *Black Empire* ix–xv.
Wintz, Cary D. *Black Culture and the Harlem Renaissance*. Houston, TX: Rice University Press, 1988.
———, ed. *African American Political Thought, 1890–1930: Washington, Du Bois, Garvey, and Randolph*. Armonk, NY: M. E. Sharpe, 1996.
Wolin, Richard. *The Seduction of Unreason: The Intellectual Romance with Fascism from Nietzsche to Postmodernism*. Princeton, NJ: Princeton University Press, 2006.
Woodson, Jon. *To Make a New Race: Gurdjieff, Toomer, and the Harlem Renaissance*. Jackson: University Press of Mississippi, 1999.
Wright, Richard. *Black Boy*. 1945. New York: Perennial Classics, 1998.
———. *Black Power: A Record of Reactions in a Land of Pathos*. 1953. New York: Harper, 1995.
"Blueprint for Negro Writing." Gates and McKay 1380–88.
———. "How 'Bigger' Was Born." 1940. *Native Son*. New York: Perennial Classics, 1998. 431–62.
———. "I Tried to Be a Communist." *Atlantic Monthly* August–September, 1944.
———. *Lawd Today!* 1963. Boston, MA: Northeastern University Press, 1993.
———. *Native Son*. 1940. New York: Perennial Classics, 1998.
———. *The Outsider*. 1953. New York: HarperPerennial, 1993.
———. *Pagan Spain*. 1957. Jackson: University of Mississippi Press, 2002.

———. *12 Million Black Voices*. 1941. New York: Thunder's Mouth Press, 1988.
———. *White Man, Listen!* 1957. Westport, CT: Greenwood Press, 1978.
Yarborough, Richard. Introduction. *Uncle Tom's Children*. New York: Harper-Perennial, 1993. ix–xxix.
Young, James O. *Black Writers of the Thirties*. Baton Rouge: Louisiana State University Press, 1973.
Žižek, Slavoj. "Fantasy as a Political Category: A Lacanian Approach." *The Žižek Reader*. Ed. Elizabeth Wright and Edmond Wright. Malden, MA: Blackwell Publishers, 1999. 87–101.

Index

Adamson, Walter L., 40
Adell, Sandra, 151
Adorno, Theodor W., 29, 47, 81, 82, 191n17
Africa, 7, 8, 20, 45, 60, 72–74, 77–79, 84, 106, 124, 141, 183n8. *See also* Ethiopia; Garvey, Marcus, vision of Africa; Hurston, Zora Neale, use of Mosaic myth; Liberia
African Blood Brotherhood, 94, 190n6
Agamben, Giorgio, 65; state of exception 132, 198n26
Althusser, Louis, 57, 58, 199n38
"America," lyrics to, 5
Anderson, Benedict, 8; theory of imagined community, 34
Anderson, Jervis, 10
anti-Semitism. *See under* Black Arts movement; black intellectuals; Garvey, Marcus; Hamid, Sufi Abdul; McKay, Claude; Schuyler, George S.
Antliff, Mark, 38
Arendt, Hannah, 51, 105, 193n14, 196n12–13

back-to-Africa. *See* Garvey, Marcus
Balch, Emily Greene, 13
Baldwin, James, 173, 174, 196n7
Baldwin, Kate A., 20
Bamberry, Chris, 173

Baraka, Amiri, 176–78, 182; and Black Nationalism, 176
Bataille, Georges, 34, 66, 89, 185n35
Baudrillard, Jean, 197–98n24
Benjamin, Walter, 29, 30, 75, 132, 194nn16–18; on fascism and the work of art, 29, 30
Berghahn, Marion, 9
Bergson, Henri, 199n40
Berman, Russell A., 34, 35
Black Arts movement: and anti-Semitism, 178, 181, 182; and black fascism, 174, 178, 179, 182; compared to historical fascism and neofascism, 178–82
black Atlantic, 8, 24–26; relationship to black fascism, 24. *See also* Gilroy, Paul
black Communism, 1, 2
black diaspora, 7, 48, 60, 108. *See also* black Zionism; Ethiopianism; Pan-Africanism
black fascism: and the black Atlantic, 24–26; compared to generic fascism, 2, 7, 27–29, 43; relationship to black radicalism, 1, 21, 27; relationship to Marxism, 23, 24, 27; theory of, 24, 27–29. *See also* black fascist aesthetics; black fascist state; black fascist text; black literary fascism; Garvey, Marcus; Gilroy, Paul;

225

black fascism (*continued*)
  Hurston, Zora Neale; McKay, Claude; Schuyler, George S.; Wright, Richard
black fascist aesthetics, 41, 44. *See also* black fascist text; black literary fascism
black fascist state, 43, 44
black fascist text, 22, 27, 42–44. *See also* black fascist aesthetics; black literary fascism
black intellectuals, 1, 25–28, 92, 99, 109, 110–13, 190n12; and Communism, 20, 21; on Communism versus fascism, 27; on Haitian independence, 16; on the New Negro, 25; in relationship with racism and anti-Semitism, 28
black-Jewish relations in Harlem, 12, 100–102, 107, 111, 112, 116
black labor, 190n11, 191n15, 191n22, 192n30; black labor unions, 190n8. *See also* Harlem: black labor movement in; McKay: and black labor in Harlem
black literary fascism, 2, 21, 42–44, 182
black Marxism, 1, 2, 21, 22, 184n20
black modernism: relationship to European, Euro-American modernism, 26
black Moses, 9, 24. *See also* Hurston, Zora Neale, use of Mosaic myth
Black Nationalism, 1, 2, 6, 19, 20, 22–24, 27, 43, 107, 115, 176, 184n8, 191n15; as class consciousness, 20; and Communism, 19–22; and Haiti, 13, 14; relationship to Ethiopianism and Ethiopia, 8–10, 183n8. *See also* Baraka, Amiri; Garvey, Marcus; Hurston, Zora Neale; Wright, Richard
Black Power, 178
black radicalism, 1, 2, 4, 183n1; and black fascism, 19–27; black Zionism, 7, 8, 48, 183n5; relationship to Communism, 19–21

Boas, Franz, 125, 136–38, 193n6, 195n23
Bontemps, Arna: *Drums at Dusk*, 17; on Haiti, 16, 17; on Richard Wright's *The Outsider*, 143, 149
Briggs, Cyril, 94
Brownshirts, 25
Bunche, Ralph, 1

Camus, Albert, 150, 197n17
Canetti, Elias, 103
Carver, George Washington, 77
Césaire, Aimé, 1
Chirenje, J. Mutero, 8
Christophe, Henri, 15, 16
Clifford, James, 26
Coles, Robert A., 152
Communism, 19–23, 25–27, 175, 176; connection to Harlem riot, 11; on the Negro question, 19, 20. *See also* black intellectuals, and Communism; Black Nationalism, and Communism; black radicalism, relationship to Communism; Garvey, Marcus, and Communism; McKay, Claude, relationship to Communism; Schuyler, George S., and Communism; Wright, Richard, on relationship between Communism and Fascism
Cooper, Wayne F., 11, 94
Coughlin, Father, 25
Cox, Oliver, 1
Cronon, Edmund David, 45
Cruse Harold, 191n26

Dash, J. Michael, 14, 15
Debord, Guy, 98, 198n33
de Felice, Renzo, 52
Deleuze, Gilles, and Félix Guattari, 34, 68, 115
Denning, Michael, 26
Derrida, Jacques, 187n21, 194n16, 197n19
Dessalines, Jean-Jacques, 15
Diedrich, Maria, 124, 125
Divine, Father, 11, 92, 108

Index 227

Double V campaign, 196n1
Du Bois, W. E. B., 1, 5, 23, 42, 77, 104;
    Dark Princess, 5; on Haiti, 15, 16;
    Souls of Black Folk 104
Durkheim, Emile, 194n19

Eatwell, Roger, 63
Eliot, T. S.: *The Waste Land*, 40
Ellison, Ralph, 20, 125, 190n10, 195n28, 196n7
Esedebe, P. Olisanwuche, 183n7
Ethiopia, 7–9, 24, 46–49, 51, 52, 56, 58, 68, 69. *See also* Ethiopianism; Garvey, Marcus; Italo-Ethiopian conflict; Schulyer, George S.
Ethiopianism, 7–9, 74, 86, 183n7. *See also* Schuyler, George S.
existentialism. *See* Sartre, Jean-Paul; Wright, Richard

Fabre, Michel, 17
Falasca-Zamponi, Simonetta, 37
Falange, 147. *See also* Spanish Fascism
Fanon, Frantz, 199n37
fascism. *See* generic fascism
fascist aesthetics, 34–44, 186n43; fascist use of myth, 29, 30, 32–37, 41, 42, 53; fascist appropriation of art and aesthetics, 29, 30, 33–35, 37, 39–41; fascist literary text and work of art, 34–42; use of images and ideograms, 30, 35, 36, 39–41. *See also* black fascist aesthetics
fascist authoritarian state, 1, 3, 30–33, 41, 66. *See also* Garvey, Marcus, and the black fascist state *and under* Hurston, Zora Neale
fascist imperialism. *See under* Garvey, Marcus
fascist misogyny and gender politics, 30–32, 34, 189n12
fascist modernism, 35; relationship of fascism to modernism "proper," 36–39
Foucault, Michel, 34, 55, 70, 198n34
Franco, Francisco, 28, 147

Frazer, Sir James George, 194n19
Freud, Sigmund, 105, 125, 193n5, 197n15;
    Civilization and Its Discontents, 29
Fromm, Erich, 52, 197n14
Führerprinzip. *See under* Hurston, Zora Neale

Gaines, Kevin K., 184n8
Garnet, Henry Highland, 117
Garvey, Amy Jacques, 52
Garvey, Marcus, 1–3, 6, 19, 22–24, 41, 43–72, 76, 77, 88, 92, 103, 104, 107, 115, 117, 122 123, 145, 174, 186n2, 187n12, 187nn18–19, 188n26, 190n5, 192n30; and anti-Semitism, 45, 46, 52–54, 56–58, 186nn8–9; attitudes toward Mussolini and Italian Fascism, 48, 51–53, 58, 59, 61–67, 69, 186n10, 187n20; back-to-Africa, 43, 49, 70; and the black fascist state, 47, 55, 56, 59, 60, 62–64, 66, 70; and Communism, 19, 22, 61; on the corporatist state, 61–63; criticism of Haile Selassie, 46–49, 51–58, 69, 72, 186n5; and Ethiopia, 46–49, 51, 52, 56, 58, 68, 69; and fascist imperialism, 51, 59–61, 65; and Hegelian dialectics, 54; influence on black fascist aesthetics, 44, 47, 70, 71, 145, 170; and Marxism, 23, 61; *Message to the People*, 41, 47, 51, 53–57, 60–62, 64–70; and nationalism, 43, 51, 61, 64, 65, 188n22; and Pan-Africanism, 48, 60; and racial purity, 55–57, 67, 70; relationship to (black) fascism, 3, 43–47, 49–53, 55–63, 65–70; in relation to Hitler and Mussolini, 6, 45–47, 53, 186n1; use of the Bible and Christian theology, 51–55, 58, 59, 62–70, 107; view of war and violence, 68, 69; vision of Africa, 45, 46, 49, 50, 52, 54, 55, 59–62
Garveyism, 19, 20, 22, 23, 46, 47, 49–51, 60, 72, 76, 94, 104, 115, 122, 123
Gates, Henry Louis, Jr., 3, 76, 77, 195n24

Gättens, Marie-Luise, 32
Gayle, Addison, Jr., 180, 181
generic fascism, 1–3, 7, 10, 14, 21–24, 28–30, 41, 43, 46–50, 52, 53, 57, 63, 65, 118, 123, 126, 171–78, 185n36, 188n23, 197n16; influence on black intellectuals, 18, 27. *See also* Italian Fascism; Nazism; Spanish Fascism
generic fascist ideology, 2, 22, 27–29, 76, 118, 123, 126, 185n38, 188n5, 193n11. *See also* generic fascism; Payne, Stanley G.
Gentile, Giovanni, 59, 64
Gentile, Emilio, 53
Gide, André, 112
Giles, James R., 12
Gilroy, Paul: *Against Race*, 26; *The Black Atlantic*, 24, 196n6; on black fascism, 2, 22, 24; on Garvey and Garveyism, 22, 46, 55; on Hurston, 121; theory of black Atlantic, 24–26; on Wright, 196n6
Girard, Rene, 193n13, 198n31
Golsen, Richard J., 40
Gramsci, Antonio, 89, 98, 110, 191n24
Great Depression, the, 25–27, 44, 111
Greenberg, Cheryl Lynn, 11
Greenberg, Robert M., 95
Gregor, A. James, 49
Griffin, Barbara Jackson, 96
Griffin, Roger, 29, 34, 52, 64
Gruesser, John Cullen, 77

Haiti: influence on African American political and cultural imagination, 13–17, 24, 185n27; as model for black fascism, 3; U.S. occupation of, 2, 13, 14, 74, 75, 184n17. *See also* Christophe, Henri; Dessalines, Jean-Jacques; Hurston, Zora Neale, on Haiti; L'Ouverture, Toussaint
Hakutani, Yoshinobu, 152
Hall, Stuart, 27
Hamid, Sufi Abdul, 3, 6, 12, 86, 98, 190n12; "Don't Buy Where You Can't Work," 10, 91, 115; use of anti-Semitism 6, 10–12, 91, 99–102; use of Nazi rhetoric, 6, 12, 100, 102. *See also* McKay, Claude, on Sufi Abdul Hamid
Hansberry, Lorraine, 150
Harlem, 4, 19, 25–28, 44, 87–116, 190n12; black labor movement in, 6, 10, 11, 13. *See also* McKay, Claude
Harlem Renaissance, 18, 24, 44, 115, 123, 186nn44–45
Harlem riot (1935), 2, 3, 10, 11, 44, 184n13, 190n10. *See also* McKay, Claude
Hatlen, Burton, 39
Heidegger, Martin, 106, 187n21
Heinl, Robert Debs, and Nancy Gordon Heinl, 15
Henderson, Stephen, 181
Herf, Geoffrey, 49
Herndon, Angelo, 158, 165
Herscovits, Melville J., 195n27
Hewitt, Andrew, 36
Hicks, Granville, 148
Hill, Robert A., 45, 47
Hill, Robert A., and R. Kent Rasumussen, 6, 78, 79
historical fascism. *See* generic fascism
Hitler, Adolf, 6, 38, 110, 111, 118, 119, 124, 127, 133, 147, 160, 161, 163, 168, 170, 174, 175. *See also* James, C. L. R., comparison of Marcus Garvey and Hitler; Garvey, Marcus, in relation to Hitler and Mussolini
Hobbes, Thomas, 198n36
Hopkins, Pauline E., 183n8
Horkheimer, Max, 63; and Theodor W. Adorno, 68, 100
Hubert, Henri, and Marcel Mauss, 138, 139, 194nn19–20, 195n25
Hughes, Langston, 188n2; on Haiti, 15, 16; *I Wonder as I Wander*, 15, 16
Hugo, Victor, 184n18
Hurston, Zora Neale, 1, 3, 70, 71, 117–42, 192n2, 194n22, 195n27,

195n29; and black fascism, 71, 142, 170, 174; and Black Nationalism, 3, 118, 120, 122, 123, 126, 136, 139, 140, 142; and the Book of Thoth, 139–41, 195n25; and fascism, 118, 121–32, 136, 138, 140–42; and the fascist authoritarian state, 118, 128, 130, 131, 133–36, 141, 142; and the *Führerprinzip*, 118, 126, 132, 133, 135, 141; on Haiti, 3, 16, 17, 119, 121, 122, 136, 139, 141, 192n1; and Judaism, 117, 125, 127–31, 133–42; *Moses, Man of the Mountain*, 3, 41, 117, 118, 120, 123–43; and racial purity, 119–21, 125, 134; on the relationship between European Jews and African Americans, 123, 124, 126, 128, 136; relationship to Nazism and the Nazi myth, 3, 123–26, 128–31, 134, 135, 139, 141, 143 192n3; representation of Egyptians and Egypt, 118, 125–42, 194n21; and sacrifice, 129, 133–135, 138–42, 193n13, 194n19, 195n25; *Tell My Horse*, 3, 16, 119, 121, 122, 192n1; use of Mosaic myth, 117–42, 192nn3–4, 193n5, 193n8; use of myth, 119, 120, 123, 128, 129, 131, 142; and Voodoo, 119, 136. *See also* Boas, Franz; Garvey, Marcus; Wright, Richard

Islam, 106, 114. *See also* Nation of Islam
Italo-Ethiopian conflict, 2, 3, 6, 7, 9, 46, 72–77, 79, 85, 184nn9–10, 188n2
Italian Fascism, 9, 10, 28, 42, 51, 53, 57, 59, 84, 89, 172, 186–87n10. *See also* Garvey, Marcus; generic fascism; Mussolini, Benito

Jackson, Blyden, 118, 195n29
Jacobs, Sylvia M., 9
James, C. L. R., 1; comparison of Marcus Garvey and Hitler, 50
Jenkins, David, 8
Johnson, Barbara, 124, 125, 193n5

Johnson, James Weldon, 14; on Haiti, 14, 184n18
Jünger, Ernst, 29, 30

Kafka, Franz, 197n19
Kalaidjian, Walter, 26
Kantorowicz, Ernst H., 130
Karenga, Malauna, 181
Kelley, Robin D. G., 1, 7, 19
Kierkegaard, Søren, 151
Kinnamon, Kenneth, and Michel Fabre, 147, 148
Knox, MacGregor, 51
Kracauer, Siefried, 80
Ku Klux Klan, 25, 48, 49, 92, 93, 190n5

Laclau, Ernesto, 33, 34
Lacoue-Labarthe, Philippe, and Jean-Luc Nancy: on the Nazi myth, 32, 33, 56, 64, 70, 187n21, 193n14
Lagarde, Paul de, 193n12
Langbehn, Julius, 193n12
Laqueur, Walter, 175, 176
Lawrence, Jacob, 17
Lemke, Sieglinde: *Primitivist Modernism*, 24
LeSeur, Geta, 96
Levecq, Christine, 125, 126
Levine, Lawrence W., 46
Lewis, David Levering, 11, 91
Lewis, Rupert, 45, 46
Lewis, Wyndham, 26, 37–39, 41
Liberia, 73, 74
Linz, Juan, 50, 60
"Literary Garveyism," 3
Locke, Alain, 125
L'Ouverture, Toussaint, 15, 17, 116, 117, 119
Lukács, Georg, 108, 192n28
Lyotard, Jean-François, 197n23

Maduka, Chidi, 153
Mailer, Norman, 181
Malcolm X, 174
Marcuse, Herbert, 58, 189n13

Martin, Elaine, 32
Martin, Tony, 3, 46, 49, 122
Marxism, 21–27, 44, 108; account of fascism, 23. *See also* black fascism, relationship to Marxism; black Marxism; Garvey, Marcus, and Marxism
Mauss, Marcel. *See* Hubert, Henri
Maxwell, William J., 26, 143
McDowell, Winston C., 12, 125
McKay, Claude, 1, 3, 5, 6, 27, 70, 71, 87–116, 143, 174, 190n3, 191n20; and anti-Semitism, 3, 99–102, 111; *Banana Bottom,* 94, 95; and black fascism, 3, 88, 104, 109, 111, 116, 142; on black intellectuals, 92, 99, 109–13; and black labor in Harlem, 87–97, 106–16, 183n2, 192n28; and fascism, 87, 88, 93, 95, 98, 99, 102, 107, 108, 111–14, 143; on Marcus Garvey, 103, 104, 106, 107, 116; and Mike Gold, 191n26; on Sufi Abdul Hamid, 3, 11–13, 28, 88, 90–93, 96, 99–102, 104, 106, 107, 109, 111, 114–16; *Harlem: A Negro Metropolis,* 3, 12, 92, 93, 96, 99; *Harlem Glory: A Fragment of Aframerican Life,* 41, 71, 88, 95, 96, 104–16, 162; on Harlem riot (1935), 88, 96, 97, 101–3, 111; "Harlem Runs Wild," 3, 11, 88, 96–103, 181, 182; *Home to Harlem,* 95; *A Long Way from Home,* 3, 88–90, 94, 96; and Nazism, 5, 6; relationship to Christianity and Catholicism, 87, 88, 96, 106, 107, 114; relationship to Communism, 3, 11, 12, 13, 19, 20, 88, 93, 94, 104, 108–12, 114; on George S. Schuyler, 72, 73, 116, 190n2. *See also* Schuyler, George S., on Claude McKay
McLeod, Marian B., 95
Mencken, H. L., 74
Menelik II, 9, 10, 86
Mitchell, Angelyn, 179
modernism. *See* black modernism; fascist modernism

Moore, Richard B., 51
Morris, Robert J., 125
Morrison, Paul, 38
Mosaic myth. *See under* Hurston, Zora Neale
Mosse, George, 57, 58, 188n24, 191n19, 191n23
Mullen, Bill V., 21
Mussolini, Benito, 5–7, 9, 25, 37, 38, 59, 64, 66, 72, 76, 77, 86, 110, 111, 147, 160, 161, 168, 175, 189n6. *See also* Garvey, Marcus; Pound, Ezra
myth: fascist use of, 29, 30, 32–37, 41, 42, 47, 53, 56; the Nazi myth, 32, 33, 56, 64, 65, 70; relationship to ideology, 33, 34. *See also* Hurston, use of Mosaic myth; Hurston, use of myth; Lacoue-Labarthe, Philippe, and Jean-Luc Nancy

Naison, Mark, 6, 10
Napoleon, 160
Nation of Islam, 173, 174
Nazism, 5, 6, 18, 25, 29, 32, 40, 42, 51, 52, 84, 92, 98, 99, 105, 113, 114, 116, 123–26, 128–31, 143, 145, 163, 172–75, 185n39, 187nn10–11, 189n9, 189n14, 191n19, 192n29, 193n14, 198n27, 198n32. *See also* generic fascism; Hitler, Adolf; Hurston, Zora Neale; Wright, Richard
Nelson, Cary, 26
Nembhard, Lens S., 48
neofascism, 172–78, 197n21
Nicholls, David, 14
Nolte, Ernst, 23
North, Michael, 26

Ottley, Roi, 149

Padmore, George, 1
Pan-Africanism, 7–9, 48, 72, 74, 77, 183n7, 188n2. *See also* Garvey, Marcus
Passmore, Kevin, 30, 31

Payne, Stanley G., 29, 66, characteristics of generic fascist ideology, 29, 185nn37–38, 186n40, 188n5
Pittsburgh Courier, 3, 6, 72–75, 85–87, 189n1, 190n2, 196n1
Plummer, Brenda Gayle, 14
Pound, Ezra, 26, 37–39, 41; *Cantos* as fascist art, 38, 39; on Mussolini, 25, 38, 39
Powell, Adam Clayton, Jr., 10, 12
Prescott, Orville, 148
Prince Hall, 117
Prowe, Diethelm, 174

racial purity. See Garvey, Marcus; Hurston, Zora Neale
Randolph, A. Philip, 191n22
Redkey, Edwin S., 8
Reich, Wilhelm, 29, 46
Renda, Mary A., 14
Riefenstahl, Leni, 34, 41, 193n15
Robinson, Cedric J., 19
Roediger, David, 184n16
Rugoff, Milton, 150

sacrifice, 193n13, 194n19, 194n20. See also Hubert, Henri, and Marcel Mauss; Hurston, Zora Neale
Sartre, Jean-Paul, 198n35, 199n37; on anti-Semitism, 191n14. See also existentialism; Wright, Richard, and Jean-Paul Sartre
Schmitt, Carl, 157, 199n39
Schopenhauer, Arthur, 198n28
Schuyler, George S., 1, 3, 27, 41, 70, 72–88, 189n7, 189n11, 190n12; *Black Empire*, 3, 6, 7, 18, 27, 41, 70, 72, 73, 76–86, 87; black fascism, 3, 84–86, 142, 174; and Communism, 73, 74; relationship to Marcus Garvey, 3, 72, 76–78; and Ethiopianism, 74, 86; on Claude McKay, 87, 189n1, 190n2; on the New Negro, 75, 76; an Pan-Africanism, 72–74, 77; support of Haile Selassie, 72; use of fascist ideology, 72, 73, 75–86, 189n11. See also McKay, Claude, on George S. Schuyler
Selassie, Haile. See Garvey, Marcus, criticism of Haile Selassie; Schuyler, George S., support of Haile Selassie
Sewell, Tony, 49, 50, 186n2
Sherry, Vincent, 39
Smith, David Lionel, 178, 179
Smith, William Robertson, 194n19
Socialism, 30, 109, 111
Solomon, Mark, 12, 19
Spackman, Barbara, 189n12
Spanish Fascism, 28, 147, 183n4. See also Falange; Franco, Francisco
Speer, Albert, 189n9
Stalin, Joseph, 160, 161
Stein, Judith, 48
Stephens, Michelle A., 94
Sternhell, Zeev, 123
Styron, William, 181
Sundquist, Eric J., 8

Tarchi, Marco, 62
Theweleit, Klaus, 30, 81, 82
Thomas, Lorenzo, 180
Tillery, Tyrone, 12
totalitarianism. See under Wright, Richard
Tucker, Jeffrey A., 77
Turner, Darwin T., 151
Tylor, Edward B., 194n19

United Negro Improvement Association (UNIA), 6, 19, 45, 46, 49, 53, 190n5. See also Garvey, Marcus

van den Bruck, Moeller, 193n12
Van Vechten, Carl, 123
Vincent, Stenio, 14–17, 121

Washington, Booker T., 21, 77
Weisbord, Robert G., 7, 11
Welles, Orson, 14
Williams, John A., 77
Wolin, Richard, 172–74
Woodson, Jon, 189n7

Wright, Richard, 1, 4, 17, 20, 70, 71, 143–70, 196nn2–3, 196n9, 196n11, 197n15, 197n24, 198n28, 198n33, 199n38, 199n40; and black fascism, 4, 143, 146, 156, 164, 165, 169, 170; and Black Nationalism, 145, 146, 153; and existentialism, 143, 144, 147–53, 170, 196n12, 197n17, 199n37; and fascism, 144, 145, 147, 148, 154–65, 167–71, 196n4; "How Bigger Was Born," 17, 18, 144–46; *Native Son,* 4, 147, 150, 151; and Nazism, 143, 155, 163, 167; *The Outsider,* 4, 41, 70, 142–44, 147, 149–70, 196n6, 196n7, 197n20; on relationship between Communism and Fascism, 17, 18, 27, 144, 145, 151, 153–56, 158–60, 162–69, 172; and Jean-Paul Sartre, 147–52, 170, 199n37; and totalitarianism, 144, 148, 153–55, 157–59, 162, 164–66, 168, 197–98n24; Wright-Hurston debate, 143

Žižek, Slavoj, 33, 65

www.ingramcontent.com/pod-product-compliance
Lightning Source LLC
Chambersburg PA
CBHW031709230426
43668CB00006B/160